BETRAYING
THE
GOSPEL

The C.S. Lewis Centre Library

BETRAYING
THE
GOSPEL

MODERN THEOLOGIES AND
CHRISTIAN ◆ ORTHODOXY

ANDREW WALKER

BRISTOL
BOOKS®
WILMORE, KY 40390

In memoriam
C.S. Lewis 1898-1963

BETRAYING THE GOSPEL
Copyright © 1988 by The C.S. Lewis Centre
Published by Bristol Books

First United States Edition, March 1990

First published in Great Britain as *Different Gospels* by Hodder and Stoughton Ltd, Mill Road, Dunton Green, Sevenoaks, Kent TN13 2YE. ISBN: 0-340-42631 4

Library of Congress Card Number: 88-82619
ISBN: 0-917851-47-1

BRISTOL BOOKS
An imprint of the Forum for Scriptural Christianity, Inc.
308 East Main Street • Wilmore, Kentucky 40390

Acknowledgements

R. J. Berry's essay, 'Miracles: Scepticism, Credulity or Reality?' which appears here by permission of Macmillan Magazines Ltd, is a slightly amended and revised version of his essay, 'What to believe about miracles', which originally appeared in *Nature* Vol. 322, No. 6077, 24 July 1986, pp. 321-322, copyright 1986 Macmillan Magazines Ltd, and was also used as an appendix in his book *God and Evolution* (London: Hodder & Stoughton, 1988).

Peter L. Berger's essay, 'Different Gospels: The Social Sources of Apostasy', was originally the Erasmus Lecture, January 1987, delivered at St Peter's Lutheran Church, New York City (hence the opening words). It was then published in *This World* 17 (1987), pp. 6-17, and appears in Richard Neuhaus (ed.), *American Apostasy: The Triumph of Other Gospels* (Grand Rapids: Wm B. Eerdmans, 1988). It is printed here, with only minor changes, by permission of Richard Neuhaus and Peter L. Berger.

Message from
Cardinal Johannes Willebrands,
President of the Secretariat for
Promoting Christian Unity,
to Dr. Andrew Walker,
Director of the C.S. Lewis Centre

The establishing of the C.S. Lewis Centre and the publication by the Centre of the volume *Betraying the Gospel* are to be welcomed by all Christians.

The voice of atheistic and materialistic philosophies in the world today compels all of us who confess the truth of Christ to bear united witness to that truth. Such witness depends precisely on unity in the profession of faith. For this reason it is important and most welcome that the C.S. Lewis Centre, which will concern itself with studying and addressing the philosophies that have grown up in our modern culture and which prescind from the Christian tradition, should be ecumenical in its foundation and its operation.

It is my hope that the Centre may be a context for the furthering both of ecumenical dialogue and of the evangelisation of contemporary culture. The Centre and all who will work for it have my prayers and warm good wishes.

Johannes Cardinal Willebrands
Vatican City

A Note on References

The citation style used in the text is an adaptation of the Harvard system. References are generally to authors and dates (the additional digits being to page numbers) and are linked to an alphabetised Bibliography at the end of the volume. Thus a reference such as (Lewis 1943:37) would be to C.S. Lewis' book *The Abolition of Man*, page 37.

Where in the text it was neither practical nor desirable to give the full reference, but an item nevertheless appears in the Bibliography, the date is simply given in brackets. Thus in a line where a series of authors are mentioned (*e.g.* 'Pannenberg (1968), Moltmann (1974) . . .') the relevant literature can easily be identified.

CONTENTS

EDITOR'S PREFACE

Andrew Walker

This collection of interviews and essays will be of particular interest to all those Americans and Europeans who are concerned with what appear to be alternative gospels to that of historic Christianity. It will also interest all those open-minded people who, while neither traditionalists nor even perhaps orthodox believers, want to know what traditionalists and orthodox Christians have to say about modernism.

Having said that, however, many of the contributors to this volume would not particularly want to be associated with a label that confined them only to traditionalism. Perhaps there is an acceptable interface between the traditional and the modern: hybrids can be stronger than pure breeds. Nevertheless, that being so, it is a question of discernment as to how far historic Christian thought and theology can have truck with modernist thought. It is the underlying conviction of the C.S. Lewis Centre that we have gone too far. At what stage openness to new things becomes a betrayal of the gospel (see the interview with Metropolitan Anthony, p. 41), and hence of our calling as Christians, is perhaps one of the great questions that all churches are now having to face.

Again and again throughout this collection we return to the Enlightenment as the backdrop against which modernism comes into full focus. Without an understanding of the dualistic modes of thought that dominate modernity it is difficult to make sense—let alone plot the course—of modern theologies.

We have self-consciously limited ourselves in this volume to essays and discussions aimed at the intelligent reader, not the academic and theological specialist. Clearly this opens us to the charge of over-simplification and caricature. To a certain extent it is a charge that we accept, for all true scholarship is subject to a thousand caveats. Nevertheless, if we were to write only for specialists we would end up speaking only to ourselves. It is the policy of the C.S. Lewis Centre to try to speak from a base in sound scholarship, but in a manner that is accessible to a wide audience.

Much of the material here has been worked and reworked, in print and in the classroom, by many of the contributors over the years. This collection is therefore somewhat of a 'sampler' or a 'taster' in hope that the issues we raise will lead the reader to a search for a fuller and more satisfying scholarship than we are offering here. Therefore, in some cases, where the contributor has written more extensively on matters dealt with in the interviews or essays, readers are directed to such material (see also the Notes on the contributors, which also contains such information).

It would be dishonest, however, to pretend that even these generalist essays are easy to digest for everybody. They will be of most interest to those with some higher education; it is hoped, however, that their appeal will extend beyond those in the universities and seminaries to all who are concerned to understand the influence of modernism in the church today.

The contributors have been free to express their views within the boundaries of a broad trinitarian orthodoxy. In this respect, such a collection may offend those people who would want to see adopted here a much firmer constituency and confessional stance. So, for example, this book is not intended specifically to defend the principles of the Reformation (though a fair number of writers here would describe themselves as 'Reformed'). Neither is *Betraying the Gospel* an attempt to defend Catholicism, Eastern Orthodoxy or open such a broad constituency as Evangelicalism. Our distinguished writers write as communicators of the historic faith but from their own confessional stances. Clearly, also, some of the contributors would consider themselves more liberal than others. But the issue here is not are some authors more or less conservative: The issue is that men of good will and common concern for the gospel have come together to defend creedal Christianity against 'different gospels'.

Like Billy Graham in his foreword (p. 15) the C.S. Lewis Centre does not expect our readers to agree with everything written here. But if we had begged Prof T.F. Torrance not to offend some Evangelicals, or Prof Berry not to offend some Catholics, or perhaps again ask Prof Berger that he tone down his right-wing views and insist that Prof Heron say nothing to suggest that C.S. Lewis was not a brilliant New Testament scholar, then *Betraying the Gospel* would have ended up as nothing but bland, courteous but limp, friendly but without vigor.

When Christians take the risk of 'mucking in' together they must be prepared to dirty their hands. Those who are too 'pure' to join in will do what the pure always do—shout the odd from the touchline.

Not only did we think it improper to insist that our contributors agree on everything, but we thought it unrealistic, also, to try to insist that so many eminent scholars and churchmen should write to some predetermined level of popular writing. This means (in reference to the matter of 'digestibility' mentioned above) that some of the essays are more 'meaty' (or more difficult) than others. Furthermore, Professor Alan Torrance and Dr Gavin D'Costa were asked in particular to pay greater attention to detail in their essays (pp. 201-223 and pp. 224-242), as they deal with two major theological issues that have become of great concern to orthodox Christians in the last few years. Their knowledge of, sensitivity to and empathy with their respective subjects make their criticisms all the more devastating.

Where it is the case that material used here has appeared in print before and is reproduced here in an altered form, due acknowledgement has been made. Given the nature of the collection, the essays have been kept to below nine thousand words and footnotes have generally been avoided, relevant and essential bibliographical references being incorporated in the text according to a modified version of the Harvard system (on which see the separate explanatory note, p. 7).

The structure of *Betraying the Gospel* is divided between interviews with eminent churchmen from four different traditions and essays from leading or rising Christian scholars. (Our intention was to have five interviews, but unfortunately Lord Michael Ramsey, the former Archbishop of Canterbury, who had initially agreed to be interviewed, had to bow out because he felt too unwell to participate. The death of Lord Ramsey earlier in 1988 was a great loss to us all.) The interviews are reflections by elder statemen of Christendom upon the state of Christianity today. They lead on to a fuller treatment in the essays of aspects of historic Christianity and the significance of modernism of the contemporary Christian church.

We decided to subdivide the essays into two sections: The first section deals specifically with theological concerns, and the second and smaller section is an attempt to show that modernism has implications not only for academic theology but also for the church and the world. We have deliberately started these essays with a strong trinitarian affirmation, without which orthodox Christianity has no radical gospel for our contemporary world, and ended the collection with an assessment of the social factors involved in the growth of 'different gospels' which in its turn issues a call to distinguish the true gospel from its contemporary alternatives, and to maintain fidelity to it. (Readers who are disappointed that there is no evaluation of post-modernist theology in this section should take heart, for there will be a future C.S. Lewis Centre symposium on this racial development in theological thinking.)

My grateful thanks go to Metropolitan Anthony, Bishop Lesslie Newbigin, Professor Thomas F. Torrance and Cardinal Leon-Joseph Suenens, who allowed me to invade their homes and their privacy in order to conduct the interviews. Their hospitality was most appreciated.

I would also like to thank the many members of the advisory board of the C.S. Lewis Centre who have contributed to this volume, and in so doing have demonstrated their commitment to the recovery of our historic faith.

Special thanks must go to David Mackinder, who works as a free-lance religious books editor and is now a member of the editorial board of the C.S. Lewis Centre. His expertise, both theological and editorial, was invaluable in bringing this collection together into its final form.

FOREWORD

Billy Graham

It is entirely fitting that this significant collection of essays, committed to defending some of the essential beliefs of the historic Christian faith and their implications for our lives, is being published under the auspices of a research centre which is named after one of the twentieth century's most articulate and perceptive Christians.

C.S. Lewis was truly a remarkable individual—brilliant scholar and professor, renowned science fiction and fantasy writer, sensitive observer of the human scene, close friend and colleague of some of his generation's best-known literary figures. First and foremost, however, Lewis was a Christian, deeply committed to Jesus Christ and profoundly convinced that only in Christ 'are hidden all the treasures of wisdom and knowledge ... For in Christ all the fulness of the Deity lives in bodily form' (Col 2:3, 9).

As is well known, Lewis had not always held those convictions; *Surprised by Joy* (Lewis 1955), his personal chronicle of his long pilgrimage from atheism through agnosticism to faith in Christ, has deservedly taken its place among the classics of Christian autobiography. Like Augustine and countless others before him, once Lewis had become convinced of the truth of the gospel he knew there was no turning back, and that the formidable intellectual gifts God had given him must now be used solely for the glory of God. From his pen came a steady stream of incisive works which sought to explain and defend the central truths of historic Christianity. A major concern became the communication of the gospel to those who rejected it, or who at least did not understand it. He also accurately perceived the threat to biblical

Christianity from philosophies and theologies which claimed to be
Christian but were in fact thoroughly secular, and he sought—
without being vitriolic or arrogant—to counteract their influence
through his writings.

I vividly remember having lunch with him in Cambridge
during one of my several visits to the university where he was
professor. I went, frankly, with some trepidation; what could I
possibly say to someone of such rare genius? And yet he made me
feel at ease the moment we met. My overwhelming memory is that
he was one of the most genuinely humble and unassuming men I
have ever met. The gospel's truth clearly had touched not only his
mind but his heart and life—as it must with all who truly follow
Christ.

Since his death in 1963—the same day President John F.
Kennedy was assassinated—C.S. Lewis' influence has grown
dramatically. In fact, I think he probably would be a bit embar-
rassed (and surprised) at the number of people today who would
claim him as their intellectual and spiritual mentor. His books have
been translated into a number of languages and continue to sell at
a rapid rate. The small community where I live has its C.S. Lewis
Society; a nearby high school regularly performs plays based on
some of Lewis' works.

Beyond that, however, Lewis has become one of the truly
ecumenical figures of our generation—a Christian for all Christians. Lewis refused to be pigeon-holed into any single denomina-
tional or traditional stereotype. Instead, his goal was to return to
the core of the historic Christian faith—to God's revelation of
himself in Jesus Christ and in the pages of the Bible. As a result
he has appealed increasingly to Christians who come from a wide
spectrum of backgrounds, but who share his concern to defend the
Christian faith, especially in the face of militant secularism and
antisupernatural philosophies.

This concern is clearly mirrored in the following collection of
essays, drawing as it does upon theologians from several countries
and many church traditions who, in spite of their differences,
nevertheless see themselves as those who stand for the foundational truths of the gospel. Since it is a diverse collection, no reader
will fully agree with everything that is said here. But that must not

divert us from the significance of their effort.

The importance of this book lies in the common commitment of its contributors to explain and defend intelligently 'the faith that was once for all entrusted to the saints' (Jude 3). In an age marked by confusion and doubt and the clash of competing ideologies, the timeless truth of the gospel of Jesus Christ—the *euangelion*—needs to be proclaimed with clarity and boldness as never before. We read of the apostles that 'Day after day, in the temple courts and from house to house, they never stopped teaching and proclaiming the good news that Jesus is the Christ' (Acts 5:42). As individual Christians we may be called by the Holy Spirit to different tasks within the body of Christ, and we may use many different methods of declaring the gospel. But the essential message has not changed, nor has the mandate to 'go and make disciples of all nations' (Matthew 28:19). May this volume confront each reader with the message of the living Christ, and the mandate to follow him and declare his truth to our world.

I commend the work of the C.S. Lewis Centre as it seeks to defend and elucidate the historic Christian faith. This volume is a worthy step toward that goal.

INTRODUCTION

Andrew Walker

Orthodoxy and modernism

We live in a fashionable age. In the 1960s we were all tempted to become liberals. The temptation in the late 1980s and into the 1990s is to become conservatives. There is, perhaps, a tendency for most of us as we get older to regret the follies of our youth. Getting older often seems to bring a reaction; two well-known examples would be Wordsworth and Dosto-yevsky, who both took reactionary directions in later life.

If we are Christians, however, all fashions – both liberal and conservative – come under the judgement of the gospel. It has always taken discernment to look beneath the surface texture of reality in order to read aright the 'signs of the times'. In the light of the gospel, we have sometimes been called to stand firm against prevailing philosophies and intel-lectual movements that are not only against the Christian church but also against humanity.

Who can now doubt that Fascism, for example, was one of the greatest evils of the modern era? And yet in the 1930s many saw it as a useful bulwark against Bolshevism. Lloyd George, that great champion of parliamentary reform, even praised Hitler (as did so many Americans) for his successful policy of full employment. Nobel prize-winners such as Lenard and Stark joined the Nazi Party in the 1920s and supported the doctrines of Nordic racial superiority. British intellectuals such as D. H. Lawrence became enamoured with the pseudo-psychology of German fascism, praising the superiority of 'blood knowledge' over rational enquiry (Lawrence 1961). And in the very heartland of the Protestant Reformation, in the Lutheran church itself, Bishop Müller and other senior churchmen of the German national church were to deny the humanity of Jesus by taking away his Jewishness and sub-stituting in its place an unreal and docetic flesh that owed more to the milk-and-water Jesus of Wagner's antisemitic imagination than to the Christ of the New Testament.

It is easier than we like to admit to get carried along by the current tide of intellectual and political fashions.

We are, of course, all immersed in a culture, and cannot step outside of human language and society in order to understand it more objectively. Living in the modern world as we do, however, we *can* step outside our contemporary culture in the sense of moving out of the dominant secularist worldview of our advanced industrial nations and into an alternative *weltanschauung*. Recently, for example, Allan Bloom has analysed the subjectivity and relativism of American society from the standpoint of classicism (Bloom 1988), and Gabriel Josipovichi has brilliantly viewed the modern novel from the perspective of the medieval artist (Josipovichi 1971).

In this collection of essays we are approaching the modern world, and in particular modernist thought in theology, from the standpoint of Christian orthodoxy. To do so is to run the risk not only of being accused of being part of the fashionable trend towards conservativism in the West but also of being antiquarian and reactionary. There is no doubt that every age is capable of romanticising the past, and nostalgia for a supposedly stable history is never far away from any of us. But moderns are particularly prone to the converse of this prob-lem. C. S. Lewis called it 'chronological snobbery' (Lewis 1955:166) – the tacit acceptance that all modern thought and development of the present is superior to the past simply because it is new. Indeed the thrust behind modernism is the commitment to the belief that one can step outside of tradition and submit it to a rigorous critical rationality.

Strictly speaking, it is not necessary for Christians to

assume that modernist thought is always destructive. While it can be relativistic and inimical to the timeless truths of the gospel, it need not always be so. I say this because, according to the *Oxford English Dictionary*, modernism is 'a tendency or movement towards modifying traditional beliefs and doctrines in accordance with the findings of modern criticism and research'. It follows, therefore, that there is modernist art, architecture, music and literature, as well as modernist theology. They do not always have to be intrinsically bad just because they are not traditional, any more than new things are good by virtue of their newness. Classicism in philosophy and architecture is not the literal embodiment of eternal verities, nor, necessarily, even their reflection! If we understand modernism as that tendency to modify traditions in the light of post-Enlightenment thinking, then it follows that there are very few of us who are not modernist in some way or other. Indeed our universities, Bible colleges and seminaries have been enhanced by a more careful and critical attention to biblical and traditional texts.

Christian theology is not, however, predicated upon naturalistic philosophical methods or empirical enquiry, but upon revelation. The dogmas of faith are not the product of experimentation, phenomenological hermeneutics or probability theory: they are the expressed and *cataphatic*[1] certainties of the historic church (though I would want to add that there are also mystical certainties, which cannot be expressed in the language of creeds). These certainties have come to light as a result of the illumination of the Holy Spirit upon the revelation of God's person and purposes for all humankind as found in the sacred texts of the Old and New Testaments.

Such a statement is of course immediately problematic if one is a modernist. It would be a meaningless statement from a logical positivist position, for example, for it is neither a statement open to empirical verification nor does it contain any symbolic (mathematical or tautological) propositions.

[1] From the Greek *kataphatekē*, meaning here that which can be affirmed (positively said).

(Even without taking a positivistic approach to language, it contains all kinds of words and ideas that are difficult to deal with if one is modern: see what Hegel makes of 'spirit' in *The Phenomenology of Mind* (1807), for example, or how Durkheim deals with the notion of the sacred in *The Elementary Forms of Religious Life* (1915).

But now here comes the rub. Given that modernism by definition wants to scrutinise and criticise *all* traditional ways of thinking and expression – and modernism is no respecter of confessions, for all historic and traditional commitments are grist to its critical mill – is there any way we can critically evaluate modernist thought from the perspective of historic Christianity?

One thing we can do is to participate in the process of critical evaluation itself. And this collection of essays is partly a response to modernism in a rational and critical way (see in particular the contributions by T. F. Torrance, Lesslie Newbigin, Keith Ward, R. J. Berry, Alan Torrance and Gavin D'Costa). We can even go further, and utilise modernistic methods themselves in order to assert the historical reliability of the gospels (see James Dunn's essay). This may be going too far for some Eastern Orthodox and conservative evangelicals, but the point being made here is that even on modern critical grounds there is still much to be said in defence of orthodoxy. There is, however, an infinite critical regress in modernism, because there is always a further step of analysis to take (always another 'second order' view).

And so, standing within the historic Christian tradition, as all the contributors to this volume do, we want to demonstrate our commitment to go beyond rational critiques of our culture and modern thought forms – as necessary and as useful as they are – and confront modernity (our advanced societies) with the gospel. In this sense *Betraying the Gospel* is propagandist: it proclaims the great truths of the apostolic faith from the Trinity (see the essays by Tom Smail and Colin Gunton) to the incarnation and resurrection of our Lord (see Alister McGrath's essay).

Under the imperative of the historic Christian gospel, many

of us feel that we need to say that something has gone desperately wrong with our post-Enlightenment culture (T. F. Torrance, Lesslie Newbigin, Keith Ward, Alasdair Heron, Colin Gunton, Gavin D'Costa and Alan Torrance all address this issue). This is not to say that we do not recognise the Enlightenment's great achievements, but it is to say that we also believe that by the light of the gospel and Christian tradition we can see some of its dark sides too. To say, however, that we stand within the historic tradition needs some clarification (though no justification) before we look a little more closely at the Enlightenment.

Mere Christianity

As I said earlier (p. 22), modernism is no respecter of confessions. The universal threat of modernism creates its own ecumenical imperative for us: we find, Christians everywhere, that what is under attack in modernity is not Catholicism, evangelicalism, or any particular denominationalism. What is under attack is the very bedrock of *all* Christianity. It is the great foundational truths of the faith that are feeling the impact of modernist critiques: the incarnation, the resurrection, God as Trinity, the miraculous, the Bible as a sacred text, the concept and reality of revelation.

It would be ridiculous to suggest that the Christian church has always been faithful to the historic tradition 'once delivered'. It has constantly reneged on the gospel, seemingly preferring schism to unity. But what we are beginning to recognise today is that while it is true that Christianity has failed to hold together, it has, at least until the modern era, clearly shown a family resemblance, even though the family has been divided and separated. The scars of the Reformation were too deep for Protestants and Catholics to recognise just how close together they were in many ways (see, for example, the comments about devotional literature in the essay by Peter Toon and Graham Leonard). And the separation of Greek East from Latin West exaggerated the differences between the two halves of what was in ecclesial reality and eucharistic solidarity the true ecumenical church during the first Christian millennium.

But of course our historical divisions have not been only matters of prejudice, triumphalism and a failure to repent of schism (though they have so often been the spiritual causes of disruption): there have been matters of principle at stake. The Eastern Orthodox churches, for example, believed that the bishop of Rome could be considered *primus inter pares* in the Christian church, but not the overlord of the other bishops of the ancient sees. Protestantism in the sixteenth century was a revolt against the corruption of late medieval Catholicism, but it was more than merely a protest against practices: it was a concern (like the earlier Great Schism, though for different reasons) with the question of authority in the church.

Yet we find that nearly all the great historic disagreements between East and West, Catholic and Protestant, were on issues of *theologuemena* (theological opinions of great importance, but not of crucial dogmatic significance).[1] Perhaps, or so the Orthodox believe, this evaluation does not cover the still unresolved East/West dispute concerning the person and function of the Holy Spirit within the divine Trinity (the notorious *Filioque* debate, on which see the comments in Tom Smail's essay), but it does cover the majority of disagreements within Christendom. This is not to say that we do not hold passionately to our theological opinions. The creeds, for example, say nothing about the devil; neither do they tell us whether baptism is only for adults or is for children as well; nor, like the Bible itself, do they outline an inerrant theory of scripture (though they obviously reflect a 'high' view). Disparate views on ecclesiology, sacraments and authority continue to divide historic Christendom, and will probably continue to do so until the parousia. Nevertheless, our divisions and hot disagreements sometimes blind us to the fact that we have inherited together a common apostolic faith.

Never has there been a time in Christian history when it has

---

[1] And there were more issues still, that can best be described as involving 'pious opinions'.

been more vital to rediscover and reaffirm this common heritage. Not the catholicism of the Latin West or the Greek East, but the common credal truths of the historic church which all 'right-believing' Christians – Protestants, Orthodox and Catholics – recognise as the foundations of Christianity. The Reformers of Protestant Europe, for example, accepted not only the truth of sola scriptura but also the great dogmatic formulations of the early councils of the church. Luther was particularly anxious to show that he was recovering the authentic catholic tradition. Certainly it was the case that both he and Calvin accepted the Christology of Chalcedon and the Nicene and so-called Apostles' Creeds. Both Luther and Calvin, like the Puritan Divines, Hooker and Owen, loved the fathers of the early church. John and Charles Wesley, too, were closer to St Augustine and St Basil than ever they were to the new philosophers of their own century.

In the twentieth century, C.S. Lewis, in his great apologetical work Mere Christianity (1952), has insisted that there is a common path of Christianity that pilgrims down the ages have trod in the certainty that they were on firm ground. This ground was for Lewis the high road of basic orthodoxy, the great viaduct of Christendom that proudly and surely has spanned the changes and uncertainties of the centuries. Christians – mere Christians – can recognise each other on the way, and while they may argue and fail to agree on many matters, they are nevertheless travellers together on 'the main road'.

It is this vision which has given birth to the C.S. Lewis Centre. It is the same vision which captured the imagination of many of the advisers to the Centre who agreed to contribute to Betraying the Gospel Many of the scholars and eminent churchmen represented in these interviews and essays would not typically appear together between the same book covers. That they have done so is a recognition (a) that things have become so serious both in our modern culture and in our churches that we must pull together for the sake of the gospel, and (b) that we can do so in integrity because we allow each other to be ourselves, with all our unresolved and historical differences. This, then, is ecumenism, but it is not uniformity. It is togetherness for the common cause, but not compromise of cherished beliefs. What we are aiming to do, quite simply, is to speak from within the historic tradition to our contemporary world.

There is no commitment within the C. S. Lewis Centre to a lifeless formalised tradition, for without the infusion of holiness and a spiritual theology tradition is no more than dry bones. At the launch of the C. S. Lewis Centre in London in October 1987, Metropolitan Anthony in a written message said: 'Too often we hear arguments between modernists and ultra-traditionalists in all our churches. Arguments between a politically or ideologically coloured "theology" and a blind holding on to an unthinking observance of the *letter* rather than the spirit of the law lead nowhere.'

The modern world needs the proclamation of the good news and the presence of the Spirit, not medieval scholasticism or outmoded metaphysics. As Bishop Newbigin pointed out in his *The Other Side of 1984*, there can be no going back behind the Enlightenment, as if it had never happened (Newbigin 1983). We need to recapture the wonder of the Bible as a sacred text that speaks to us of God and from God through the Spirit (see Peter Toon and Graham Leonard's essay, and the essay by Alasdair Heron), but it is unlikely that we can return to an innocence that has not yet tasted of the tree of critical knowledge. A simplistic fundamentalism, with all its hallmarks of triumphalism and anti-intellectualism, will always find itself a role in modernity because it brings certainties into a world that has lost its way. But it will fail to capture the 'main road' of Christendom if it ignores the common ('mere') Christianity that is present in the historic churches as well as many of the newer ones. (Billy Graham, by contrast, has become the respected statesman and transdenominational evangelist that he is because he has appealed to mere Christians among Baptist churches, among Catholics in Poland and among Orthodox in Russia.)

Fundamentalists may rule media empires and create separatist enclaves and political caucuses, but they will not defeat the undoubted and proven power of modernism by ignoring it. They may rail – and rightly so – against 'secular humanism' from their worldly electronic stations, but modernism will never be overthrown without confronting the 'mind-set' that has become concretised in the institutions and ideologies of modernity. (The Holy Spirit wants to transform our minds as well as change our hearts.) It is this 'mind-set' – this unexamined 'fiduciary framework' – that we have inherited from the Enlightenment and which in its modernist guise stands over and against the church.

The Enlightenment and modernism

One of the problems with the word 'modernism' is that it evokes notions of contemporaneity or, at least, recent history. When people talk about liberalism in the church, for example, they tend to identify it with the recent liberalising tendencies in the larger society. In the 1960s, during the so-called 'permissive' era, when there were so many changes in social, moral and sexual behaviour, it seemed to some Christians then as if this new liberalism had spilt over into the church. This was the view in America with the publication of Thomas Altizer's *The Gospel of Christian Atheism* (1966) and his *Radical Theology and the Death of God* (1966), written with W. Hamilton, and also in England, in 1963, with the *succes de scandale* of John Robinson's *Honest To God*.

But in fact Robinson's book was a popular and bastardised pastiche of Rudolf Bultmann's demythologising theology, which had been around since the Second World War (Bultmann 1960). Altizer's thesis was even older, being an extreme (and rather silly) extension of nineteenth-century kenoticism (the renunication of the divine nature).

More recently, in the 1980s, some conservative evangelicals in Britain were up in arms over the BBC's *Sea of Faith* series and Independent Television's *Jesus: The Evidence*, as if the devil had suddenly been let loose on an unsuspecting British public with a clutch of new heresies with which to bamboozle the faint-hearted and weak-minded (see Cupitt 1984 and Wilson 1984). It may very well be that television is more devilish than meets the eye (see Walker 1987: ch. 6), but the theology that was expounded in those programmes was neither new nor did it represent mainstream academic theology. What it did do, like so much of modernist theology, was to rework themes in nineteenth-century liberalism (in the sense of the German school of Ritschl and his followers). These themes are themselves predicated upon Enlightenment presuppositions. Michael Goulder has rightly said that 'we are driving over the same course as our eighteenth-century forefathers, only at four times the speed' (Goulder & Hick 1983: 88).

It is perhaps a sobering thought that modernism began some three hundred years ago, yet this sobriety will help us to see that there is no new crisis in theology and the Christian faith, in the sense that some flood of alien gospels has suddenly and unexpectedly burst upon us. What has happened is less dramatic but perhaps more damaging. We have all been caught in a flow-tide of change that has gradually but relentlessly eroded traditional and historic Christianity (the rhythmic lapping of the waves gently lulling us to sleep). Today we are waking up and seeing that the erosion of the centuries has worn away much of our heritage until we now find ourselves cut back to the bare rock – the foundations – of the faith.

For some of us the shock of being awakened from our somnambulism and seeing for the first time the situation as it really is has had the same (and sobering) effect as if we really had just been caught in the icy deluge of strange gospels.

If we want to turn the tide (and not merely swim against it, as Keith Ward has recently suggested we may be doing, Ward 1986), we have to realise that we are called to 'earnestly contend for the faith' through mission and evangelism not only to our people but also to our culture. The presuppositions of our modern thought need to be baptised and cleansed in an altogether different fountainhead and we must stem the poison streams flowing from the Enlightenment itself.

Of course we must acknowledge that there are 'healing waters' and life-giving tributaries that flow from that great source of modern knowledge also (see Colin Gunton's essay): the Enlightenment is not the origin of all our ills any more than it is the watershed of all that is good in modernity. No doubt many of us are glad that we are living on this side of the Enlightenment. Not only has it brought us critical tools that have helped us to understand the universe and our social world more richly, it has also brought with it a new and vital vision of freedom and autonomy for human beings. The Enlightenment offered us the chance to be free from a 'moral law' imposed from above, outside and against ourselves. It seemed to offer us freedom from a God who throughout the Middle Ages had become increasingly autocratic and dictatorial. (The loving Father had become identified with absolute monarchy, and despite the Reformation some Puritan versions of Calvinism had turned the monarch into lawgiver and judge, stern and unapproachable – law preceded grace and the *pantokrator* superseded Christ, the suffering and redemptive servant.)

But tragically, as Colin Gunton's essay demonstrates, the desire for freedom did not free us to be ourselves, rather it led to a more terrible tyranny: the insistence – the demand – that we be free to control our own destiny, knowledge and morality. Is not the Enlightenment another bright Eden where again, dazed by the glittering angel, we believe with all our hearts that we can 'shuffle off this mortal coil' and be as the gods? So, for example, the deists of the late eighteenth century cast the transcendent and holy God out of the heavens and immanentised him in nature or history. It seemed better to bring God down to earth, or to heel, making him one of us, or we part of him, than to tolerate his radical otherness. (Is not this Hegel's solution to what he saw to be the tyranny of God? See p. 190).

The freedom to be ourselves is indeed a gift from God, but to be free is not to free ourselves from him like the prodigal

son, who demanded his inheritance from his father as a right
(a right which was not his to claim, as the father was not yet
dead). The language of rights becomes, after the Enlightenment, both the demand for justice and the demand for
autonomy. The demand for autonomy, to be free from God,
is also a demand to be free of each other, to be our 'own man',
free of community restraints and fellowships. The language
of rights is the assertion of individualism (at least for Kant
and Locke in Europe and Franklin and Jefferson in the
New American Republic). And so the failure to find a
personal bond between the collective and the individual
has been one of the dominant problems in advanced
industrial societies, both socialist and capitalist (again,
see Colin Gunton's essay, and the comments in Alan
Torrance's essay about the individual and the community,
pp. 218-223).

To identify freedom as both a positive gift of the Enlightenment and yet also a gift that is tainted with a strident and
selfish assertionism is to recognise that good and evil are often
poured out together upon the world. To return to our earlier
extended metaphor, we can say that the healing and poison-
ous streams from the Enlightenment flow out together, but by
their very nature cannot join up together. And it is here that
we detect the dualistic flow of thought that has provided
both the greatness and the destructiveness of our modern
era.

It is a truism that much classical thought attempted a
unitary grasp of realities (see the interview with Tom Torrance). The macrocosm and microcosm of Neoplatonism and
the eternal verities of Aristotelianism were common features
of medieval scholasticism. But if we take an example from
traditional Christology, we can see here that Christians
faced with the absolute otherness of God and his radical
separation from his creatures nevertheless saw that in
the incarnation something unique, miraculous, hitherto
thought impossible had happened: spirit and matter, otherness and givenness, knowing and unknowing, subject and
object were integrated into one indivisible unity. Putting it

more theologically: God and man, creator and creature, joined together without confusion in the person of Jesus of Nazareth.

Post-Enlightenment thought cannot conceive of (nor permit) such a unity, for it operates with a dualistic concept of reality: that which can be known in the phenomenal world (science and self-conscious knowledge), and that which exists in the noumenal world (of ideas) but which cannot be known objectively. Such a radical dualism, exemplified by Kant's *Critique of Pure Reason* (1787), leaves traditional metaphysics in one realm and history, experience and matter in another. At a stroke Jesus is torn apart, leaving us with his historical location and humanity to be investigated in the phenomenal world but banishing his divinity to an unknown and unknowable shadowland of ideas.

It is no coincidence that the rush to find the historical (and hence truly authentic) Jesus had its heyday in the nineteenth century and still features in twentieth-century modernism (see, for example, Cupitt 1979). And so (as T. F. Torrance says, p. 61) since the Enlightenment we have a world 'split in two', a world in which we have both a measurable and quantifiable universe open to scientific investigation and a world which is not measurable, not quantifiable. In the unmeasurable world (later positivists were to say the meaningless world) room is made for faith, feeling, subjectivity, opinion and traditional metaphysics. In the empirical, measurable world there is no room for miracles, revelation or divinity. Such a dualism renders patristic thought untenable (see Alasdair Heron's essay, p. 142), and with it the unitary thrust of Christian orthodoxy.

If Kant's thought led to the severing of the umbilical cord that bound the noumenal and the phenomenal, the majority of the writers in that by now notorious book *The Myth of God Incarnate* (Hick 1977) were simply following through that fatal manoeuvre to its final and deadly conclusion (see Alister McGrath's essay): God is not after all joined to his creatures in solidarity and love (though Hick, like others before him, is quite happy for God to be in all of us as long as he is neither radically other than us nor uniquely joined to humanity in the person of Jesus).

But also stemming from Kant we do not merely inherit a dualism that divides physics from metaphysics, measurability from immeasurability: we inherit a commitment to what Kant (*Critique of Practical Reason*, 1788) wants to call *autonomy*. This is the arena of thought and action which is under our personal control and the only sphere in which faith, moral actions and practical reasoning can legitimately be exercised. *Heteronomy*, on the other hand, Kant saw as objectivised reality over and against our freedom as rational and autonomous beings. It is not to be seen as synonymous with the noumenal world (though they often overlap) because it is *any* source of knowledge external to ourselves. Heteronomy could be the dogmas of Christianity, the systematic metaphysics of a Thomas Aquinas, or the laws of natural science in the phenomenal realm.

And so, by implication, Kant's severance of the noumenal from the phenomenal, and his insistence that we should look for morality and faith in ourselves (autonomy), cut Christianity off from the objective revelation of God in Christ and raised the issue that the scriptures themselves are over and against us until we assent to them and make them our own. Kant remained a rationalist and an idealist, but in opposing autonomy to heteronomy he opened up the possibility that faith for us may now be predicated upon experience, personal moralism, self-consciousness, emotion or will, but certainly not on outmoded (and now cut off) metaphysics and tradition. And it is the 'father of modern theology', Schleiermacher (1821), who, accepting Kant's strictures on the noumenal world, and yet wishing to avoid a purely phenomenalist and heteronomous (empiricist and external) basis for knowledge, opts to build a modern systematic theology on experience rather than revelation (see Gavin D'Costa's essay, p. 238).

Modernist theology proper takes its assumptions from Kant, Schleiermacher and Hegel (see Colin Gunton's essay, p. 191). Hegel at least saw the problem inherent in Kantian dualism. He attempted to describe the whole of reality as a synthesis of the objective and the subjective, the metaphysical and the historical. Dialectic was an attempt to articulate the necessary harmony of these apparent oppositions. As Gunton points out, however (p. 190), Hegel takes the radical otherness of God and brings him into history as the *geist* of progress who, like some Platonic demiurge, seeks to realise himself by coming to be. Conversely, we find that we creatures, pictured as separated from God by nature in the Christian schema of salvation, are now ourselves capable of divinity, not because of what God in Christ has done for us but because we are potentially (if not intrinsically) divine: we too can become part of the divine by virtue of being caught up in the process of the laws of history (heteronomy) in their movement to their utopian consummation.

Tragically Hegel, the apostle of freedom and synthesis, bound us, as Kierkegaard saw only too plainly, to a philosophy of unfreedom where men and women are subject to the iron laws of history. As every sociologist and student of socialism knows, Marx tried to turn Hegel on his head and ground his metaphysics in the concrete world of economy and society (but he could never shake off his Hegelianism): the totalitarianism of Marxist systems is inextricably bound up with the totalitarianism of Hegelian metaphysics.

But if Hegel at least saw the problem of the Enlightenment, it has been more typical in modernity that philosophical and theological thought have tended to oscillate between heteronomy and autonomy. Kantian dualism led to the horns of a dilemma, and few besides Hegel have attempted to grasp them both. Various thinkers have either tried to hold on to an idealism 'out there', despite Kant's strictures on the noumenal (the English idealist T. H. Green comes to mind), or more typically to the heteronomy of science. The positivism of Comte and the mechanistic determinism of Bernard probably had more of an effect on nineteenth-century thought (outside of Germany) than did Hegelianism. Positivism and what elsewhere I have called scientism (Walker 1987: ch. 7) squeeze out free will and human imagination from reality and replace them with laws of nature. In this respect positivism bound humankind by the iron laws of nature every bit as much as men and women were bound by the inexorable unfolding laws of Marxist history.

Science was so powerful because it was both phenomenalist (in the Kantian sense I have outlined here) and a source of dogmatic truths. Its very objectivity (its facticity and measurability) pushed the noumenal world even further away from consciousness. And yet the modernist search for authenticity from Schleiermacher onwards has tended to ignore heteronomy and ground its truth in experience and self-consciousness. Existentialism and Heideggerian (and Husserlian) phenomenology would be paradigm examples of this approach, though we also find both Ritschl in Germany and Tolstoy in Russia falling back upon moralism (albeit a moralism stripped of revelational and supernaturalist truths) in their search for authentic faith.

In practice what has happened in all areas of intellectual thought, but particularly in theology, is that scholars have tended to accept the heteronomy of science and taken it as given (how mechanistic and absolute was Rudolf Bultmann's trust in science, for example). Having accepted that side of the Kantian dualism they then turn to autonomy (to the subjective sphere) in order to deal with those other issues of faith and destiny, morals, and beliefs, about which science has nothing to say (see R. J. Berry's essay). Kantian dualism really has the upper hand here, because although the objective reality of science is accepted without question (because it is within the phenomenal sphere), the objectivity of, say, moral law is rejected out of hand as irredeemably lost in the cast-off noumenal universe. The noumenal now seems to be a sort of alternative cosmos where the outdated intellectual furniture of pre-critical days drifts aimlessly in conceptual space: a little scholasticism here, some patristics over there, and in the far distance the outmoded dogmatics of Chalcedon.

Heteronomy is dangerous and leads to unfreedom and tyranny; but autonomy, lacking any objective standard, is not only obviously subjective but is also open to the possibility of anarchy and nihilism. Once heteronomy is rejected, autonomy runs the risk of being seen as inauthentic – an illegitimate attempt to impose a subjective meaning on a meaningless universe. At best, finding itself free from the constraints and laws of heteronomy, autonomy can find no common ground for human society and morality. Autonomy (as we have seen) is really a recipe for individualism, and it is no coincidence that the Kantian dualism also splits the individual from the larger community (see Colin Gunton's essay, pp. 193-194).

If to our other dualisms we were to add the division between mind and body that we find in Descartes, that precursor of the Enlightenment, we would perhaps be adding more dualisms than we can cope with in such a short space (though do see Alan Torrance's essay, pp. 218-223)! But we ought at least to recognise that modernist theology is in thrall to the dualistic agenda of Enlightenment thought. Schleiermacher, Ritschl and Bultmann, for example, are theologians of the autonomous, but they also genuflect to the heteronomy of science. Liberation theology, too, is in danger of veering towards heteronomy (see Alan Torrance's essay), though, as with the process theology of Hartshorne (1941), we can see here a tacit Hegelianism: progress through becoming in history.

Ironically it could be argued that biblical fundamentalism may itself be modernistic,[1] for it no longer treats the Bible with the unitary sensitivity with which the early fathers approached their Christology and the scriptures (as well as Lesslie Newbigin's and T. F. Torrance's interviews, see Alasdair Heron's essay). For the fathers the Word made flesh was both truly human and divine, and so was the New Testament. The word of God in some nineteenth-century conservative evangelical circles, however, comes dangerously close to being divinely dictated notes, with virtually no human interference: the scriptures become a version of positivism where reality is just read off without due exercise of the imagination, human engagement with the text, or divine inspiration. Today in the United States the cult of Reconstructionism (Clapp 1987) and

---

[1] Fundamentalists, unlike modernists *per se*, are basically orthodox; but the question arises: Is inerrancy a dogmatic question or one of *theologoumena*?

many literalist forms of dispensationalism smack more of
heteronomy than of autonomy. (What on earth would the
Reformers John Wesley and Jonathan Edwards make of modern
dispensationalist theories of history?)

Perhaps one could argue that while this talk of dualism and
modernity is all very well for intellectuals, it really has little or
no relevance for the ordinary man or woman in the pew. But, on
the contrary, it does. Dualistic patterns of thought permeate the
whole of our culture, not just our universities. We see a passionate concern for human rights and justice in our societies,
but from what does it stem? What common standards of
morality or rules of evidence can be evoked? Some people insist
on public morality – and we still have a sort of civil religion that
insists on a penal code and acceptable rules of behaviour
(though jurisprudence seems to be moving away from natural
law to precedents these days). But there seem to be no agreed
standards of moral behaviour in private life.

I think that the public/private split in our modern societies
is analogous to Kant's heteronomy/autonomy split. (But I do not
mean to suggest here that there is any logical relationship
between these two – more what Max Weber would have called
an 'elective affinity'.) Public life is for society – which is seen
to have its own 'needs' and functional prerequisites – and
private life is for the self-fulfilment of individuals.

The public world is that objectified world 'out there'; it is
a world of government, bureaucracies, work and institutions. It
is a world of legal and rational activity, as exemplified in the
banking system, city finance and the forces of law and order.

On the other hand there is the private world of leisure,
the family, church, and voluntary associations. Here individual autonomy rules. Personal preferences, private
moralities, relativistic philosophies and traditional beliefs
jostle for attention. But this autonomous province is the land
of opinion, not truth. The familiar riposte 'But that's just
your opinion' is a tacit acceptance that one opinion is as good
as another and that truth (in the autonomous world at least,
if not in the law courts!) means 'your truth' but not necessarily 'my truth'. Subjective relativism dominates in this world, so

that it becomes taboo to insist that a truth such as the Christian gospel transcends our many versions of reality and truth-telling (although the taboo does not mind you holding such an opinion so long as no absolutist claims are made for it! See, in this regard, Gavin D'Costa's treatment of the presuppositions of pluralism). Different gospels, we need to remember, have their social origins as well as their intellectual ones (see Peter Berger's essay).

It goes without saying that all the above remarks on modernist dualisms are worthy of a thousand qualifications. To offer a general account is inevitably to speak in generalisations that need grounding in further scholarship and more specialised study. One of the causes of modernistic dominance, however, is brought about by the separation of scholars into discrete and neat territories (see Alasdair Heron's comments on this in his essay, pp. 158-159). In this respect I do not agree with the comment of the Dean of Salisbury, when he said that 'we have come to the end of Renaissance man' (Newbigin 1983:1) – he has been moribund for a long time. The Enlightenment has not in fact been a flowering of a high and rounded culture. We have moved in two directions at once, as befits a dualistic and bifurcated community. On the one hand we now live in the age of the specialist. In theology, like science itself, we are trained in different methods and totally different presuppositions; is it so surprising that we Christians are so divided in our faith when we do not even share a common language? The age of specialism has become so complex and compartmentalised that the Renaissance figure who was deeply grounded in all aspects of intellectual thought and cultural knowledge is now probably an impossibility.

On the other hand the need for the intellectual generalist has become even more urgent in a world of a thousand specialities than ever it was for the aristocratic dilettantes of the eighteenth century. So modern society has responded with the polyglot and smatterer (see Solzhenitsyn's article 'The Smatterers' in Solzhenitsyn 1976). The mass media and journalism now use the language of 'speakeasy' in order to offer the general public – who now share little culture in common in the pluralist world in which we live – a kind of plastic Esperanto.

This collection of essays, coming as it does from different disciplines and from various theological standpoints, cannot pretend to form a unitary whole (or to be entirely free of smattering). We are ourselves heirs of the Enlightenment, and no doubt we too reflect the bifurcation of reality that dominates modernity. Nevertheless we are also 'mere Christians', and as such believe that there is a gospel that transcends the dualisms of our contemporary society and modernistic theology. In the light of this gospel it seems to many of us that we have expected too much from the Enlightenment. It is to be hoped that our culture has now become mature enough to sift the chaff from the wheat and to hold on to only that which is life-giving and to discard the rest. We must accept that we cannot go back to the innocence of Eden (back behind the Enlightenment); but on the other hand we must recall that the timeless truths of the gospel never call us to look back – they call us instead to look *up*. We cannot slink away to some illusory safety or allow ourselves to slouch towards a new secular order still waiting to be born (though we may be called to live through it). Neither do we have to plod worthily along for ever and ever (see Lesslie Newbigin's comments on pp. 58-59 of his interview) with existential grit and stoic determination: we who have heard and responded to the gospel of hope are marching to Zion.

Part One

INTERVIEWS

Interview with

METROPOLITAN ANTHONY OF SOUROZH

Andrew Walker: Metropolitan Anthony, you've been in England now since 1948, when you first came here as the Chaplain to the Fellowship of St Albans and St Sergius. That means that for forty years you've been in Britain and have obviously seen an extraordinary number of changes in Christianity since you've been here. On the whole, do you feel that these changes have been for the better or for the worse?

Metropolitan Anthony: My general impression is that it is for the worse.

On the one hand, society at large has become a great deal more secular. Not that it has acquired a secular ideology, but it could be defined a little in the way in which St Paul defined people by saying, 'Their god is their belly.' It is not a *new* theology, it is simply a lack of ideal, a lack of ideology, of faith.

But what I feel is much worse, is that the church, in order to try to keep within its boundaries as many people as possible – whether they are believers or half-believers, or no believers at all – has watered down its message to the point of no longer expressing the message of the gospel. And this, I feel, is a betrayal of Christ and a betrayal of the gospel, and also a failure to fulfil our mission, because it is not by a watered-down Christianity that one can save the world, it is by presenting *all* the message of Christ in all its majestic and awesome greatness, and also in its extraordinary *human* quality.

AW: I know that C. S. Lewis would often use the expression 'Christianity and water' as a means of saying that, for many years now, Christianity has been presented in a form which modern Christians seem to think secular people need. There is this idea, isn't there, that we need to 'make the gospel relevant'. Of course, Lewis' argument is that in trying to make it relevant we water it down. But what sort of examples of watered-down Christianity have you in mind?

MA: One could give a great many examples.

What strikes me most, because it is a more accessible example, is the attitude of so many theologians and preachers to the person of Christ. (Problems of trinitarian theology are far more remote from people's concrete perceptions, but the question about Christ is absolutely crucial.) Is Christ 'God become man' – true God and true man – or is he a remarkable man who in an allegorical sense was the Son of God more than anyone else is a son of God?

This question leads us a long way. On the one hand, if Christ is *not* the Son of God become the Son of Man, all the gospel falls, and the door is open to identifying the Christian message with all religious messages of the world – Christ becomes one of the many preachers or wise men. While, on the other hand, the crux of Christianity is our proclamation, our passionate conviction, that in Christ the fullness of the Godhead has abided in the flesh; that it is a historical event; that God has entered the world and is now in the world; that in a way, one may say, the end has already come with the incarnation, and we are expecting the end as a glorious advent of Christ at the end of time. (However, the end is not to be understood as a point in time, but as a fulfilment, and it is already there for us to see.) In Jesus we have got before us the only real true man, because to be real and true as a human being means to be at one with God; short of this we are subhuman.

AW: Do you feel, then, that many of the modern gospels – the watered-down gospels – simply do not have a gospel for modern man?

MA: No, I don't think they do have a gospel for modern man, because gospel means 'good news'. And what is the good news that one can find in watered-down Christianity?

When I discovered the gospel as a teenager, what struck me was that it is a message about God being so close, so deeply concerned with *us*, and also – simultaneously and inevitably – that man is so great. I'm reminded of the phrase of Angelus Silesius, who says that 'I am as great as God, God is as small as I' – and this is a vision of *man* as well as being a vision of God. And I feel that unless we have got an ideal that is vast enough, great enough, challenging enough, there is no point in having Christianity as one of the possible world outlooks.

AW: But of course what happens so often today is that you hear this sort of line: 'Well this is all very interesting, but it is extremely primitive. It's the sort of thing you could have talked about before the philosophical Enlightenment, but now that we live in a scientific age, when we know miracles don't occur, how can we possibly talk in this outdated metaphysical language?' When you hear those sorts of things, which I hear all the time, what sort of replies do you give?

MA: I don't know anything about metaphysical language. What we say about Christ is experiential. We could say, in the same terms as St Paul said, that we know the risen Christ. I know that God exists because I have *met* him. It is not a fairy tale or something I have inherited – or we have inherited – from our grandmothers, it's a personal experience about *knowing* him. And so it is as certain, to those of us who believe, as so many other things which are not rational but which are both reasonable and real. We do not speak of beauty or of love in other terms than we speak of God. It too is a direct experience. It *cannot* be proved. It is known only from within.

AW: Is there perhaps, as some people might say, a danger that if we overstress the experiential side of our faith, which is so important to us personally, we may make our experience the test of the authority of scripture?

MA: Of course there is a danger. The two must coincide.

The test of our experience is in the scriptures, not the other way round. But if the scriptures remain an ancient document which we examine (as one can examine old parchments and try to date them) without any way of relating to the event described, it remains a dead letter. While in the early Christian age, what is striking is that a message reached people indeed. Believing comes from hearing . . . but at the same time this hearing opened up the mind and the heart to an understanding.

I think that what is essential in the hearing – in the gospel, in the message of the apostles, in the message of the saints – is that it speaks truth that reaches us, and to which we can respond by saying, 'Yes, that *is* the truth; that *is* beauty; that *is* something which has disclosed to me a depth which I vaguely perceived within me, but which I could not comprehend; and there it is – opening up, light shining, something blossoming out – a victory of life and truth within me, which convinces me of what the gospel says.'

There is a passage in one of the ascetics of the early years of the church that says, 'If God himself stood before you and said do this or do that, yet if your heart could not say "Amen" to it, don't do it, because God does not need your doing, but the harmony that can be established between you and him.' (I'm not quoting exactly, but that is the thought.) And the message of the gospel, if it doesn't awake in us a sense of being *the* truth, is vain.

AW: All right, let's move on to something else.

If it is the case, as you have put it, that we are not really hearing the gospel today, but we are listening to watered-down gospels – gospels which are not really a gospel for modern man – what do you think is the way forward, given the fact that, of course, God has ways which we know not of? What do you think Christians should be doing in the face of these watered-down gospels?

MA: I believe there are two things.

The one is to go back to the gospel as it stands, and proclaim the gospel that was lived and manifested by Christ, seen and proclaimed by the apostles, and then by their disciples.

But there is also another side to it. St Paul already said that 'the name of Christ is reviled because of us', and when we look at the history of Christianity we can say that the Christian world has proclaimed and spoken of the gospel, at times with great eloquence and truth, but that at large the Christian world has not *lived* the gospel, and certainly not built a world that is worthy of the faith which we proclaim. And when we think that we are coming ever nearer to the two thousandth anniversary of Christianity, we can say that we have betrayed the gospel by the kind of world we have built, in *all* its parts.

AW: It is certainly true, I believe, that we have perhaps stressed 'orthodoxia', and not 'orthopraxia', to such an extent that people are not very impressed these days by our beliefs unless they can see something in our lives. In this respect, do you think it is perhaps the case that a great deal more emphasis needs to be given in the Christian life to holiness and prayer?

MA: I am quite certain of that.

I remember a saying, an old saying, of Christianity to the effect that no one can turn away from the secular world towards eternity if he has not seen in the eyes or in the face of at least one person the shining of eternal life. Also, I remember that in a broadcast made during the war C. S. Lewis said that when people see a believer, what they *should* say is, 'Look, statues are coming to life!' Well, we *are* statues – and not always the most beautiful ones – and yet people meeting *us* cannot say that here are beings of another world, possessed of another dimension than anyone else, which is a significant thing.

I'm not talking of trying to build a city of men that is more palatable or less monstrous than the one we have already built. The city of men which we are called to build should be coextensive to a city of God in which the first citizen should be Jesus of Nazareth, both God and man – vast enough, deep enough, to contain the whole of the divine mystery. And this is what we are not doing.

AW: Do you think that there has been too much emphasis on church unity on the basis of togetherness, and not enough emphasis on repentance? I say this because we hear a great deal about ecumenism in terms of trying to arrive at common statements of agreement, but do you think that what is needed more in a divided Christendom is for people to repent?

MA: I think that if you take the word 'repentance' in the way in which most people understand it, as bewailing one's past, instead of doing anything about one's present and future, it's not the kind of thing we need. But if by repentance you mean turning away from the twilight towards the light, turning Godwards and *moving* Godwards, then indeed we need repentance in that sense. And this can be done, as you said before, in terms of prayer, in terms of a deeper spiritual life, because it will direct us Godwards and it will be born of our communion with God.

To attempt unity on terms which are *less* than the gospel is a betrayal of Christ. There is nothing else to be said from my point of view about it, because it is totally indifferent whether the Christians of the world are at one or not if they are not truly Christian. And there is no other way of being a Christian than to be Christian according to the gospel in the image of Christ – singly and, in the image of the total Christ, collectively.

AW: A few years ago, at an ecumenical gathering I attended, a senior churchman said that he didn't know that we could even say what it means to be a Christian.

You have talked a great deal about the gospel, the primitive gospel. What does it mean, according to the primitive gospel, to be a Christian?

MA: Ultimately, to be Christian means to be such a person that anyone meeting us should have met Christ himself.

This is a very radical claim. Of course we are not full light, but a twilight; but people meeting us should say, 'I have seen the light.' That *is* being a Christian.

AW: I wonder if I could ask one question to add to that? I suppose people might say, 'Well, if that's what being a Christian is, how do I become one?'

MA: You don't try to become one. One doesn't try to become a saint; one doesn't try to become a ray of light. One simply tries, from the twilight in which we are, to enter into God's light in adoration, in worship, in prayer, in obedience. And it just happens. Because anyone who would set his mind towards becoming a saint would end in nothing but pride and silliness. Humility is part of it, and humility means being capable of listening to God, and doing and being what he expects us to be, without asking more. What happens next is God's.

AW: Thank you very much, Metropolitan Anthony.

Interview with

BISHOP LESSLIE NEWBIGIN

Andrew Walker: Bishop Newbigin, in recent years you have turned your attention particularly to problems of Western culture – here I'm thinking mainly of your Warfield Lectures given at Princeton Theological Seminary (Newbigin 1986) and also of your booklet for the British Council of Churches, *The Other Side of 1984* (Newbigin 1983). Would it be correct to say that you think that advanced Western industrial societies took a wrong turn with the Enlightenment?

Bishop Lesslie Newbigin: I became involved in these questions basically because I was a foreign missionary in India and have been through the experience of seeking, as an Englishman, to communicate the gospel across the cultural divide that separates our countries. And therefore I have had to reflect about the way that one communicates the gospel in a culture whose presuppositions simply make it incredible.

Having spent most of my working life in India and then come back, I have discovered – in a way, to my own astonishment – that one faces the same problem here, and that one is again in a culture where, when you attempt to communicate the gospel, you are going completely against the stream.

What has troubled me greatly is that the response of the churches on the whole has been so timid – that there is a tendency to feel that when somebody says, 'But I can't believe that!', then you hoist the white flag and say, 'Well, of course we can't expect you to!' As a foreign missionary, on the other hand, one is accustomed to the situation where you know that what you're saying runs counter to the dominant culture, but nevertheless you have to say it.

AW: Let me be clear about this: are you saying, in effect, that when you came back to 'the mother country' that sent you out to mission 'the heathens', that you came back to a land of heathens?

LN: Well, yes, in a sense. By which I mean that I had been accustomed, like all of us in the 1960s, to talking about the secular society and its great values and so on. (I was to a considerable extent conned by the dominant theology of the 1960s and thought that secularity was one of God's great gifts – and there is a real truth in that.) But it didn't take long to discover that we are really not in a secular society but in a pagan society – not a society which has no gods, but a society which has false gods. I came to feel that more and more.

AW: If you think then that we're in a society that has false gods as opposed to no gods, what are these false gods?

LN: Well, very obviously, at a superficial level they are money, sex, prestige, power – all those things. But at a more fundamental level, I think there hides a concept of reality which is supposed to be beyond question.

As you know, the sociologists like Peter Berger talk about 'plausibility structures'. In any society there is a plausibility structure – things within that are immediately believed; things that contradict it are simply not believed. Now we have a plausibility structure which, broadly speaking, is the result of the whole immense shift of thought that took place at the Enlightenment, with all its positive elements.

But what people fail to see, of course – and one does fail to see it if one has never moved outside of it – is that every plausibility structure rests upon faith commitments.

What I find so difficult is that we're in a society here where if

you make statements which are within that plausibility structure, you're OK – no questions are asked, you can say what
you like. But if you make, for example, a Christian statement,
then that's not acceptable in public life – it's not acceptable in
politics, it's not acceptable in the university essay – because
that represents a particular faith commitment and therefore it
is ruled out . . . omitting to note that our accepted plausibility
structure also rests on faith commitments.

What I feel, and have felt, is the need to encourage my
fellow churchmen to be less timid in challenging the plausibility structure that dominates our society, to be ready to say,
'Yes, what I'm saying rests upon other faith commitments,
but that doesn't make it untrue.'

AW: Well, let's take up, then, what the faith commitment
behind the present plausibility structure is. Are we talking
about a commitment to what Karl Popper would call 'critical
rationality', or the scientific worldview, or what?

LN: I think it is the belief that the scientific method – which
has been so enormously fruitful for human life – is the only
reliable way of understanding the total human situation.
That's what I think one has to challenge.

The difficulty I feel is that when Christians are unwilling to
challenge that, then the gospel becomes either (a) just something that is helpful (you know, 'It helps me in my personal
life') or (b) something which degenerates into mere moralism
('This is what you ought to do') – so that preaching becomes
either telling people what they ought to do, or lambasting
people because of what they do do – or (c) something which just
offers people some kind of personal 'spiritual' consolation,
but does not challenge people's understanding of what is the
real world they have to deal with.

AW: I know that Professor Jim Packer has sometimes used
the phrase 'scaled-down Christianities', by which he seems to
mean that we cut our gospel down to fit the secular climate in

which we find ourselves. Is that what you think is the most negative aspect of modern Christianity?

LN: Yes. And you see this is the kind of issue that one faced in trying to communicate the gospel in India, because you obviously had to take seriously the whole Hindu worldview, with its great elements of rationality and strength (which I found enormously impressive).

In that kind of situation you have to ask yourself, not 'How can we fit the gospel into this?', but 'At what points does the gospel illuminate this, at what points does it question it, at what points does it contradict it?' But one has to express those things in a way which the listening Hindu will recognise as his own language. That's the crucial thing.

And that I think was the difficulty, because if you're going to use another language, you're at least provisionally accepting the way of understanding the world which that language embodies, and you therefore have to commit yourself to the other worldview, at least up to that point – but in order to challenge it.

AW: This idea of challenging the worldview with the gospel is obviously a crucial concern to you; but if we go back to the Enlightenment, isn't this precisely where things started to go wrong?

For example, I believe it was Luther who took the view that the gospel was always above us and we should submit ourselves, as it were, to the gospel. But on the other hand doesn't Kant in *The Critique of Practical Reason* (Kant 1788) make it fairly clear that anything which is external to us, even the scriptures, should be submitted to our *own* personal and autonomous reason and moral choice? By following this Enlightenment reversal of the Reformers' view, haven't we, as it were, turned the gospel into something to be dissected and determined by *us*, rather than submitting ourselves to the gospel? Do you think that's a fair comment?

LN: Yes. I'm not a trained philosopher, but I think that way of describing the difference is absolutely right.

I recently read a long interview with the person who has just come as the head of the Central Mosque here. He had had the experience of studying Islam in both a madrassa and in a modern Western university, and he brought out very vividly the contrast between studying the sacred books of Islam from within that faith in order to understand it – which does not at all preclude asking critical questions, but at least means you are studying it with the provisional assumption that it is true, and that you want to understand it – and, on the other hand, taking a stance right outside it and looking at it as an example of a religious experience.

My training in theology was very largely of the second kind – a lot of the biblical studies that I did as a theological student looked at the text as it were from the outside. Now, I think there is a difference between that and the study of the Christian tradition, the scriptures and the founders of the Christian tradition from within – which *doesn't* exclude asking critical questions, but is based on the assumption that one can find truth there.

AW: Again, don't we go back to a post-Enlightenment position, which is that after Kant (and following Schleiermacher) – by virtue of the fact that we're now looking at the scriptures as something outside of us, which we are looking down upon – there has been a switch from saying, 'Here is the sacred text to which we give heed' to saying, 'Here is a collection of interesting objects which we must now dissect to see which we can authenticate'? I mean, isn't that a classical shift?

LN: Indeed it is. And of course it's part of that shift that I'm talking about – because you're then studying the scriptures from within another set of faith commitments.

The problem is that people do not recognise that they are faith commitments. If you take a Christian stance, then that is a faith commitment; but if you take a 'modern scientific critical approach', that is not taken to be a faith commitment but just a reading off of what is the case.

All fundamental worldviews have to rest upon faith commitments which cannot be demonstrated from outside of those views. And the problem that one has is not that people should *have* presuppositions and prejudices, but that they should be unaware of them.

Prejudice has become a bad word in our culture, but in fact you don't learn to know anything without at least an initial prejudice in favour of your teacher or in favour of the text book. It's not having prejudice that's wrong; it's being unaware of the fact that you are prejudiced which is wrong.

AW: Do you have a prejudice against a great deal of modern theological scholarship in the sense that you think a lot of modernist scholarship undermines the Christian faith?

LN: I think there is a lot of scholarship that does that.

I would want to insist that we have a duty to exercise our critical faculties upon everything that we try to understand. But the question is, 'On what basis are the critical questions asked?'

No criticism – I learnt this from Michael Polanyi – no criticism is possible except on the basis of beliefs which, at that moment, you do not criticise. You cannot question the truth of a statement except on the basis of a statement which you believe to be true.

It's the question of what is the stance from which one exercises one's critical faculties that is the crucial question. But my other problem would be that so much of what exercises the minds of theological scholars is relatively trivial, is relatively predictable.

I remember a vivid experience from my own theological training, when our New Testament professor spent two and a half hours discussing the question whether the Last Supper took place on the fourteenth or the fifteenth Nissan, which is a matter upon which one can display an immense amount of brilliant scholarship. He then disposed of the resurrection in twenty minutes, and a student asked him, 'Sir, do you mean that Jesus did rise from the dead or that he didn't?' And the professor replied, 'That's too big a question to go into in this classroom.' That's what I mean: the first kind of study provides a field for the display of the kind of scholarship that gets one professorships, but it is trivial from the point of view of the Christian faith.

AW: Couldn't one also argue that a good deal of modern scholarship is a lot more subjective and relativistic than at first it appears?

Let me give an example. At the turn of the century it was the consensus of opinion within a great deal of scholarship that the resurrection could be explained by recourse to redemption myths that were rampant in the Middle East at that time. Yet here we are, a hundred years later, and there are very few 'liberal' scholars who would give any credence to that view at all. In other words, one of the things that always frightens people on the outside when they first start looking at modern scholarship is that it seems to be so rational, so scientific – but very often it turns out to involve a great deal more subjective interpretation than it initially appears to. Do you think that's so?

LN: Is that not another way of putting the point that I was trying to make earlier?

All knowing involves – does it not? – both a subjective and an objective pole. If it is real knowledge then it is knowledge of that reality out there; but if I *know*, then my knowing is part of the operation, and my knowing will be shaped by my mind, which is shaped by all its previous experience and educational training and what not.

So the crucial question always is (granted that we have the duty to exercise the critical reason on everything that claims to be true): 'Upon what basis is your criticism founded?' That is because, as I said before, you can only criticise on the basis of something which you believe to be true.

Now if you believe it to be true that there were redemption myths rampant throughout the whole of the Hellenistic world at that time, then that will be part of the knowing person approaching the text – but then you need also to be able to exercise your critical faculty in relation to that assumption.

The problem concerns the assumptions that you take for granted without questioning. And that brings us back to what I would call the modern scientific worldview, which is enormously important, enormously fruitful, but also needs to be subjected to critical examination.

AW: Given that you obviously are not against critical examination *per se*, how do you answer people when they say to you, 'Why, Bishop Newbigin, do you believe in the incarnation and the resurrection of Christ?' I mean, how would you suggest to a modern world that such a belief is credible?

LN: Well, ultimately, of course (and here we see my Reformed background), I come to the doctrine of election. I mean that by his mysterious grace God took hold of me, an unbelieving, pondering person, and put me in a position where the reality of Jesus Christ, crucified and risen, became for me the one clue that I could follow in making sense of a very perplexing world.

The test, of course, can only come at the end. I would want to claim that that clue ultimately gives one a kind of rationality that is more inclusive of the whole of human experience than the real, though limited, rationality of the reductionist and rationalist scientific point of view. But at the end of the day we have to wait for the day of judgement.

There is an element of risk, there is an element of commitment involved where you don't pretend to *have* something – that is, if there were some way by which I could prove the authority of Jesus Christ from outside, then *that* would be my authority and not Jesus Christ. I can only point to him.

AW: Given that you can point to him, do you think it reasonable or unreasonable to suggest that to be a Christian does involve some minimal amount of beliefs?

LN: Oh yes, surely it does.

AW: I mean, if somebody was to come here, put you into a corner and say, 'Now look here Bishop, what have you got to believe to be a believing Christian?' What would you say were the basics?

LN: I would simply say, 'Jesus Christ, the final and determinative centre around which everything else is understood.' If that is there, I am not enthusiastic about drawing exact boundaries.

I think you can define an entity by its boundaries or by its centre. I think that Christianity is an entity defined by its centre. So provided a person is, as it were, 'looking to Jesus' and seeing him as the central, decisive, determinative reality in relation to which all else is to be understood, then (even if his ideas are weird or off-beat) I would regard him as a brother in Christ. (Though I might argue with him; I might tell him I think he's wrong; I might rub his nose in the New Testament and tell him, 'Look, you're misunderstanding Jesus', and all that.)

But once you start trying to define Christianity by its boundaries, you'll always come up against some kind of legalism. You know: 'Has he been baptised? Has he been confirmed? Was the bishop who confirmed him in the apostolic succession?' and so forth. Or 'Has he had the right kind of religious experience? Was his conversion datable? Did he have those kinds of feelings at that time?' and so on. You always finish up with some kind of legalism, whereas I think Christianity is to be defined by its centre.

AW: If we're going to define Christianity by its centre, in what ways can you say that Jesus Christ is still 'good news for modern man'?

LN: Because death is conquerable; because the crucified is risen; because not just anyone rose from the dead, but this one who went down to the very depths of the human situation; because *he* is raised.

I see Christianity as a kind of fall-out from an original explosion of joy. But of course you don't just communicate it simply by arguments. It's an existential reality present in a believing, worshipping community, and the only ultimate hermeneutic for the gospel is a believing community.

AW: Do you think that we are living in a fallen culture in which it is becoming increasingly difficult for a believing community to survive?

LN: All human life is after the fall, so all human life – and therefore all human culture – is corrupted by human sin.

Yet I think there are good elements in our culture. Some of my Third World friends still comment on things they find here which are obviously results of our long Christian schooling and for which we ought to be thankful. I think those are elements of mutual trust, of mutual courtesy and so forth, which are tremendously precious – and of course the great gift of freedom, of freedom of thought, which we owe to the Enlightenment.

But on the other hand there are obviously very, very dark elements in our culture. What for me is the most tragic thing is the loss of hope – the loss of any sense of a meaningful future – which expresses itself in the mindless vandalism that we see so much around us. Why do people just smash up things for the fun of smashing them up? Because they see no future, I think – and in that sense that's where I would put the finger.

AW: Would you not say then that this loss of hope may perhaps even be some sort of evidence that we're coming to the end of an Enlightenment culture which has always stressed progress and optimism?

LN: Yes, in that sense I do think we are at the end of an era. Even when I was a schoolboy we believed in progress. The sort of schooling that I had led me to believe that you could understand human history as a continuing progress and that we were part of it. But I don't think any of us believes that now. In that sense we are at the end of a culture.

AW: What are your hopes for the future as far as the church is concerned? What do you look for generally and hope for as the way forward?

LN: You may think that I'm evading your question, but I do believe fundamentally that the horizon for the Christian is not some prospect, some bit of futurology – either for his own personal life or for the life of his society.

The horizon for the Christian is 'He shall come again' and 'We look for the coming of the Lord.' It can be tomorrow or any time, but that's the horizon. That horizon is for me fundamental, and that's what makes it possible to be hopeful and therefore to find life meaningful.

As regards what we can in our fallible human guesswork anticipate, I don't know. The one thing that strikes me about all the futurological essays one reads is that after ten years we realise that they were wrong.

Our capacity to forecast the future is very limited. All I can say is that one sees signs of hope, one sees signs of growth. I often liken the church to a bush that's been very hard pruned: I think there are buds, and though they are very small I think they are signs of hope.

AW: That you can see hope in the fact that we await the return of Christ really does alter our basic perspective on life, doesn't it?

I remember C. S. Lewis in one of his articles points out that if you believe that one day history will end, it alters everything that you do – it alters your attitude towards progress, towards morals. Do you think that we've lost that eschatological sense of the church?

LN: Yes, yes. I get fed up with those theologians who tell me that of course Jesus expected the end of the world soon, but that he was mistaken and that the New Testament believers had to learn to do without it, and that we must just plod along. I think this is nonsense.

The words of Jesus do contain statements of that tremendous sense of immediacy, but they also contain statements of 'You don't know' and 'Not even the Son of Man knows.' So we are called upon to live day by day in this expectation of the great and glorious climax, but not just sort of plodding along for ever and ever.

When we invest in some particular programme the kinds of hopes that properly belong to the ultimate consummation, we get a destructive fanaticism and are always disappointed.

AW: Thank you, Bishop Newbigin.

Interview with

PROFESSOR THOMAS F. TORRANCE

Andrew Walker: Professor Torrance, you are the first theologian to be the recipient of the Templeton Foundation Prize for Progress in Religion, and you can rightly claim to be Britain's most distinguished theologian since the Second World War. You've seen many changes in theology in the last thirty years – are they primarily changes for the better or for the worse?

Professor Thomas F. Torrance: Well, I think I have to say that there have been ups and downs.

In certain respects there have been changes for the better, because it is now clearer than before what the really fundamental issues are. And also it is clearer that theology cannot be conducted in the abstract or in separation from the whole universe that God had made and which we know about more and more in our science. So, in one respect, then, theology is much better because real theologians now perceive the depth of the problem and they try to think out the relation between it and the world, the created order which God has made.

On the other hand, since the war we have seen backlashes in several respects, in which people have tried to make the gospel 'relevant' and in point of fact have made it irrelevant because they have simply catered to certain superficial ideas. So we've had flashes of fashion here and there which, in the end, have been superficial. And that has often tended to dominate the scene.

But all the time there has been burrowing through, a deeper issue. For example, people are beginning to come to grips with the works of Karl Barth, who is undoubtedly the greatest theologian that the world has seen for many centuries. So the people who really think are making great advances. Also, and I think this is *very* important, the main believers in the world are often scientists, hard scientists – and that is, I think, an indication of the fact that pure, deep theology and rigorous science are much closer than they have ever been before, and that seems to me an enormous advance.

AW: It's interesting that you should see a convergence between what you call 'hard' science and theology. But isn't it the case that in many people's minds they tend to see them as in opposition to each other? You get these sorts of statements being made: 'Science has shown that miracles are impossible' or 'Science makes it impossible to believe in the resurrection.' And, incidentally, many theologians say this sort of thing too, don't they? What do you think of this sort of view of science?

TFT: Well, I think that is the case, but this is one of our basic problems. In the Western world, in Western science since the Renaissance and the Enlightenment and the rise of modern mechanics, we have split the world into two – a world that is measurable, or quantifiable, and a world that is not measurable, or not quantifiable; a world that you can grasp in visible data and a world you cannot grasp in that way.

Now, in that situation, the old scientific world has unfortunately become a closed system of cause and effect, so it rules out automatically anything like revelation or God or miracles or incarnation. And on the other side, everything is only subjective, that is, in terms of what *you* experience or what *you* feel. That view has dominated the scene, and it still dominates the split culture. And that's why we have the huge gap today between the social sciences and the hard sciences, because the social sciences are still tied up with that obsolete notion of science and the phenomenalist approach, whereas the hard scientists are not. They are at grips with nature in its depths, in its real intelligibilities and, therefore, when they do that, they are much more open to theology.

Let me give you an illustration of this.

A friend of mine in Princeton once heard Richard Feynman, who was one of the great authorities on the nature of physical law (and who was not, he says, a believer) speaking about the nature of physical law and its open structure – something quite different from the Newtonian kind of law which excluded miracles. And in order to illustrate this he said: 'You know, this would not be hostile even to Christian views of incarnation and resurrection.' That to me is a staggering instance, if an extreme one – but that's what I find now among physical scientists.

AW: Let us take up, then, the issues of resurrection and incarnation as perhaps two of the 'stumbling-blocks' that the modern mind – very often the theological modern mind at least – seems to find in present-day belief.

Recently, for example, we've heard from a number of theologians and bishops, particularly through the media, that the resurrection need not be understood as a historical and physical event. What do you think of these views?

TFT: People who talk like that use a Newtonian notion of science, with an idea of the universe as a closed determinist system, so that supernatural events break that – are a violation of it – therefore there's no miracle or resurrection.

But actually, if you have a notion of the resurrection as something that is not a physical event and is merely a subjective event – if it has nothing to do with space and time – that is scientific nonsense.

Any event that is scientifically apprehensible is an empirical *and* a theoretical event – it is physical and yet it is intelligible beyond itself. So it is only a concept of the resurrection which takes space and time seriously that is really scientifically respectable.

I'll give you an illustration about this.

Several years ago, when *Concilium* first opened its doors to

Protestants, I was invited to share a platform with Hans Küng on the subject of the resurrection. And when Hans Küng – whom I've known since he was a fairly young man – talked about it, to my astonishment he denied the physical side of the resurrection. So I challenged him and said, 'Why?' And he replied, 'Because you can't talk like that in the modern scientific world.' But I said, 'The exact opposite is the case: only if you speak of the resurrection in terms of an empty tomb, of an event that is physical *and* a direct act of God [the two correlated together] can it scientifically be respectable, can you communicate about it.' And up jumped a physicist, who supported me against Hans Küng.

I think that is typical of what we have today.

AW: I think it's an extremely good example, because I think that one of the things that worries many ordinary people who don't understand science very much is that they simply don't know what theologians *mean* when they say a resurrection can be something other than a physical event – it seems to them to be a nonsense. For example, a man in a church once said to me, 'What on earth does a non-physical resurrection look like?'

Do you think there is a sense in which common sense is perhaps nearer to the truth here, and closer to the scientists, than some of our modern theologians?

TFT: I think so. The common man knows that ghosts don't rise again from the dead. To talk about the resurrection of a ghost or a spirit is just a contradiction in terms.

But of course there's something here very deep that I think we have to appreciate: the modern scientific world looks upon all nature as contingent – that is to say, it's not necessary, it didn't have to happen, and it is open in its structure. And that concept didn't arise out of science; it is a direct product of the Christian doctrine of the incarnation and of the doctrine of the creation of the world out of nothing – that God created not only the physical world but also the intelligible world out of nothing.

For a millennium and a half we lost that notion of contingency, but modern science has resurrected it. Therefore science is now at grips with the very basis which was produced for it by the Christian faith. So today we see this understanding of nature and the doctrine of the incarnation and creation coming very close together.

AW: It's very interesting that we've now moved from the resurrection to the incarnation, because in recent years, as well as hearing – primarily through media reports rather than through serious scholarship – that the resurrection should be understood as a non-physical event, we have also been told that the incarnation is not a historical reality, is not an intervention in history, but is some form of mythology (I'm obviously thinking here of the publication in 1977 of J. Hick (ed.), *The Myth of God Incarnate*).

I suppose a straightforward question to you as a theologian would be, 'Can one be a Christian and not believe in the incarnation?'

TFT: Immediately a question like that is asked, my mind goes back to fundamental texts in the early church which said quite clearly that the Christian and the Catholic faith is one in which we believe not only in God, but in the incarnation and the Trinity, and that if you don't believe this, you can't be a Christian.

I would say that the incarnation is at the heart of the Christian faith.

Let me put it this way.

There have arisen in history – in ancient times, unfortunately (as the fathers knew), in medieval times and in modern times – habits of thinking which tear apart what should be *united*: that is to say, dualist ways of thinking. Now when these dualist ways of thinking take over and you look at Jesus, what do you do? The dualist patterns of thought we are working with tear Christianity apart from Christ – they tear Christ apart from God, then they tear Christianity apart from Christ.

That dualism is the root of all our modernistic error, and it is the essence of the great battle the early church fought out when they said, 'When Jesus says "Your sins are forgiven," is that the word of God or just the word of man?' Now, if it's only the word of man, then there is no forgiveness, there is no validity in it. The same problem arises when we ask, 'When Jesus died for us and made atonement for our sins, was that God acting or was it just a man?'

If you cut the bond between Jesus Christ and God, the very essence of the gospel drops out – Christianity has lost its substance. So you cannot really believe, 'be a Christian', without believing in the incarnation.

Now, of course, we have to think out, 'How do we think "God and man together in Christ"?' – and that's our central theological problem. But for me this is much easier in the modern scientific world than it was in the early world of Newtonian tyranny, of a deterministic concept of the universe.

So I would say, 'Yes, properly speaking you cannot be a Christian without believing in the incarnation,' for in the incarnation you believe in the inner connection between the person of Jesus and God, and therefore you believe that the acts of Jesus are acts of God – and what God does we have in Jesus, and there is no God 'behind the back of Jesus'.

Now that's the essence of Christianity: 'I am the way and the truth and the life. No-one comes to the Father except through me.'

AW: You won't mind me saying this, but if that most famous theologian of the twentieth century, Karl Barth, was here, he would have agreed with every word of that: in many ways it's an echoing of his own statements (Torrance 1986).

And so we must ask a very serious question: Considering that for many years – certainly since the 1940s – we have been seeing what you earlier referred to as 'backlashes' of earlier nineteenth-century closed, deterministic views (or various forms of subjectivism), why is it that Barth, who was the champion of the traditional gospel, has often been seen by many Protestant evangelicals not as an ally but as an enemy?

TFT: I think the reason he has been seen as an enemy by many people, and not just evangelicals, is due to a misunderstanding of Barth's thought about rationality and the uncongeniality of his opposition to dualism.

Let's take the second point first.

All Barth's theology rests on a basis where the kind of dualism that we've been talking about is cast aside: he works on a unitary basis. In Germany that's been very difficult to accept, because all German thought is governed by the massive genius of Immanuel Kant, and Kant's thought was dualistic – he tore the noumenal and the phenomenal apart. In the post-war period Barth's thought fell out of favour in Germany because there was a strong backlash in favour of *German* thought – in favour of Kantian and Hegelian thought. Now, of course, the situation has improved somewhat and his theology is perhaps more acceptable.

As to evangelical opposition to Barth, perhaps I ought to describe some of his thought and then make two points.

Barth said that the church has on two great occasions in the past had to struggle for its very existence in holding on to the deity of Christ. And this it achieved at the Council of Nicea (325). This meant that the church believed that God himself is the content of his revelation, and that what God reveals of himself is not something *about* God, but *God* – the Word of God *is* God. And that unity between God and his revelation is the very essence of the gospel. (We've seen it beforehand in relation to the incarnation, the Word made flesh.) The other thing that Barth emphasised so much (it comes in the early church also, in the doctrine of the Holy Spirit) is that the *gift* of God and the *giver* are one and the same – that the grace that God gives is not something detached from God, but *God himself*, giving himself. Now that, of course, was the great message of the Reformation: salvation by grace alone. Also tied up with both of those is that the *being* of God and his *act* are at one – so there is a unity between God's being and his act.

At this point evangelicalism, which is tied to a dualist pattern of thinking, finds that Barth undercuts it.

First, it doesn't like it when Barth says that the word of God is not the scriptures *as such*, but that the Word which we really hear of God (that God himself is his Word) we meet in holy scripture.

Second, Barth also says that the grace of God that is given is identical with God in Jesus Christ – therefore justification means that God justifies me *in Christ*, and that in myself I am shown to be wrong: 'Let God be true and every man a liar.' Now the fundamentalist orthodox wants to boast of his orthodoxy; but according to Barth he is a liar, because only God is true.

So, if you take these doctrines seriously they turn us inside out and they question us inside out. That questioning of us is, I think, the real reason why Barth is so opposed, even by some evangelicals.

But now take the other side.

Why is it that the so-called modernists oppose him? The reason for this is a different form of the same thing. Our modern culture, our modern society – and until recently this was true of our modern science too – is tied up with the Enlightenment, when we separated faith and reason, when we separated the physical, the visible and the invisible. When that happened reason was turned in upon itself, so that it was now by thinking in terms of one's own reason that one established the truth – in science or in theology.

Now to my mind Barth is the only great theologian in the whole history of modern thought who has insisted on thinking out what is the nature of reason – he laid hold of the concept of reason and rethought it radically from the bottom. Barth's radical rethinking of intelligibility and of the nature of reason – in which you can't separate the mind from the intelligible world that God has created – conflicts with the rationalists. (Again it is the physical scientists, the mathematicians and the chemists whose views are much more in agreement with Barth at this point. Whereas Barth undertook his revolution in the light of Jesus Christ, in the light of the incarnation, of God's self-revelation, the modern scientist has to do it in the light of what God has actually made in creation – yet the two are very close together.)

From this it is clear that Barth is not, as the modernists and the evangelicals allege, an irrationalist – he is more profoundly rational than either of them. Here we have an extraordinary irony: they accuse him of being irrational, of not being concerned with reason, but the exact opposite is the case – the point is that he is so deeply rational that they are incapable of comprehending him properly.

AW: With Barth's high view of the nature and content of revelation, do we not see – perhaps for the first time since the predominantly rationalistic approach of nineteenth-century theological liberalism – theology once again being done 'from above'? Yet it seems to me that in many British and American universities we still have an awful lot of examples of people trying to do theology 'from below'.

Do you think that theology from below can actually succeed? Can one, as it were, get to the content of true theology, that is to God himself, from human reasoning – or does one have to work from revelation first, 'down to' our reasoning?

TFT: I don't think we can theologise from below upwards or from above downwards, and once again there is an analogy I draw from scientific method.

The day used to be when scientists' methods were polarised: on the one hand, there were those who used to say, 'Let's make our empirical observations, gather the empirical data, and then we can deduce theories about it'; on the other hand, there were people who thought first of all in theories, and then tried to apply them to the empirical. This meant you were either an empiricist or a rationalist. But actually neither was right, because in science we start right away, at every level, with an understanding of nature which is at once empirical *and* theoretical.

That's how Barth starts, you see. Right away he asks, 'Who is Jesus Christ?' and 'What is revelation?' For him revelation is always divine and human: God and man. So you start off, therefore, with the unitary fact of Christ – neither from below nor from above. And you allow that fact to talk to you out of its inner reason, out of the inner depths of intelligibility, and that is God's Word, God's revelation.

AW: Given that, does it not follow, though, that one has to start with a fundamental datum of revelation, otherwise one starts with nothing?

TFT: Oh yes, because you can't know God behind his back – you can only know God when he shows *himself* to you. What we have in revelation is God talking to us, revealing himself to us, and making his Word incarnate. But it is the *incarnate* Word, the Word become flesh, the Word become man, it's from that unity that we start – so that we can take the divine and the human, and the human and the divine, together, and *out* of that unity we have our theology.

AW: OK . . . Can we perhaps now go back to an earlier question I asked you about the evangelicals?
   Do you think it is still the case in large sections of the evangelical world (and here I'm thinking particularly of the southern states of the USA) that people confuse God's revelation with the words about revelation in scripture?
   I ask that because I feel that that position is a misunderstanding of Barth which is still committed by many evangelicals – they think he is not a biblicist because he doesn't address himself to the words of scripture, he addresses himself to the revelation from scripture.

TFT: Yes, of course, the point that you're making is quite right. (Although some evangelicals, such as Bernard Ramm in the States, would argue (Ramm 1983) that Barth is the most biblical theologian there has been for hundreds of years.)
   You see, in their dualist way of thinking, evangelicals divide God from holy scripture. And then, to make holy scripture

divine, they identify the words of scripture with the words of God – as though God in himself spoke a human language. In a way that's a mythologising, an anthropologising, of God.

This means, therefore, that they don't interpret the holy scriptures as referring to truth independently of the scriptures, and therefore they have deified the scriptures. In turn, that means that you end up with God versus scripture or scripture versus God – and that Barth won't have. In a way, it's a kind of positivism of holy scripture.

AW: It could be argued, despite the fact that there are so many different strains of it, that a lot of modernist theology has tended to take the teachings and the message of Christ away from Christ himself.

Do you feel that, in a way, what is perhaps missing most of all in modern theology is the person of Jesus himself – the person and his acts together?

TFT: Oh I agree, but you see the person of Christ himself is *God* become man, *God* meeting us in our humanity, face to face with humanity. But if you detach Christianity from Christ, then it becomes attached to society; then it is immediately engulfed in the whole socio-political world, so that then you've got a radical secularisation of Christianity.

Now that is what Barth fought with. When he was fighting the Nazis, he took his main stand, in the Barmen Declaration (1934), on the words of Jesus: 'I am the way and the truth and the life. No-one comes to the Father except through me.' If you lose that then you secularise the church.

But I'm afraid that today many have jumped on to the bandwagon of phenomenology, sociology and politics, and so they've secularised the church.

And what have they been doing? Let me put it quite frankly.

Historically speaking, Jesus was crucified because he refused to play the role of a political Messiah. They wanted him to be the political hero, the Messiah, so much so that Jesus could hardly use the word Christ (Messiah), because they would misinterpret it. And so he was crucified because he wouldn't do that.

But *today* the church is crucifying Christ again by turning him into a political Messiah. Yet that's the *opposite* of what he came to do. (Now, of course, the power of the cross, the power of Christ, is much greater than all that – it turns the whole world upside down.) And also, because the modern church doesn't believe in the power of the cross, it has to create its own Holy Ghost, and so it has recourse to social temporal power or economic pressures, in order to bring Christian ideas into effect, whereas that can only be brought about through the incarnation and through the Holy Ghost in Christ. So they do not really believe that the cross of Christ is the power of God that upsets all the principalities and powers of the world.

That is my main problem with the modern church – its secularisation and its being engulfed and lost in the whole mass of modern socio-political thought because it has departed from the controlling centre of God's self-giving and self-revelation in Jesus Christ.

AW: Do you think we could say, as a result of that, that perhaps one of the things that the church needs a great deal more of – in a word – is evangelism?

TFT: Yes, I think this is absolutely central – because what we need is an evangelical relation between people and God. It's in that evangelical relation, that is to say, through Christ and his gospel, that man is put in the right with God. And only in that evangelical relation with God can we have a proper understanding of ethics and morals, for example.

Take the enormous problem we have today as a result of the permissive society that grew up in the 1960s – and before that – when people developed a concept of ethics that was entirely subjective, on its own, but detached from God. Now that has become quite corrupt, and there's no way of curing that except by bringing people back to God – because God is the only source of what is true or right. It's in the evangelical relation that we link up people with God, and so link them up with the very source where even their moral life and their thought, as well as their intellectual life, is rejuvenated and recreated.

So I would say that, from the whole social/moral point of view, the country needs more than anything an evangelical relation with God.

This to me is one of the great contributions of Karl Barth. God for him had an evangelical relation with the whole of our life and thought – even, as I said earlier on, with reason and things like that, but also with ethics. Now how can we recover that? Because the church has no message, for example, to AIDS, or to the permissive society, except 'Do good . . . Do good . . . Be good . . .', and that's boring. But if they know God in Christ, then their whole life is transformed and the whole ethical foundation will transform.

AW: Thank you, Professor Torrance.

Interview with

CARDINAL LEON-JOSEPH SUENENS

Andrew Walker: Cardinal Suenens, although you have in recent times been linked with the charismatic renewal movement, you have of course been a major architect for reform within the Catholic Church for many years. In particular, you were partly responsible for the structure and outline of the Second Vatican Council, and served as one of its four moderators. Looking back, what do you think Vatican II achieved?

Cardinal Leon-Joseph Suenens: Well, I believe that we affirmed the apostolic tradition, but were prepared to begin reforming some of our less historic traditions. We brought back the diaconate as a major institution open to married men, and insisted on the compulsory retirement of bishops at the age of seventy-five. More importantly, we stressed the importance of collegiality in the church and the necessity for greater lay participation.

AW: You do not view Vatican II, then, as some do, as the beginning of theological liberalism in the Roman Catholic Church and the undermining of the historic tradition?

L-JS: Not at all. Pope John XXIII initiated a new sense of collegiality, seeking dialogue between the primacy and the bishops. Vatican II has been likened to the opening of a window which let in fresh air and light. We were very well aware of the Protestant theology of the death of God, and other non-traditional theologies making their presence felt, but this was not a feature of the Vatican Council itself.

If I had to make a major criticism of the Council, it would be that we did not go far enough in encouraging all our people to witness to Jesus Christ in word and deed. We did not do enough to insist on the necessity of evangelisation. Our people have become passive and mute, and need to be turned into active Christians.

AW: What do you think most threatens Christianity today?

L-JS: Major sociological factors have changed the situation. Once Christians were carried along by a culture that sustained and nurtured faith. This is no longer so. Because we cannot rely any more (and this now includes Catholic as well as Protestant countries) on a Christian culture, we can no longer afford the luxury of timid and nominal Christians. A personal conversion is now a necessity for modern Christians. Experience is the key that unlocks the treasures of tradition and theology. We need a new Pentecost, a revival of our baptism vows – a new Upper Room. If we are going to prepare Christians for the future, then we must say 'yes' to the Spirit, 'yes' to Pentecost, but 'no' to Pentecostalism.

AW: If you think that sociological factors have led us away from Christian culture, do you think that modern theologies threaten the church? Liberation theology, for example?

L-JS: Liberation theology in South America springs out of an underground of genuine religiosity. The problem is that Europeans interpret it in intellectual ways that are alien to the experience of Latin Americans. I am more concerned by those theologies that deny the physical resurrection of Jesus. The resurrection is the key to Christianity. Resurrection is not reanimation, but a miracle that demonstrates God's love for us. God always does the unexpected. The resurrection, like all miracles, cannot be demonstrated in terms of causality; they are God's surprises.

AW: In your book *Renewal and the Powers of Darkness* (Suenens 1982), you seem to want to affirm the reality of the devil as well as God. Why is this?

L-JS: We cannot explain redemption without the devil – remove him and all the powers of darkness, and the Christian story no longer has meaning. We need to discover today the reality of the angels of God and the angels of darkness. We need the Spirit, not only to equip us to be holy, active Christians, but also to combat the spiritual forces that are opposed to Christ and his church.

AW: If we are to stand against the devil and against the sociological and philosophical attacks upon the gospel, does this not demand that we come together in unity? What do you understand true ecumenism to be?

L-JS: I believe unity needs to be down-to-earth. As Christians, we must come together to stress our similarities. Fraternity demands that we recognise each other's identity and yet be prepared to come together and live our Christian lives together. My hope is in the Holy Spirit. The renewal movement surprised us, and the Spirit has more surprises in store.

On a practical point, which is also spiritual, I would like all the bishops of the main historical denominations to come together to seek for a new Pentecost, an Upper Room experience which would bind us together. We have to be aware of the dangers of sects and extremism. As I think I have said before, we need Pentecost, but not Pentecostalism.

I think also that we should not worry about turning Christians into a majority in our secular world. What we want is a fervent minority to be salt and leaven in society. Authentic Christianity is what is needed. Some one godly person can become a Moses or David. I confirmed about 250,000 children in my life as a bishop, and I knew that many of the children I laid hands on would never go to mass again. This will no longer do. Christians in all our denominations need Jesus to come alive for them in a real way so that his presence is sought and experienced every day. These are the sort of Christians we should be seeking to bring together. Christians who are alive to God's grace and power need each other so that the institutional dimension of the church can be opened up to the mystical and charismatic dimension. Ecumenism without the charismatic dimension is dead. Charismatic Christianity without the institutional framework is unrealistic.

AW: Cardinal Suenens, do you have any specific hopes for the future that you would like to share with us?

L-JS: I have fears as well as hopes, but I am not a prophet and cannot see into the future. However, I do dream of a better tomorrow, and I pray for us all. My hope rests in Jesus, not in predictions. Perhaps I can give you a prayer that I wrote recently that expresses my hope?

AW: Thank you, Cardinal; this would seem an appropriate way to bring our conversation to a proper end.

Prayer for the year 2000

Looking at the world . . .

Lord, we are afraid to face the world of tomorrow;
We have lost faith in ourselves;
We no longer believe in that boundless progress
Which was supposed to ensure our future happiness;
Nor do we believe any longer in science as the salvation of
    mankind;
Nor do we believe that man is the supreme end of man,
Nor that death is the last word of life.

And we know, too, that if tomorrow there were to be
Another nuclear disaster such as Chernobyl,
Whether by accident or design,

There could be an apocalyptic explosion
From which none of us would survive,
No one even to number and bury the dead . . .

Looking at the church . . .

Lord, if I turn my eyes to the church,
Who received from your Son the promise of eternal life,
I feel how poor and weak, we, your disciples, are today,
So poor and poorly Christian;
But I hear on every side
The pressing call of our pastors
For a new and second evangelisation
To make us true and faithful Christians,
Conscious of the imperatives of our baptism.

Help us to discover the fervour of the early Christians
And the power of the first evangelisation,
That morning of Pentecost, as it started
In the cenacle of Jerusalem
Where your disciples, with Mary, gathered in prayer,
Awaited, Father, the fulfilment of your promise.
Give us the grace to be renewed
'In the Spirit and in fire.'
Teach us to speak to the world in tongues of fire,
Let us bring to an end this time of uncertainty
Where Christians are timid and mute
Discussing anxiously problems of today,
As in the past on the road from Jerusalem to Emmaus,
Without realising that the Master is risen and alive.

Prayer for the future . . .

Lord, open our hearts to welcome your Holy Spirit;
Teach us to await his coming, as Mary did, at the time of the
    annunciation

And again at Pentecost – the nativity of the church –
When she became also our mother.
Teach the coming generations that your Son, Jesus Christ,
    remains
For ever and ever, the saviour of the world.

Help us to proclaim, loudly and boldly,
That he is 'the way, the truth, and the life'.
The way, which leads us towards our final destiny.
The truth, which lights our way through the night.
The life, which gives us a profound peace, serenity and joy
Which nothing created can destroy.

May your disciples, on the eve of the third millennium,
Hasten their steps, to obey the order given by the Master,
To be 'one' in the unity of the Father, the Son, the Holy
    Spirit.
And may they approach the Lord together,
Radiant with his light,
With no shadow on their face,
So that the whole world will recognise Jesus Christ alive in
    his disciples,
Now and for ever.

                    Amen

Part Two

DOCTRINAL ISSUES IN THE LIGHT OF MODERNIST THOUGHT

THE HOLY TRINITY AND THE RESURRECTION OF JESUS

Thomas A. Smail

Many modern Christians do not know what to make of the doctrine of the Trinity. Although they profess it in their creeds and liturgies and in their hymns sing about the God who is Father, Son and Holy Spirit, three persons in one God, they would find it hard to explain why they said these things or what they meant by them. To say that God is somehow both three and one at the same time can easily look like a highly incomprehensible kind of metaphysical mathematics which is entirely remote from the biblical gospel, our own living relationship with God and our life in the world.

The evidence suggests that an understanding of and an enthusiasm for the doctrine among clergy and ministers are in many cases not much higher. In a recent survey quite a lot of ordained leaders said they found Trinity Sunday the second most difficult day of the year – after Remembrance Day – to know what to say. All in all it does not look as if the central Christian assertion about God – that he is Father, Son and Holy Spirit – is either understood or cherished in pulpit or pew.

There are many reasons for this neglect. Undoubtedly the fault lies at least in part with the way in which the doctrine of the Trinity has sometimes been expounded in the past, in rarified terms of theological speculation which do indeed make it hard to see how it is connected with the New Testament gospel, so that it looks as if you could ignore or even drop it without losing anything from the vital heart of Christian faith.

But the chief fault certainly lies in the ways of thinking of modernity, which for the last two centuries and more have powerfully influenced the whole Western world, Christians included. Modernist thinking and trinitarian thinking do not easily combine. Biblical criticism, strongly influenced as it has been by modernist presuppositions, has eroded the authority of the scriptures and in particular has cast doubt on the authenticity of those texts on which the doctrine of the Trinity was traditionally based.

More generally, the prevailing tendency of all modern thinking, when it deals with God at all, is to rely upon reason and experience rather than upon the Bible and God's self-revelation in Christ to which it bears witness. If, as a child of modernity, I want to know what can be known about God, I will turn to my own rational processes or my own religious experiences rather than to what God shows me about himself through the prophets and apostles and supremely through Jesus Christ. I will believe as much of the Bible as agrees with my own understanding and my own experience and dismiss the rest.

If the Bible and God's revelation in Christ are treated in that way, it is no wonder that the doctrine of the Trinity soon begins to look irrelevant. The only reason for believing in a trinitarian God is that it is that sort of God who reveals himself in Christ. It therefore follows that if we are not prepared to take the Christian revelation seriously we shall not take the doctrine of the Trinity seriously either.

We are however living at a time when the presuppositions of modern thinking are being challenged by scientists and philosophers alike, so there is a chance to escape from a framework that devalues the Christian revelation and its trinitarian understanding of God to a new framework of thinking that puts them both at the centre once again. This has been happening in much of the theology of the last fifty years. Karl Barth on the Reformed side and Karl Rahner on the Roman Catholic side are two eminent Christian thinkers who evolved two very different theologies which nevertheless have in common the centrality of a trinitarian doctrine of God arising from and being a key to the understanding of the biblical gospel.

In this paper my purpose is to show the connection between the doctrine of the Trinity and the New Testament in relation to one of the central assertions of the New Testament, namely that on the third day the crucified Jesus of Nazareth rose again from the dead. I shall be trying to indicate that we can make full sense of the biblical account of the resurrection only if we see it as an act in which God reveals himself as Father, Son and Holy Spirit, each acting in a distinctive way but in the closest possible relationship and indeed unity with one another. The resurrection needs to be understood as the act of three divine persons who are one God.

Before we can proceed with that main purpose we must first, however, say what we mean by the resurrection. What we think actually happened at Easter will affect whether we think that the event contains a revelation of a trinitarian God. To take an extreme example, if Easter is only about the rising again of the faith of the disciples rather than about the rising again of Jesus, since such an event tells us nothing about Jesus it is hardly likely to tell us anything about God.

My own understanding of Easter, which there is no room to defend in detail here, is much more conservative and traditional. The gospel writers seem to me to ring entirely true when they portray the risen Jesus not as the subject of some ethereal vision, but as the same Jesus of Nazareth who died on the cross, totally transformed indeed, but still a real man who can be touched and handled in space and time, to whom all power has been given on earth as well as in heaven. One does not have to accept the historical accuracy of every detail of the gospel accounts to believe their central assertion of the continued bodily identity of Jesus and his divine-human lordship over the created world. It is such a realist understanding of the resurrection that, we shall be arguing, contains within itself a revelation of Father, Son and Holy Spirit.

It is also important for our purposes that we should understand the resurrection in an integrated and inclusive way. In
other words it includes not just the discovery of the empty
tomb on Easter morning and the appearances of Jesus to his
disciples that followed, but also the ascension and exaltation
of Jesus to the Father's right hand and the imparting of the
Spirit to the church. Under the influence of the church's
liturgical year, based as it is on Luke's timescale of events, we
tend to think of resurrection, ascension and Pentecost as
three events separated in time from one another, each with its
own distinct significance. But we need to remember that John
and many of the other New Testament writers draw into the
closest theological association the three events that Luke
holds temporally apart. For John the lifting up of Jesus to
reign with the Father in his ascension is seen in the closest
connection with his being lifted up on the cross to die and his
being lifted up from the grave to live (John 12:32). For John
also the Holy Spirit is breathed out upon the disciples, to
equip them for their mission, on Easter evening and not fifty
days later (John 20:22).

Paul and the writer to the Hebrews also think of Easter in
this inclusive and integrated way. In the early Christian hymn
that Paul quotes in Philippians 2, the resurrection as such is
not mentioned, but simply assumed as part of the exaltation
of Jesus, 'He . . . became obedient to death – even death on a
cross! Therefore God exalted him to the highest place' (Phil
2:8–9). The same thing happens in Hebrews, which has only
one explicit reference to the resurrection (Heb 13:20), but
whose whole teaching depends on the fact that 'we . . . have
such a high priest, who sat down at the right hand of the
throne of the Majesty in heaven' (Heb 8:1). We are therefore
on good New Testament ground when we deal with the whole
Easter complex of events in this inclusive way. To do so will
enable us to see that it is the whole Easter mystery, compris-
ing resurrection, ascension and outpouring of the Spirit,
considered in its wholeness, that reveals God as Trinity.
As we look at it in this way we shall see Father, Son and
Holy Spirit in action, each in a distinct way and yet in the

closest possible relationship and indeed unity with one another.

First, then, *as regards God the Father: it is consistently clear throughout the whole Easter event that it is the Father who is both the initiating source and the ultimate goal of all that happens in relation to the raising of the Son and the sending of the Spirit. It is from the Father that it all starts and it is to the Father that it is all to return.*

'Praise be to the God and Father of our Lord Jesus Christ! In his great mercy he has given us new birth into a living hope through the resurrection of Jesus Christ from the dead' (1 Pet 1:3). That verse is typical of many others in different parts of the New Testament in which the resurrection is seen as the distinctive personal act of God the Father, his justifying vindication of Jesus in the face of his crucifiers. Men put him to death, but he appealed his case to his Father (Luke 23:46) and in response God said his own great Yes to all that Jesus had lived and died for by raising him from the dead. Walter Künneth has the weight of the biblical evidence behind him when he says, 'it is decisive to recognize that *God is exclusively the subject of the action in the resurrection of Jesus*' (Künneth 1965: 128). Jesus rises because he has been raised up by his Father, he acts because he has first been acted upon by God. He is the resurrection and the life (John 11:25), not in and by himself but because he has received this from the Father.

What is true of his resurrection is also true of his exaltation. He does not exalt himself – that would be against his whole character – it is his Father who exalts him to his own right hand. His Father's act is of course grounded in what Jesus has done. As Paul puts it in the passage we have already quoted, 'he . . . became obedient to death – even death on a cross! *Therefore* . . .' (Phil 2:8–9). Nevertheless his exaltation remains the distinctive personal act of God the Father, '*God* exalted him to the highest place and gave him the name that is above every name' (Phil 2:9). The authority in heaven and on earth that has been given to him (Matt 28:18) is to be exercised in a way that glorifies and serves the purposes of the

Father who gave it (Phil 2:11). In the end indeed, also according to Paul, that kingly authority has to be surrendered back to the Father who gave it, so that God may be all in all (1 Cor 15:24–28). The primary agency of the Father, as the ultimate source and goal of the resurrection and exaltation of the Son, emerges as an emphasis that is persistent in the writings of Paul and that characterises the way in which all the other New Testament writers understand what Easter means.

The same emphasis is equally apparent when we turn to the post-Easter outpouring of the Holy Spirit. Acts 2:32–33 is highly important in this connection. Peter is speaking: 'God has raised this Jesus to life, and we are all witnesses of the fact. Exalted to the right hand of God, he has received from the Father the promised Holy Spirit and has poured out what you now see and hear.' Here we have the clear beginnings of a fully trinitarian understanding of what happened at Pentecost. The Holy Spirit did not come on his own, he was poured out by Jesus after and as a result of his resurrection and his exaltation to God's right hand. Yet even Jesus is not the ultimate origin of the newly poured out Spirit. He gives him only because he has first received him from the Father. Here again the primacy and priority of the Father are very clearly asserted and we are given good biblical support for our attempt to understand the Holy Spirit in a fully trinitarian way. Here is one point at least where Luke – who often holds resurrection, ascension and Pentecost apart – begins to integrate them theologically, and it is highly significant that he does so in such a trinitarian way.

When we come to John's teaching about the coming of the Spirit, we see the same trinitarian insights being worked out in a more explicit and indeed sophisticated manner. We cannot do that teaching full justice here, but must content ourselves with pointing to a few significant verses.

In John 14:16 Jesus says, 'I will ask the Father, and he will give you another Counsellor to be with you for ever – the Spirit of truth.' Here both Father and Son are involved in the giving of the Spirit. The giver is the Father, but he gives in response to the prayer of the Son. So also John 15:26 (a verse that was at the centre of much controversy in medieval times between Eastern Orthodox theologians on the one hand and Western Catholic theologians on the other), 'When the Counsellor comes, whom I will send to you from the Father, the Spirit of truth who goes out [proceeds] from the Father, he will testify about me.' Here it is Jesus who immediately is going to send the Spirit upon his disciples, but it is from the Father that he sends him, it is from the Father as his ultimate source and origin that he proceeds. To summarise, for John as for Luke the sending of the Spirit is an act that involves in different ways both the Father and the Son; in other words it is a trinitarian act. It is the Father who gives the Spirit, but he gives him in the closest connection with the person and the completed work of the Son (*cf.* John 16:7–8; 20:22).

As we have already hinted, it was disagreement about the part of the Father and the Son in sending the Spirit that was a chief cause of the division between the Eastern Orthodox and Western Catholic Churches that came to a head in 1054, a difference that is still reflected in the different forms in which these two bodies of Christians say the third article of the Nicene Creed down to the present day. In the Orthodox East they say, 'We believe in the Holy Spirit, the Lord and Giver of Life, who proceeds from the Father' and in the Roman Catholic and Protestant West they say, 'We believe in the Holy Spirit . . . who proceeds from the Father *and the Son*.' And because the words 'and the Son' are in Latin *Filioque*, the disagreement is commonly referred to as 'the *Filioque* controversy'.

If we compare the two competing positions with the teaching of John we have just outlined, we can see that, as is so often the case on such occasions, there are strong and weak points on both sides.

The East has the New Testament behind it in insisting that ultimately and primarily the Spirit comes from and is sent by the Father. To say he comes from the Father 'and the Son' is to obscure that fact. At the same time the Eastern failure to say anything at all in the creed about the Son's part in the sending of the Spirit is to leave out what for John is a vital factor in the whole matter.

The West on the other hand is in line with John's teaching in holding that the Son has an essential part in the sending of the Spirit, but the formula it uses does not make it clear that the Spirit the Son gives us is the Spirit that he himself has first received from the Father. It is through the Son – and in no other way – that the Spirit reaches us, but the one from whom he comes through the Son is the Father.

It is sometimes suggested nowadays that the old controversy could be ended in a way that is faithful to the New Testament and that guards the important points that both sides were making, if we all confess, 'We believe in the Holy Spirit, the Lord and Giver of Life, who proceeds from the Father *through* the Son.'

In this whole section, however, what we have been emphasising is that everything to do with the resurrection of Jesus and the sending of the Spirit has its origin in God the Father. It is he who raises Jesus from the dead to his own right hand, and it is he who through his exalted Son sends the Spirit to the church at Pentecost.

Now mainline Christian theologians have down the centuries maintained that, through Jesus Christ and in the Holy Spirit, God shows himself to us as he really is. As you can see what a man is like in his inmost being by how he reveals himself in his outward actions, so by contemplating what God does among us in human history, you can see what he is like in his own life and being from eternity to eternity.

Applying that principle, we can say that in God's action in the resurrection of Jesus we are shown a Father who sends his Son and his Spirit to us, and a Son and a Spirit who come from that Father and in their distinctive ways do his will, serve his purpose and glorify his name here on earth. So, according to that principle, if God is like that in his actions towards us, he is also like that in himself. God *is* Father, Son and Holy Spirit and, within his own divine life, the Son and the Spirit are what they are not from themselves or in themselves, but from the

Father. He does not come from them, but they come from him.

In the resurrection of Jesus we see the Father giving life, power and glory to the Son and breathing out the Holy Spirit. That is what he does in his own life; the Father is the giver of life to the Son and the breather out of the Holy Spirit. In the Holy Trinity the Spirit and Son in their different ways owe their life and their being to him alone. Within the life of God the Father is the source and origin of his Son and of his Spirit.

Second, *as regards the Son: the integrated Easter event that proclaims the primacy of the Father equally clearly proclaims what we may call the derived deity of the Son*.

When the Father raises his Son from the dead to his own throne, he is telling us something not just about himself, but about that Son, namely that he belongs not just with us on the human side of reality, but with God himself on the divine side of reality. Jesus of Nazareth who is our brother is also the eternal Son of God. It was chiefly in the light of Easter and what followed after that he was so revealed and proclaimed.

The New Testament writers, each in their own way, make it clear that it is to himself that the Father exalts his Son, because it is with himself, on the divine side of reality, that the Son eternally belongs. The name that the exalted Jesus is given is (again according to Paul in Philippians 2) the name that is above every name, the name *Kurios*, 'Lord', which is God's own name. The divine honours that according to Isaiah 45:23 are to be paid to the Lord Yahweh alone are now to be paid to the exalted Jesus. At his name every knee shall bow and every tongue confess that he is *Kurios*. Moreover, this confession of the divine lordship of Jesus, far from detracting from or being in competition with the glory of the Father, is actually the appointed way to glorify him.

Furthermore, the exaltation of Christ at his ascension is in this very passage seen to have astounding implications for the understanding of the being of God himself. The Philippians hymn makes it clear that the place and the name to which Jesus ascended are the place and the name that have from eternity belonged to him, that have always been his within the life of God himself. The historical exaltation of the Son is, in exact accordance with the principle that we were expounding at the end of the last section, read back into the being of God himself. Jesus is confessed as *Kurios* because that is what he is. The one to whom every knee bows and whom every tongue confesses (Phil 2:10–11) is the one who is 'in very nature God' (Phil 2:6). Or, to speak the language of Ephesians, 'What does "he ascended" mean except that he also descended to the lower, earthly regions?' (Eph 4:9). His exaltation to God is seen to imply that his work and his person have their eternal origination within God's own life.

We can see the same process taking place within the other strands of New Testament Christology. In Hebrews the exalted high priest 'who sat down at the right hand of the throne of the Majesty in heaven' (Heb 8:1) is also the eternal Son 'through whom [God] made the universe', who is 'the radiance of God's glory and the exact representation of his being, sustaining all things by his powerful word' (Heb 1:2–3). The exalted Christ is again presented as one who shares the deity of the Father, but it is all the time taken for granted that his is a deity that is derived from and dependent upon that of the Father.

It is however in Johannine Christology that the connection between the resurrection and exaltation of Jesus and his eternal relationship to the Father is most clearly asserted. At the end of the gospel, as soon as Thomas is convinced about the resurrection, he confesses in the most unambiguous terms the deity of the risen Christ, 'My Lord (*kurios*) and my God (*theos*)!' (John 20:28). If Jesus is Lord and God in his resurrection and exaltation, that means for John that he is also, within the life of God himself, the eternal Son who is 'in the bosom of the Father' (John 1:18, RSV) and the Word (*Logos*) who is eternally with God and is himself God (John 1:1) and his partner in all his works (John 1:3). All this, however, is said on the clear assumption that it does not threaten the primacy of the Father. The Son is Son because on the one hand he is all that the Father is, he is of the very stuff of the

Father's deity, but on the other hand all he is and all he has he owes not to himself but to the Father (John 5:19).

In these different ways the New Testament authors register their conviction that the exalted Christ reveals himself, in what he is and what he does, to be of the very being of God, and it is that distinctively Christian post-resurrection insight that generates a drastic revision in their whole understanding of God, which results ultimately in the developed trinitarian doctrine of the later creeds, but is present already within the New Testament itself at different stages of development.

There is of course no going back on the fundamental Old Testament faith that God is one, but that oneness is now seen in a different way. God is one not so much in the way that a solitary individual is one, but much more like the way in which a human family is one or a husband and wife are one flesh. It is a oneness that contains within itself the sort of relationship that Jesus had with his Father on earth, that he continues to have with his Father in his exaltation to heaven, and that he has always with his Father from eternity to eternity. Within the life of God there is one who is called Father and another who is called Son, two centres of personal being and action who relate to each other in mutual love and self-giving, as we see in the human life and death of Jesus. The Father is called Father because the Son derives all that he is from him, but the Son shares totally the divine nature of the Father: he is not a creature, but (as the creed puts it in an attempt to say the unsayable) 'eternally begotten of the Father, God from God, Light from Light, true God from true God, begotten not made, of one Being with the Father'.

That is the attempt of the creed to define what we have called the derived divinity of Christ, which says on the one hand that he is of the same being and nature as the Father, but nevertheless has that being and nature not in and from himself but from his Father. The risen Son of God shows himself to be not only our brother, but God's eternal Son, who is to us and does for us what only God can do. Yet at the same time he is to be differentiated from God the Father, as the one who is sent is to be differentiated from the one who sends him, the one

who obeys from the one whom he obeys, the one who is raised
from the one who raises him.

The doctrine of the Trinity depends upon our believing in
the divinity of the risen and ascended Lord. That is why it has
always been misunderstood and attacked by Jews and Muslims who could see in Jesus nothing other than a human
prophet and teacher, someone not in any essential way
different from those who went before him and those who
came after him. There are also in our day liberal and radical
Christians who dispute the New Testament estimate of Jesus
and seek to understand him as a man in whom the Spirit of
God resided as he does in all of us – only to a far greater
degree – rather than as one who, as well as being wholly man
and our brother, is also wholly God as God's Son.

On that modern radical view of Jesus there is of course no
need for a trinitarian doctrine of God. Jesus so understood is
man and not God. Whether we need a trinitarian doctrine of
God or not depends on whether with Thomas and the vast
multitude of Christians down the centuries and across the
continents we will confess Jesus as Lord and God. It is
impossible to go into the matter further here, except to
register my own firm conviction that the confession of Jesus as
divine Son made man is essential to the New Testament
gospel, which soon falls apart without it. Only if he is God can
he make an absolute claim on my obedience and worship.
Only if he is God can he be the source of forgiveness, new life
and salvation to those who believe in him. But if he is indeed
God, then it takes something very like a trinitarian doctrine of
God to express his relationship to his Father. In the end we all
have to answer for ourselves his question, 'Who do you say I
am?' (Matt 16:15). The authentic Christian answer, which the
church has always given and goes on giving today, is: 'You are
the Christ, the Son of the living God' (Matt 16:16). It is that
answer, when it is worked out fully, that requires a trinitarian
understanding of God.

So far we have spoken as if it was enough to talk of God the
Father and God the Son – the Father who has divine life in and
from himself, and the Son who has the same divine life in

himself but has it from his Father. This is indeed the God who is at work and who reveals himself in the exaltation of Jesus. If we stopped there, however, we should speak only of a God who is two in one, in a *bi*nitarian rather than a fully *tri*nitarian way. We need now to remind ourselves that included in what we have called the integrated Easter event is what happened at Pentecost when, as a direct result of the resurrection and exaltation of Jesus, the Holy Spirit was poured out on the apostolic company. We need to ask ourselves now what we can learn from that about the relationship of the Spirit to the Father and the Son within the trinitarian life of God.

Our third and final thesis is therefore: *the integrated Easter event that reveals the primacy of the Father and the derived deity of the Son, also reveals the mutual interdependence of the Son and the Holy Spirit.*

The New Testament never delineates the distinct person-hood of the Holy Spirit as clearly as it does that of the Father and the Son, but it says enough to indicate that in the great events of the life, death and resurrection of Jesus there is at work a third personal agent (usually identified as the Holy Spirit) who, as at the baptism of Jesus, comes from the Father to the Son to empower him for his work, and who at Pentecost and after comes to the church to enable us to know and confess the Father and the Son and to participate in their life, love and power. The Spirit does his work in a way that draws attention not to himself but rather to the Father and to Jesus, and that is why he is the most difficult of the three to identify.

It is not possible here to deal with the rich New Testament teaching about the Spirit, so we must confine ourselves to his activity in connection with the resurrection of Jesus. Here we can see a twofold relationship. On the one hand it is through the activity of the Spirit that Jesus is raised, and on the other hand it is through the risen Jesus that the Spirit is sent to the church at Pentecost.

To take the latter point first, the dependence of the coming of the Holy Spirit upon the resurrection and exaltation of Jesus is emphasised in many parts of the New Testament. We have only to recall Acts 2:33, '[Jesus] . . . has poured out what you now see and hear', and John 16:7, 'Unless I go away, the Counsellor will not come to you; but if I go, I will send him to you.' For Paul also the dependence of the work of the Spirit upon the work of Christ is so close that at some points (although not by any means always) he seems to identify the one with the other. According to 2 Corinthians 3:18, one of the central Pauline statements on this subject, the business of the Spirit is to transform Christians into the likeness of Christ, so that their lives as well as their lips proclaim that he is Lord (*cf*. 1 Cor 12:3). In other words the Holy Spirit does nothing of his own that is apart from or beyond what Christ has done. He simply takes what is in Christ and so works in us that it becomes ours also. That is what is said explicitly in John 16:14–15, 'He will bring glory to me by taking from what is mine and making it known to you. All that belongs to the Father is mine. That is why I said the Spirit will take from what is mine and make it known to you.'

There is thus a dependence of the work of the Spirit upon the work of Jesus. In accordance with the principle that we enunciated earlier (that the way God acts among us reveals what he is eternally in himself) trinitarian theology, especially in the West, has therefore concluded that the Spirit comes eternally from the Son as well as from the Father. That is why the Western form of the Nicene Creed affirms that the Holy Spirit 'proceeds from the Father *and the Son* [*Filioque*]'.

We have already seen that this Western formula is open to criticism because it obscures the primacy of the Father over the Son in the sending of the Spirit. But even if we amend it to read '. . . who proceeds from the Father *through the Son*', it is still not entirely acceptable, because it suggests that there is a one-way dependence of the Spirit and his work upon the Son and his work. This is to leave out an important strand of New Testament evidence about the activity of the Spirit, as we shall now see.

The New Testament provides considerable support for the trinitarian statement that the Father raises the Son from the dead through the activity of the Holy Spirit (*cf*. Rom 1:4; 1 Cor 6:14; 1 Tim 3:16; 1 Pet 3:18). If that is so, then it is the Son who is dependent upon the Spirit in his reception of resurrection life from the Father, just as he was dependent upon the Spirit for his human birth from Mary (Luke 1:35) and for his endowment with messianic power in his baptism. For the New Testament writers the Father incarnates, empowers and raises up his Son through his Spirit. In the story of Jesus it is not just that the Spirit comes through the Son, but equally that the Son comes through the Spirit.

Thus, the relationship between Son and Spirit that is brought to light at the resurrection of Jesus is not a one-way dependence of the latter upon the former, as Western trinitarian thought has often suggested, but rather a mutual interdependence of the one upon the other, the Son upon the Spirit and the Spirit upon the Son. The two-sided mutuality of that relationship is classically expressed in the words of John the Baptist in John 1:33, 'The man on whom you see the Spirit come down and remain is he who will baptise with the Holy Spirit.' At his baptism Jesus receives the Spirit and all that he brings from the Father for his own work; at Pentecost he sends that same Spirit from the Father to empower us in our work for him.

We may therefore conclude that, if the relationships between Son and Spirit in the eternal life of God are as they are revealed in the life and especially in the resurrection of Jesus, we need to speak of a mutual interdependence of the one upon the other and of the dependence of both of them upon the Father from whom they come and whose being and nature they share. The second-century theologian Irenaeus of Lyons put it well when he said that the Son and the Spirit are the two hands of God. As such they work in the closest co-ordination with each other and neither has priority over the other.

If we were therefore to amend the creed to reflect this relationship we would need to say about the Spirit that 'he proceeds from the Father *through the Son*'; but we would also need to say about the Son that he is 'eternally begotten of the Father *through the Spirit*'. In that way what we say about the relationships of Father, Son and Spirit in God would more faithfully reflect what the New Testament obliges us to say about the relationships revealed in the life and in the resurrection of Jesus.

The primacy of the Father, the derived deity of the Son, the mutuality of Son and Spirit, these are the consistent patterns of trinitarian relationships that characterise the interactions of the three divine persons as portrayed in the Easter gospel. These three are one because they share the same being and nature, the same will and purpose in all that they do: they so give themselves, the one to the other, that they mysteriously interpenetrate and indwell one another in all that they do and are. This is what we mean when we speak of Father, Son and Holy Spirit, three persons and one God.

If we do our thinking about God within the presuppositions of modernity, we shall have little time for such trinitarian mysteries, but if, as Christians have always done, we defy the presuppositions of the thinking of our day and look to Jesus Christ – incarnate, crucified and risen – to learn what God does and who he is, then, as we have tried to show, we shall be led to the same insights as the first Christians and see that the God who raised Jesus from the dead has to be confessed in his triune glory as Father, Son and Holy Spirit, to whom indeed be glory for ever.

RESURRECTION AND INCARNATION:
The foundations of the Christian faith

Alister E. McGrath

> The doctrine of Christ's divinity seems to me not something stuck on which you can unstick but something that peeps out at every point so that you'd have to unravel the whole web to get rid of it. (C. S. Lewis, letter to Arthur Greaves, 11 December 1944; Hooper 1979: p. 503)

For C. S. Lewis, the coherence of Christianity was such that it was impossible to eliminate the idea of the divinity of Christ without doing such damage to the web of Christian doctrine that the entire structure of the Christian faith would collapse. Far from being an optional extra, something which had accidentally been added and which now required removal, it was an essential and integral part of the authentically Christian understanding of reality. Modernism, however, has laid down two fundamental challenges to this view.

First, that it is *wrong*. Our growing understanding of the background to the New Testament, the way in which Christian doctrine has developed, the rise of the scientific worldview, and so on, force us to abandon the idea that Jesus was God in any meaningful sense of the word.

Second, it is *unnecessary*. Christianity can exist without the need for such obsolete and cumbersome ideas as God becoming man, traditionally grounded in the resurrection of Jesus Christ and expressed in the doctrine of the incarnation. In a world come of age, Christianity must learn to abandon these ideas as archaic and irrelevant if it is to survive.

In the present essay we wish to suggest that the only way in which Christianity is likely to survive in the future is by reclaiming its incarnational heritage as the only proper and legitimate interpretation of the significance of the history of Jesus of Nazareth.

It will be obvious that it is impossible in this brief essay to do justice either to the objections raised against the traditional understandings of the resurrection and the incarnation, or to recent responses to these objections. The present essay is concerned to indicate briefly the *ineffectiveness* of recent criticism of these doctrines, and the *inadequacy* of the proposed alternative explanations of the identity and significance of Jesus Christ. We begin by considering the objections raised against the resurrection and the incarnation.

Objections to the resurrection and the incarnation

Three criticisms of the resurrection

The New Testament is permeated by references to the resurrection of Jesus of Nazareth. The consequences of this event for both the personal experience of the first Christians and their understanding of the identity and significance of Jesus himself dominate the horizons of the New Testament writers.

It was on the basis of the belief that the one who was crucified had been raised by God from the dead that the astonishing developments in the perceived status and identity of Jesus took place. The cross was interpreted from the standpoint of the resurrection, and Jesus' teaching was accorded reverence on account of who the resurrection disclosed him to be. Jesus was worshipped and adored as the living Lord, who would come again – not merely revered as a dead rabbi.

The tendency to 'think of Jesus Christ as of God' (2 Clement 1.1) is already evident within the New Testament. It cannot be emphasised too strongly that the most important developments in the Christian understanding of the identity and significance of Jesus Christ took place not during the patristic period but within twenty years of the crucifixion itself.

1. The first Christians were mistaken

Of course, the modern critics of the resurrection point out, it was easy for the first Christians to believe in the resurrection of Jesus. After all, belief in resurrections was a commonplace at the time. The first Christians may have jumped to the conclusion that Jesus was raised from the dead, when in fact something rather different actually happened.

Although the crude charges of yesteryear (for example, that the disciples stole the corpse of Jesus from its tomb, or that they were the victims of mass hysteria) are still occasionally encountered, they have generally been superseded by more subtle theories. Thus, to note the most important, the resurrection was really a *symbolic* event which the first Christians confused with a *historical* event on account of their uncritical presuppositions.

In response to this, however, it may be pointed out that in Jesus' day neither of the two contemporary beliefs about resurrection bore any resemblance to the resurrection of Jesus. The Sadducees denied the idea of a resurrection altogether (a fact which Paul was able to exploit at an awkward moment, Acts 23:6–8), while the majority expectation was of a general resurrection on the last day, at the end of history itself.

The sheer *oddness* of the Christian proclamation of the resurrection of Jesus in human history, at a definite time and place, is all too easily overlooked by modern critics, even though it was obvious at the time. The unthinkable appeared to have happened, and for that very reason demanded careful attention. Far from merely fitting into the popular expectation of the pattern of resurrection, what happened to Jesus actually contradicted it. The sheer novelty of the Christian position at the time has been obscured by two thousand years' experience of the Christian understanding of the resurrection – yet *at the time* it was wildly unorthodox and radical.

To dismiss the Christian understanding of the resurrection of Jesus because it allegedly conformed to contemporary expectations is clearly unacceptable. The suggestion that the resurrection of Jesus may be explicable as some sort of wish-fulfilment on the part of the disciples also strains the imagination somewhat. Why should the disciples have responded to the catastrophe of Jesus' death by making the hitherto unprecedented suggestion that he had been raised from the dead? The history of Israel is littered with the corpses of pious Jewish martyrs, none of whom were ever thought of as having been raised from the dead in such a manner.

2. The New Testament writers used pagan and gnostic myths
The second attack on the historicity of the resurrection of Jesus mounted in recent years is based upon the parallels between pagan myths of dying and rising gods and the resurrection of Jesus.

In the first part of the present century a substantial number of scholarly works appeared which drew attention to these pagan and gnostic myths. (Perhaps J.G. Frazer's *Adonis, Attis, Osiris* (1907) is the most famous of these in the English-speaking world.) And so it was argued that the New Testament writers were simply reproducing this myth, which was part of the intellectual furniture of the ancient world. Rudolf Bultmann was among many scholars who subsequently argued for such influence (deriving from the Mandaeans) upon the resurrection accounts and beliefs of the New Testament, and then proceeded to take the logically questionable step of arguing that such parallels discredited the historicity of the resurrection of Jesus.

Since then, however, scholarship has moved on considerably. The parallels between the pagan myths of dying and rising gods and the New Testament accounts of the resurrection of Jesus are now regarded as remote, to say the least. For instance, the New Testament documents with some care indicate the place and the date of both the death and the resurrection of Jesus, as well as identifying the witnesses to both. The contrast with the ahistorical narrative form of mythology is striking. Furthermore, there are no known instances of this myth being applied to any *specific historical figure* in pagan literature, so that the New Testament writers, had they utilised it, would have given a stunningly original twist to this mythology. (It is at this point that the wisdom of C. S. Lewis – who actually knew something about myths – must be acknowledged. Lewis intuitively realised that the New Testament accounts of the resurrection of Jesus bore no relation to 'real' mythology, despite the protests of some theologians who had dabbled in the field.) Perhaps most important, however, was the realisation that the gnostic redeemer myths – which the New Testament writers allegedly took over and applied to Jesus – were to be dated later than the New Testament itself. The gnostics, it seems, actually took over Christian ideas.

The challenge posed to the historicity of the resurrection by these theories has thus passed into textbooks of the history of ideas. But an important point must be made before we proceed any further. We have seen how allegedly responsible academic scholarship, regarded as competent in its own day, was seen to pose a serious challenge to a central aspect of the Christian faith. It was taken seriously by theologians and popular religious writers. Yet the sheer *provisionality* of scholarship seemed to have been ignored. Scholarship proceeds by evaluation of evidence and hypotheses, a process which takes decades, in which what one generation took as self-evident is often demonstrated to be in error. The fate of the resurrection myth is a case in point: in 1920 it was treated virtually as an established fact of serious and responsible scholarship; in 1988 it is regarded as an interesting, if now discredited, idea.

How many more such theories, which now seem to be persuasive and to pose a challenge to the Christian faith, will be treated as discredited and obsolete in fifty years' time? For example, in *The Myth of God Incarnate* Michael Goulder

(Hick 1977: 64–86) seriously expected Christians to abandon faith in the incarnation there and then on account of his
ingenious, if improbable, theory about its historical origins!
Christianity can hardly be expected to abandon its proclamation of the risen Christ as Saviour and Lord on such flimsy
grounds – it has a duty to speak for two thousand years of
history, as well as for an untold period in the future, in
refusing to allow the short-term preoccupations of modernity
to dictate its character for posterity.

3. There is no historical analogue to Jesus' resurrection
A third line of criticism of the historicity of the resurrection is
due to the German sociologist Ernst Troeltsch (1902), who
argued that, since dead men don't rise, so Jesus couldn't have
risen.

The basic principle underlying this objection goes back to
David Hume, and concerns the need for present-day analogues for historical events. Troeltsch asserted that since we
have no contemporary experience of the resurrection of a
dead human being we therefore have reason for supposing
that no dead man has ever been raised. But of course, as
Christianity has insisted that the resurrection of Jesus was a
unique historical event, the absence of present-day analogues
is only to be expected.

The most vigorous response to Troeltsch's criticism has
been made by Wolfhart Pannenberg (1968), who points out
that Troeltsch adopted a remarkably dogmatic view of reality,
based upon his questionable metaphysical presuppositions,
effectively dictating what could and could not have happened
in history on the basis of his preconceived views. For Pannenberg the decisive factor in determining what happened on the
first Easter Day is the evidence contained in the New Testament, and not dogmatic and provisional scholarly theories
about the nature of reality. How, asks Pannenberg, are we to
account for the New Testament evidence? What is its most
probable explanation? The historical evidence liberates us
from the kind of dogmatic metaphysical presuppositions
about what can and what cannot have happened in history that

underlie Troeltsch's critique of the resurrection, and allows us to return to the Jesus of history. And for Pannenberg the resurrection of Jesus is the most probable and plausible explanation of the historical evidence (McGrath 1986: 83–85, 161–176). Perhaps it lacks the absolute certainty which the more fundamentalist of metaphysicians seem to demand – but, as Bishop Butler so carefully demonstrated in his *Analogy of Religion* (1736), probability is the law of religious life, whether orthodox or deist (Ferreira 1986).

Criticisms of the incarnation

The doctrine of the incarnation has also come under sustained criticism recently. Many such criticisms of the incarnation, for example those expressed in *The Myth of God Incarnate*, demonstrate a regrettable tendency to concentrate upon objections to the *idea* of incarnation, rather than the *basis* of the idea itself. After all, the idea of God incarnate in a specific historical human being was quite startling within its first-century Jewish context, and a virtual impossibility within the Greek ontological framework underlying the patristic period, so that the question of what caused this belief to arise requires careful examination. Of central importance to this question is the resurrection itself, a subject studiously ignored (along with the major contributions to the incarnational discussion by Pannenberg (1968), Moltmann (1974), Rahner (1961–81), Kasper (1976) and others; *cf.* McGrath 1986: 161–203) by most of the contributors to *The Myth of God Incarnate*. The idea of incarnation is easy to criticise: it is paradoxical, enigmatic, and so on. But everyone already knows this, including the most fervent advocates of the idea! The question remains, as it always has been, is the incarnation a proper and legitimate interpretation of the history of Jesus of Nazareth?

The fact that something is paradoxical and even apparently self-contradictory does not invalidate it, despite what many critics of the incarnation seem to think. Those working in the scientific field are only too aware of the sheer complexity and mysteriousness of reality. The events lying behind the rise of quantum theory, the difficulties of using models in scientific explanation – to name but two factors which I can remember particularly clearly from my own period as a natural scientist – point to the inevitability of paradox and contradiction in any except the most superficial engagement with reality. Our apprehension of reality is partial and fragmentary, whether we are dealing with our knowledge of the natural world or of God. The Enlightenment worldview tended to suppose that reality could be totally apprehended in rational terms, an assumption which still persists in some theological circles, even where it has been abandoned as unrealistic elsewhere. All too many modern theologians cry 'Contradiction!', and expect us all to abandon whatever it is that is supposed to be contradictory there and then. But reality just isn't like that.

Logical contradiction may pose a less than decisive challenge to the principle of the incarnation, but it may immediately invalidate an incoherent argument. An example of such an argument apparently invalidated by logical inconsistency is that developed by one of the contributors to *The Myth of God Incarnate*, Frances Young, who argues (Hick 1977: 13–47) that the patristic development of the doctrine of the incarnation inevitably led to the 'blind alleys of paradox' and 'illogicality'. Having thus dismissed this doctrine for such reasons, she affirms that 'religion is destroyed without mystery – without paradox', as she develops her thesis that we must learn to live with unresolved contradictions. It would seem that paradoxes, illogicality and unresolved contradictions invalidate the patristic idea of the incarnation, but not the modern ideas which allegedly replace it! In fairness, of course, it may be noted that Professor Young's more recent writings are much more sympathetic to the idea of incarnation.

A more serious charge against the principle of the incarnation is developed by John Hick, who asserts ('argues' is not the *mot juste*) that the idea of Jesus being both God and man is logically contradictory (Hick 1977: 167–185). Quoting

Spinoza, Hick asserts that to talk of one who is both God and man is like talking about a square circle. Hick's sensitivity at this point is difficult to follow, since he is already committed to the belief that all the concepts of God to be found in the world religions – personal and impersonal, immanent and transcendent – are compatible with each other. Indeed, such is the variety of the concepts of divinity currently in circulation in the world religions that Hick seems to be obliged to turn a blind eye to the resulting logical inconsistency between them – only to seize upon and censure this alleged 'inconsistency' in the case of the incarnation.

But Hick cannot be allowed to make this robust assertion concerning the logical incompatibility of God and man unchallenged, and his less than adequate knowledge of the development of Christology in the medieval period is clearly demonstrated in this matter. The fact that there is no *logical* incompatibility between God and man in the incarnation is demonstrated, and then theologically exploited, by that most brilliant of all English theologians, William of Ockham (McGrath 1984). Ockham's discussion of this point is exhaustive and highly influential, and has yet to be discredited.

More seriously, Hick seems to work on the basis of the assumption that we know *exactly* what God is like, and on the basis of this knowledge are in a position to pass judgement on the logical niceties of the incarnation. But this is obviously not the case! Hick may be saying that there is a logical problem involved with classical theism (a *philosophical* system) in relation to the incarnation – but this is merely to suggest that classical theism is not necessarily compatible with Christianity, a point which has been made with increasing force by theologians such as Jürgen Moltmann (1974) and Eberhard Jüngel (1983) in recent years. It is not to discredit the incarnation!

Hick may be in a position to say that God is totally unable to come among us as a human being, and that the incarnation is impossible on account of who and what God is – but if he can do so, he would seem to have access to a private and infallible knowledge of God denied to the rest of us! And do we really fully understand what is meant by that deceptively familiar word 'man'? Do we really have a total and exhaustive grasp of what it is to be human? Many of us would prefer to say that the incarnation discloses the true nature of divinity and humanity, rather than approaching the incarnation on the basis of preconceived ideas of divinity and humanity.

Historical and cultural relativism

In the present section of the essay we have sketched briefly some of the objections raised recently against the resurrection and incarnation of Jesus Christ, and indicated briefly the way in which they have been met. It has not been possible to do justice to either these objections or the responses to them, and all that we have had the opportunity to do is to note how resurrection and incarnation alike are 'bloodied but un-bowed' through recent criticisms. But one final point may be made before moving on. All too often we are given the impression that something dramatic has happened recently which suddenly forces everyone of any intellectual respect-ability to abandon faith in these matters. We are told that in a world 'come of age' ideas such as resurrection and incarnation are to be discarded as pre-modern, perhaps as vestiges of a cultic idol. We are children of the modern period and must accept our lot, bequeathed by the Enlightenment, and make the most of it. But is this really the case?

If our thinking at any one time – such as the modern period – is so heavily conditioned and determined by the prevailing cultural and historical conditions, as the contributors to *The Myth of God Incarnate* in particular suggest, we must recog-nise that we are confronted with a near-total relativism of values and thought which discredits the New Testament on account of its first-century Palestinian context, and also dis-credits modern interpretations of the New Testament (including criticism of the ideas of resurrection and in-carnation) on account of their twentieth-century Western context. Each and every historical idea is conditioned by its historical context, and cannot necessarily be regarded as valid outside that context. All possess relative, not absolute, validity. Logical consistency demands that criticism of the doctrines of resurrection and incarnation be acknowledged to be as historically conditioned as those doctrines themselves, and of no permanent or universal value. This scepticism has the virtue of consistency, but is unlikely to commend itself to most critics of the resurrection and incarnation, who appear to envisage their criticisms as establishing a new, more relevant and universal version of Christianity.

But what might this new version of Christianity be like? The inclusion of the word 'new' is deliberate and weighed: historically, Christianity has regarded both the resurrection and the incarnation as essential to its historical self-understanding, and any attempt to eliminate or radically modify them would seem to lead to a version of Christianity which is not continuous with the historical forms it has taken in the course of its development. In the following section, we shall look at the result of the elimination or radical modification of these two traditional ideas.

A critical assessment of 'new' Christianity

Modernism asserts: (a) that Jesus was not God in any meaningful sense of the term; (b) that he was a man, like us in every way, but far superior religiously and morally; and (c) that everything which Christianity has wanted to say about the significance of Jesus can be said, and said well, without the belief that he was God as well as man. Let us see if this can actually be done.

On the basis of a number of important works reflecting the spirit of Enlightenment modernism, it is clear that a central idea congenial to the modern spirit is that Jesus reveals to us the love of God. It is frequently pointed out that the modern age is able to dispense with superstitious ideas about the death of Jesus (for example, that it represented a victory over Satan or the payment of a legal penalty of some sort), and instead get to the real meat of both the New Testament (so movingly expressed in the parable of the prodigal son) and modern Christianity – the love of God for humanity. In what follows, I propose to suggest that abandoning the ideas of resurrection and the incarnation means abandoning even this tender insight.

This may seem an outrageous suggestion to make, but I cannot see how this conclusion can be avoided. How may the death of Jesus Christ upon a cross at Calvary be interpreted as a demonstration of the love of God for humanity? Remember, the idea that Jesus *is* God cannot be permitted, given the presuppositions of modernism. Once modernism dispenses with the idea of incarnation, a number of possible alternative explanations of the cross remain open.

1. It represents the devastating and unexpected end to the career of Jesus, forcing his disciples to invent the idea of the resurrection to cover up the totality of this catastrophe.

2. It represents God's judgement upon the career of Jesus, demonstrating that he was cursed by the law of Moses, and thus disqualified from any putative messianic status.

3. It represents the inevitable fate of anyone who attempts to lead a life of obedience to God.

4. It represents the greatest love which one human being can show for another (*cf.* John 15:13), inspiring Jesus' followers to demonstrate an equal love for others.

5. The cross demonstrates that God is a sadistic tyrant.

6. The cross is meaningless.

All of these are plausible, within the framework of modernism. The idea that the cross demonstrates the love of God for man cannot, however, be included among this list. It is not *God* who is dying upon the cross, who gives himself for his people. It is a man – an especially splendid man – who may be ranked with others in history who have made equally great sacrifices for those whom they loved. But the death of an innocent person at the hands of corrupt judges is all too common, even today, and Jesus cannot be singled out for special discussion unless he *is* something or someone qualitatively different from us.

A critic might, of course, immediately reply that Jesus is a higher example of the kind of inspiration or illumination to be found in all human beings, so that he must be regarded as the outstanding human being – and for that reason his death assumes universal significance. But this is a remarkably dogmatic assumption – that Jesus is unique among human beings in this respect! The uniqueness of Jesus was established by the New Testament writers through the resurrection (an assumption which modernism cannot allow), and the subsequent recognition that Jesus was none other than the living God dwelling among us. But this insight is given and guaranteed by two doctrines which modernism cannot allow. It would seem that modernists are prepared to retain insights gained through the traditional framework of resurrection and incarnation – and then declare that this framework may be dispensed with. It is as if the traditional framework is treated as some sort of learning aid which may be dispensed with once the ideas in question are mastered.

But this is clearly questionable, to say the least. If the traditional framework is declared to be wrong, the consequences of this declaration for each and every aspect of Christian theology must be ascertained. Discard or radically modify the doctrines of resurrection and incarnation, and the idea of the 'uniqueness' or the 'superiority' of Jesus becomes a dogmatic assertion without foundation, an assertion which many of more humanist inclinations would find offensive. We would be equally justified in appealing to other historical figures – such as Socrates or Gandhi – as encapsulating the desiderata of Christian moral behaviour.

This point becomes more important when we return to the question of how the death of Jesus can be interpreted as a self-giving divine act that demonstrates the love of God for humanity. It is not God who is upon the cross: it is a human being. That point must be conceded by those who reject the incarnation. It may then be the case that God makes his love known indirectly (and, it must be said, in a remarkably ambiguous manner) through the death of Jesus Christ, but we have lost for ever the insight that it is God himself who shows his love for us on the cross.

What the cross might conceivably demonstrate, among a number of other, more probable, possibilities, is the full extent of the love of one human being for others. And as the love of human beings can be thought of as mirroring the love of God it would therefore be taken as an indirect demonstration of what the love of God is like, in much the same way that countless other individuals have given up their lives to save their friends or families throughout history. But who did Jesus die to save? None, save possibly Barabbas, can be said to have benefited directly from his death.

Furthermore, it would seem that modernism would like us to understand Jesus' death as making some sort of religious point which will enrich our spiritual lives. But this is not how the New Testament writers understood his death (not least because they insisted upon interpreting that death in the light of the resurrection, a procedure regarded as illegitimate by modernists), and it is certainly difficult to see how it would have cut much ice in the hostile environment in which Christianity had to survive and expand in the first period of its existence.

Had Jesus died in Western Europe in the modern period, such an interpretation of his death might have had a certain degree of plausibility – but the historical significance of Jesus' death was determined by its historical context, and we are committing historical errors which parallel those of the ill-fated nineteenth-century 'quest of the historical Jesus' if we project modern cultural preoccupations on to the event of the death of Christ. The interpretation which modernism wishes to place upon the death of Christ is culturally conditioned by the social and personal values of Western society, and is imposed upon (rather than discerned within) the history of Jesus.

The traditional framework for discussion of the manifestation of the love of God in the death of Christ is that of God humbling himself and coming among us as one of us, taking upon himself the frailty and mortality of our human nature in order to redeem it. To deny that the lonely dying figure upon the cross is God is to lose this point of contact, and to return to the view which Christianity overturned in its own day and age – that 'God is with us only in his transcendence' (Don Cupitt).

On the modernist view a divine representative – not God himself – engages with the pain and suffering of this world. It is his love, not God's, which is shown. And to those who might think that this difficulty may be eliminated by developing the idea of God allowing himself to be identified with the dying Christ, it may be pointed out that the exploration of this idea by Moltmann and Jüngel leads not merely to an incarnational but to a *trinitarian* theology. In order to do justice to the Christian experience of God through Jesus Christ, a higher profile of identification between Jesus and God than function is required – we are dealing with an identity of being, rather than just an identification of function: Jesus acts as and for God precisely because he *is* God.

A similar point may be made in relation to suffering. Twentieth-century apologetics has recognised that any theology which is unable to implicate God in some manner in the sufferings and pain of the world condemns itself as inadequate and deficient. The twentieth century witnessed previously unimagined horrors of human suffering in the trenches of the First World War, in the extermination camps of Nazi Germany, and in the programmes of genocide established by Nazi Germany and Marxist Cambodia. The rise of 'protest atheism' – perhaps one of the most powerful sentiments to which modern theology must address itself – reflects human moral revulsion at these acts. Protest atheism has a tendency to select soft targets, and there are few targets softer in this respect than a non-incarnational theology.

An incarnational theology speaks of God subjecting himself in the grim scene at Calvary to the evil and pain of the world at its worst, bearing the brunt of that agony itself. God suffered in Christ, taking upon himself the suffering and pain of the world which he created. A non-incarnational theology is forced, perhaps against its intuitive desires, to speak of a God who may send his condolences through a representative, but who does not (or cannot, for fear of being accused of logical contradiction?) enter into and share his people's suffering at first hand.

And for a modernist, highly critical of substitutionary theories of the atonement, God can hardly be allowed to take responsibility for the suffering of the world vicariously, through a human representative who suffers instead of and on behalf of God. In 1963, the English *Sunday Observer* publicised John Robinson's book *Honest to God* with the headline 'Our image of God must go'. The image that Robinson had in mind was that of an old man in the sky. But the 'image of God that must go' in the face of the intense and deadly serious moral criticisms of protest atheism is that of a God who does not experience human suffering and pain at first hand – in short, a non-incarnational image of God. Many of those who criticise the incarnation seem to realise the force of this point, and attempt to retain it, despite their intellectual misgivings. Perhaps in the end it will not be the protests of orthodoxy which destroy non-incarnational theologies, but protest atheism, which wisely and rightly detects the fundamental weakness of such a theology in precisely this respect.

A final point which may be made concerns the permanent significance of Jesus Christ. Why is he of such importance to the Christian faith here and now, some twenty centuries after his death? The traditional answer is that Jesus' significance lay in his being God incarnate; that in his specific historical existence God assumed human nature. All else is secondary to this central insight, deriving from reflection upon the significance of his resurrection. The fact that Jesus was male; the fact that he was a Jew; the precise nature of his teaching – all these are secondary to the fact that God took upon himself human nature, thereby lending it new dignity and meaning.

But if Jesus is not God incarnate, his significance must be evaluated in terms of those parameters which traditional Christianity has treated as secondary. Immediately, we are confronted with the problem of historical conditioning: what conceivable relevance may the teachings and lifestyle of a first-century male Jew have for us today, in a totally different cultural situation? The maleness of Christ has caused offence in radical feminist circles: why should women be forced to relate to a male religious teacher, whose teaching may be compromised by his very masculinity as much as by the patriarchal values of his cultural situation? And why should modern Western humanity pay any attention to the culturally-conditioned teaching of such an individual, given the seemingly insuperable cultural chasm dividing first-century Palestine and the twentieth-century West?

For reasons such as these a non-incarnational Christianity is unable to convincingly anchor the person of Jesus Christ as the centre of the Christian faith. He may be the historical point of departure for that faith, but its subsequent development involves the leaving behind of the historical particularity of his existence in order to confront the expectations of each social milieu in which Christianity may subsequently find itself. Jesus says *this* – but we say *that*. *This* may be acceptable in a first-century Palestinian context – but *that* is acceptable in a modern Western culture, in which we live and move and have our being. Jesus is thus both relativised and marginalised. Many non-incarnational versions of Christianity accept and welcome such insights – but others find them disturbing, and perhaps unconsciously articulate an incarnational Christianity in order to preserve insights which they intuitively recognise as central.

Conclusion

In this essay we have briefly summarised the case for defending the resurrection and incarnation as proper and legitimate interpretations of the history of Jesus of Nazareth, and the case for rejecting alternative explanations as inadequate.

It is hoped that the contours of the case for arguing that the resurrection and incarnation are proper and necessary elements of the Christian faith have been sketched in sufficient detail to allow the reader to take his own thinking further.

We now end this essay with some final reflections.

Critics of doctrines such as the resurrection and incarnation tend to work on the basis of two presuppositions. First, that there exists a theological equivalent of precision surgery, which allows certain elements of the Christian faith to be excised without having any detrimental effect whatsoever upon what remains. Second, that by eliminating logical and metaphysical difficulties a more plausible and hence more acceptable version of Christianity will result. Both these assumptions are clearly questionable, and must be challenged.

To return to our surgical analogy, we are not talking about removal of an appendix (a vestigial organ that apparently serves no useful purpose), but of the heart, the life-pump of the Christian faith. Faith in the resurrection and incarnation is what kept and keeps Christianity growing and spreading. The sheer vitality, profundity and excitement of the Christian faith ultimately depends upon these. In a day and age when Christianity has to fight for its existence, winning converts rather than relying upon a favourable cultural milieu, a non-incarnational theology despoiled of the resurrection has little to commend it. It is perhaps significant that many critics of the resurrection and incarnation themselves were originally attracted to Christianity through precisely the theology they are now criticising. And what, it must be asked in all seriousness, is the *converting power* of an incarnationless Christianity?

The history of the church suggests that such a version of Christianity is a spiritual dead end. To recall the words of Thomas Carlyle: 'If Arianism had won, Christianity would have dwindled to a legend.' To its critics, incarnationless Christianity seems to be scholarly, bookish and devoid of passion, without the inner dynamism to challenge and conquer unbelief in a world in which this is essential for its survival. But this is where history will pass its own judgement, in that only a form of Christianity which is convinced that it has something distinctive, true, exciting and relevant to communicate to the world in order to transform it will survive.

MIRACLES

Keith Ward

Some twentieth-century presentations of religious faith make it solely a matter of inner personal experience or commitment. But one of the clearest facts about religion is that, whenever religious faith becomes intense and living, miracles are widely claimed to occur. Miracles are not just inner experiences; they are outward and publicly observable events, closely connected with religious faith, which seem to go beyond the ordinary processes of nature. They are, in the strict and proper sense of the word, 'paranormal' occurrences. They show, in an outward and visible way, something of the spiritual character of reality, the fact that there are spiritual forces at work in the world as well as the unconscious material laws of nature which we nowadays take so much for granted.

Most claimed miracles are miracles of healing, when some illness is cured in a sudden and unexpected way which it is beyond the present powers of medical science to explain. Of course they would not be miracles unless it was believed that God or (in the case of faith healing) some mental or spiritual agency had caused the cure. What a miracle is claimed to show is the power of mind over matter. Matter, it is alleged, can be altered by some form of psychic influence – whether it is taken to be God himself, or some saint or holy person, or merely an unknown psychic power which some individuals apparently possess.

The healing miracles of Jesus are by no means unique in kind. Similar healing powers are claimed of many holy men, and the Old Testament prophets had such powers too. In the

Christian tradition, and indeed in most religious traditions, miracles are not just said to be caused by God interrupting the natural order in a seemingly haphazard or arbitrary manner. Miracles are closely associated with holiness, with the possession of strong faith or a special sort of spiritual capacity. So we find that in the Indian religious traditions those who pursue the paths of yoga and spiritual discipline are expected to develop miraculous powers of various sorts – the ability to levitate, to stop the heart-beat for periods of time, or to seem to manipulate events around them. Yet they are encouraged to regard these powers as diversions from the real business of establishing a true relationship with God or perfect enlightenment, as it is variously described.

If we look at the case of Jesus, we find a similar phenomenon. He is reported to have had remarkable powers of healing; he practised exorcism; he could calm storms, walk on water and seemingly produce food out of nothing. Yet he refused to use these powers to convince everyone of his own spiritual status, and to some extent, according to Mark, tried to keep them secret. He certainly did not use miracles to prove his divinity – that was precisely one of the temptations in the wilderness which would have distracted him from his proper task.

It seems, then, on the New Testament understanding, that miracles are not proofs of God. They are more like natural and inevitable manifestations of holiness, of closeness to God. Some people, because of their intense love of God, are so filled with his presence that the imperfections of our physical bodies are made whole by their touch, and the internally destructive mental forces which possess us are driven out and replaced by the integrating power of forgiveness and love. If Jesus was uniquely close to God, then one might expect that his miracles would be especially clear and vivid; and so the gospels say they are.

Not all the biblical miracles are of that sort, though most of them are. There are also the major miracles which mark the beginning and end of Jesus' life, the virginal conception and the resurrection. These were not brought about by some power of Jesus himself. They are unique interventions by God in human history which establish the utter uniqueness of Jesus himself and provide the vindication of his mission as the anointed one of God. Such miracles, as direct acts of God in history, are also recorded in the Old Testament – the rolling back of the Red Sea (or 'the sea of reeds' in Hebrew) being the clearest example. On the Christian view, God is always in some way active in history. These miracles are wholly extraordinary and indeed unique historical events which help to accomplish the purpose God has for the world.

It was these miracles which gave rise to David Hume's famous definition of miracle as a violation of a law of nature by a God (Hume 1748: 114). The Bible did not see it quite like that, for its authors had little idea of laws of nature in our modern sense. But it was clear that these events ran contrary to general expectations and that they were seen by the faithful as directly willed and brought about by God. These acts again surround specific prophetic figures – Moses, Elijah and Elisha – but they are not primarily thought of as produced by those persons via some power of their own. God acts in direct and wonderful ways to free his people from Egypt and bring them to the promised land. He is recorded in the pages of the Old Testament as causing floods, destroying walls, causing earthquakes and storms, causing the sun to stand still and armies to be thrown into irrational panic. It is the Lord who fights for Israel and defeats her enemies in quite astonishing ways.

Biblical scholars differ in the view they take of such records. At one extreme the accounts would be accepted much as they stand. There was a physical pillar of cloud and flame going before the Israelites in the wilderness. There was a cloud of light filling the temple and fire consuming the sacrifices. For is not God the Lord of all nature, so that he can cause it to change in any way he pleases? At the other extreme many of these accounts would be seen as legends. Perhaps they are poetic metaphors which have been later turned into 'facts' – thus the stars did not really fight for Joshua, and the sun did not really stand still. Rather, very significant events in the history of Israel have been dramatised by giving accounts of these celestial phenomena, trying to show that the very powers of nature themselves fought on behalf of Israel.

It is probably true to say that most scholars would accept that there are elements of exaggeration and fictionalisation in the Old Testament narratives. For instance, the flood at the time of Noah did not really cover the whole earth, and the ten plagues at the time of the Exodus were not quite so dramatic and drastic as they are portrayed. But the question remains: Did God guide the Israelites to Canaan and act in special ways to ensure their inheritance of his promises?

Whatever view one takes of the particular details of the Old Testament wonders, the Bible as a whole would hardly make sense if it is not true that God acts in history to accomplish particular purposes. That indeed is the testimony of the prophets, that God judges and blesses his people; that he has a specific calling for the Israelites; and that he will ensure that his promises are fulfilled. The life of Jesus makes sense only when it is seen as a fulfilment of the prophecies of the Old Testament. If Jesus was indeed the fulfilment of prophecy, then God had ordained what would happen and had in time brought it to pass. So the biblical testimony is that God acts in history in particular and unique ways – ways which are not repeated anywhere else on earth.

Of course, that does not by itself entail that miracles occur. Perhaps God always acts in ways which are not very extra-ordinary. But that seems very unlikely when one reflects on the claims a little further. If God is thought of as acting, as bringing things about for a purpose, then an analogy is being drawn with human persons. When human beings act inten-tionally they do not have to perform miracles, and their actions are not usually thought of as 'violating the laws of nature'. If I want to write this essay, I will sit down and start to type. What happens in the world – the state of affairs consisting in my typing – will be caused by my purpose. If a physicist wished to explain this state of affairs, he could no doubt do so. But if he considered only the laws of physics and nothing else, he would always miss out something important. He would miss out my purpose, about which physics would tell him nothing; and he would miss out my awareness of what I was doing, and how that affects the whole process of thinking and typing. I am, for instance, trying to construct a logical and coherent argument. Yet no number of laws of physics will even mention the rules of logic or explain how arguments proceed. The physicist can tell you only about the 'hardware' of the programme, if you like. The whole personal dimension will be missing.

Now the physicist's account of my actions may be complete in its own terms. But it will still miss out all the elements I take to be most important about my actions, and so in that sense the physical account will be an incomplete explanation. It will provide only part of the story of what is going on in the world. Now it is possible that some extra-terrestrial physicist, who was not human, might come to earth and give a physical account of all human actions, without realising anything about consciousness, thinking, purposes and so on. He might think we were all robots. Then he might think that he had completely explained human behaviour. But we would know that he was wrong; the most important elements would still be missing.

In a similar way, when a contemporary scientist looks at the universe he may be able to explain what happens in terms of laws of physics, biology, chemistry, and so on; and he may think that is all there is to it. Yet it might still be true that God – a personal agent with consciousness, purpose and thought – is in fact acting in the world to realise his purposes. The scientist might miss out this dimension altogether, and then he would have missed out the most important thing about the world. But he might never notice what he had done, because the account seems complete to him, just because he has no direct access to the mind or purposes of God.

However, I have glossed over a very important question about this analogy. To go back to the human case, is it true that the existence of consciousness, purpose and thought makes no difference to what happens on the purely physical level? Suppose there were no thought, purpose or awareness at all. Would precisely the same things happen, in accordance with the laws of physics alone? That seems a very strange idea, because it means that our thoughts really make no difference at all, that they are totally irrelevant: we think it makes a difference what we think; but in fact it does not. That view seems to me too strange to accept; it would mean that we lived under a permanent illusion about our own causal efficacy. Our belief that we can think and so cause differences to the world is so strong, deeply rooted and important that it would take an overwhelmingly strong argument to show that we were mistaken. No such argument exists; so we are quite reasonable in thinking that our thoughts make a real difference to the world. If so, there is here a further sense in which the account of physics is incomplete. Not only does it miss out one dimension of being, but it cannot explain all that happens solely in terms of the laws of physics. For if only those laws operated, without any human action, things would not be precisely as they in fact are. That is to say, the laws of physics alone cannot predict correctly what will happen in the world. Thinking makes a real difference.

We still would not say that thinking violates the laws of physics; that seems silly. What we should say is that the laws of physics state what will happen, if and only if no other influences operate to alter the situation. However, thinking is precisely another influence; it alters the situation; so the laws of physics are not broken. They are supplemented by further causal influences with which they do not directly deal. It is not that they cease operating, it is just that other factors – other sorts of causal influence – modify the way in which they operate in these specific cases.

If we now think about the actions of God again, we would similarly expect that his purposes and actions will make a difference to the world. Things will be different than they would have been if God had not had certain purposes and put them into effect. So there will be some events in the physical universe which the physical sciences alone cannot completely predict. These divine purposes need not violate the laws of physics, because, in the way I have suggested, they can supplement these laws, adding a new causal factor which modifies the way those laws operate in particular cases. Would these instances be called miracles? At first sight it seems not. Just as human actions are not miraculous, so divine actions need not be miraculous. However, we have to remember at this point that whereas there are a great many human beings there is only one God. Because there are many human beings, we take human action to be fairly common-place. We expect people to reflect, to have purposes and to cause changes in their immediate environments. Because we expect them we do not call such changes miraculous; they occasion no surprise. But the actions of God are not common-place in the same way. So if the acts of God cause changes in the universe which would not have happened in accordance with the laws of physics alone those changes might be called miraculous. They are, after all, caused by a supernatural agency and are not wholly accountable for by using the scientific laws we have available.

In one sense all the acts of God are miraculous. But it would be silly to call them miraculous, because they are usually not particularly amazing and may even be undetectable. It may seem strange to suppose that the acts of God could be undetectable, but it is obviously true. We can say that some-thing is an action if it brings about some physical state of affairs in accordance with some intention. Intentions them-selves are not observable by others. We may have some intention for the whole of our lives, while nobody even discovers what it is. We may conceal it perfectly, and I suppose that the most successful spies, especially those who are double-agents, do so. Normally, of course, we judge a person's intentions by what they do. And although that is not always a good guide, since people may not always do what they want, we do have their bodily behaviour to observe, and that helps us to judge their intentions.

God, however, has no particular observable physical body. So we cannot pick out some piece of observable behaviour anywhere in the universe and say, 'That is the behaviour of God's body; from it we can at least hazard a guess as to his intentions.' Suppose, then, that God has the intention that some state of affairs should come about, and it does come about. As observers with no direct access to the mind of God we would not know that he had such an intention, and we would not know that he had brought it about, as opposed to its coming about by physical laws or by someone else's actions. We could never be sure of that, because we can never observe any divine body acting so as to bring a state of affairs about. If we do not know either what God wants or what he does to bring it about, it is obviously true that we do not know exactly when God is acting. He may have purposes we know nothing of – and he may ensure they are brought about in ways of which we are wholly ignorant – but we would never know.

I may be thought to have taken things too far. If we can never know when God is acting, isn't the whole idea of divine action irrelevant? There are two things to say in reply to this question. First, it might be very important that God is acting, even though we can never know it. For what we attribute to good luck or coincidence might in fact be due to the action of God. And it would be very important if God did act to ensure that in the end our lives attained the purpose he willed for them. Second, it is of course an exaggeration to say that we can *never* know when God is acting. All I suggested was that many of the acts of God are undetectable. The physical universe is so complex, so many different factors operate at any one time – the free decisions of others, the laws of the sciences, and perhaps other as yet unknown laws too – that we could not be expected to pick out God's contribution with any certainty.

Christians, however, believe that the whole point of revelation is that God should show what his major intentions are, should show how he acts in general and should make at least some of his particular actions clear. I said earlier that we have no direct access to the mind of God. That is true, unless God himself provides such access by telling us his purposes. That, in the religious sense, is the point of miracle; it is an extraordinary happening – so extraordinary that we can take it as a revelation by God of his nature and purposes. It seems to me that if there is a personal God who has a purpose for the world, we should expect there to be some miracles in this sense. It would be very odd if God never made his purpose clear at all and left his existence to be wholly a matter of guesswork.

It is true that God does not make his existence quite unambiguously clear – atheism is still a possibility for human beings. So revelation is not something which convinces everyone beyond reasonable doubt, as it could have been. If God had just wanted to convince everyone of his existence, he could certainly have performed such a miraculous act – the stopping of the sun in full view of everyone, with perhaps a message written in the clouds, would probably do. Miracles are not proofs in that sense. Furthermore, it is important to remember that they do have a religious element about them. That is, they express something of God himself and call for a response of faith.

A consideration of the central miracle of the Christian faith, the resurrection of Jesus, will make this clearer. Jesus could presumably have appeared to the Sanhedrin or to Pontius Pilate. He could have made his risen life perfectly indubitable by walking openly in Jerusalem and then ascending into heaven before a packed assembly of the priests and Pharisees. But he did not. He appeared almost secretly to the apostles, behind closed doors or in the solitude of Galilee. He left them in no doubt of his resurrection; but he was not concerned to establish it to the satisfaction of those who had crucified him.

It seems, then, that the resurrection is a testimony of faith. It is not given as a clearly attested very odd happening. It is rather that it is an objective event which transforms the understandings and lives of the apostles as it vindicates the life and teachings of Jesus, showing that he did not end defeated by his enemies. It is certainly wholly extraordinary; but it occurs only in the context of faith. Within that context it has the function of making the divine purpose clear, of testifying to the authenticity of the life of Jesus as a revelation of that purpose. God makes his purpose clear to those who respond to him in faith. Miracle is neither a proof for the uncommitted nor a purely subjective event in the mind. It is, as recorded in the gospels, an objective event which confirms faith and helps to shape it further. Those who are not devoted to God by a commitment of repentance and hope will see only a very odd event; or perhaps they will miss it altogether and hear of it only from others. But those who seek the kingdom and the new life it brings will find the purpose of God expressed in an event so unexpected and yet so 'right' – the defeat of death itself by the power of God – that it will confirm for them the commitment which might otherwise have been thrown into doubt by the crucifixion.

We might see miracles, then, as confirmations for faith of the purposes of God and also as revelations of his nature and will. If so, this helps to answer a question which is often put to those who believe in miracles: Why does God not act miraculously more often, to save his people from suffering, for instance? Do alleged miracles not seem arbitrary and much too rare? If God can heal disease, why does he not intervene much more to eliminate cancer or diabetes?

When such questions are asked there is a particular picture of God at work which makes them seem sensible and real. God is seen as an all-powerful person who would seek to eliminate suffering wherever it occurred. Being all-powerful, he can of course eliminate it whenever he wants to. So it becomes completely inexplicable that he allows suffering to happen at all. It is even worse if he sometimes acts to heal people, for there then seems to be no reason why he heals some people and not others – or why he should not heal everybody.

It is most important to see that this is a picture of God which is almost wholly misleading; and it is not at all the biblical picture of God. When we read the book of Job we have to remember that it was the friends of Job who tried to explain suffering as a punishment for sin, imposed by a powerful God. Their explanations are all rejected; and in the end Job finds that he must simply bow before the overwhelming mystery and majesty of God, confessing his own nothingness before the creator of all things. Part of the message of this strange book is that we cannot explain the acts of God as if they were those of some very powerful human person – as if we could judge him morally for his goodness. God is the source of all beings, and they exist only in total dependence upon him. We cannot understand why things are as they are; but we can know that all things derive from God. We can also know that God calls us to obey and love him, and promises the joy of his presence if we do so. The biblical view is that God is almighty – all things depend solely on his power. And God is one who brings punishment on those who hate him, but shows love to those who love him and obey his laws (Exod 20:5–6). We might put this another way by saying that God allows those who choose the way of pride and hatred to bring themselves to destruction, but he guides those who are penitent to the way of eternal life.

It is futile to set ourselves up in moral judgement of the creator. If we really see – as Job did, in the end – that we depend wholly for our existence upon God, and that he offers us eternal life, then it is no use complaining that he should not have created suffering. Suffering is an integral part of this world; without it, we would not be. God offers us final deliverance from suffering; but he does not simply remove it; for to do so would be to change the structure of the world itself.

I am not trying to justify the existence of suffering, as though I could offer some explanation of why it exists. Only God knows why it exists; but we can say that it arises from the divine being itself and that it seems to be implicit in the nature of at least this creation (there may be others, but we know nothing of them). Does it limit the omnipotence of God if suffering, or the possibility of suffering, is necessarily implicit in his own being? In some abstract logical sense, no doubt it does – God is then unable to do everything that can be consistently stated in some proposition. There will be things God cannot do – create this world without any suffering in it, for instance. Yet God may be almighty in the very real sense that there is no being which could logically have more power than he has; there is nothing which has some source other than or opposed to God himself. Moreover, one might add that God is able to bring overwhelming good out of the suffering that exists, even though, since it is necessarily involved in the very nature of this creation, he is unable to remove suffering altogether.

This seems to me a possible notion of God. It seems to be more like the biblical idea of the imageless God who rides the clouds of storm and thunder as well as liberating his people through earthquake and pestilence than it is like the philosopher's idea of a God who would never permit any suffering to exist. The point is that there may be necessities in the world of which we understand nothing. It may be true that God cannot just eliminate all suffering without destroying the world as we know it.

But does that mean that God should never perform miracles, that he should never eliminate suffering? It seems to make sense to say that God will not destroy the structures of the world he has created. He will not just arbitrarily break some of the physical laws on occasion, as David Hume seems to suggest (Hume 1748). When he acts, it will be in response to the prayer and faith of creatures. The structure of the world may, after all, be such that faithful response to the creator does open up new possibilities of unique change, a transformation of the everyday which enables it to show the divine purpose which underlies it. We need to see the physical universe as a multilayered whole, able to generate new levels of meaning which can transform the lower levels at critical points. Thus the physical level gives rise to the biological when physical elements become organised in functional wholes. The biological gives rise to the conscious level. Then purposes and perceptions affect the patterning of both biological and physical levels. May there not also be a spiritual level at which human beings relate to the spiritual forces which surround them? If we look at the biblical miracles, we find that they occur when some prophet or person of deep faith so establishes a relationship to God that they become vehicles of his purposes. Around them, we might say, the material world becomes more transparent to the spiritual. It is at such points that miracles occur, opening the physical world to spiritual powers.

Seen in this light, miracles are not just rare and arbitrary violations of physical laws by God. They are points at which the dynamic power of God breaks into the world in manifestation of his purposes; and that power is released by faith, by the relationship to God attained by Abraham, Moses, Elijah, the prophets and, most fully, by Jesus. These are not so much violations of laws as manifestations of a higher law of the spirit, taking natural objects beyond their normal modes of operation. Often this is manifested in healing, whether physical or mental. But one should not think of God just deciding to heal John and not Mary, when he could easily have healed both. Rather, healings occur as part of the natural processes of the world when and in so far as they become transformative points, points where the power of the spirit breaks in through prayer and faith. God does not contradict the nature he has created. He fulfils it when it is brought to the point at which it is ready for such fulfilment.

Miracles are from faith and for faith. They occur when faith has brought a particular moment of history to the point at which it can embody the divine power. And their point is not primarily to eliminate suffering, much less to prove the existence of God to all. It is to show that suffering is not final defeat, to confirm the purpose of God to save, to make whole those who turn to him in penitence and faith. For Christians, the greatest miracle of all is the raising of Jesus from the dead. This miracle was from faith; for the whole life of Jesus had been one of total devotion to the will of the Father, and his life was in itself a prefiguring of that wholeness of being to which all are called. And it was for faith; for it assured the apostles that their discipleship had not been in vain. The way of Christ was still the way of the cross – pain was not eliminated. But victory was assured; and that is the Christian gospel, which makes faith powerful and effective for salvation.

Miracles are very important for the Christian religion; if Christ was not truly raised from death, then Christian faith is vain. A Christian faith without miracles is like a house without foundations. It may look very fine; but it will not stand for long. So it is important to have some idea of what miracles are, and to know whether they can occur. I have suggested that, in the broadest sense, a miracle is an extraordinary event, inexplicable on the known laws of physics, which is caused by some paranormal mental power or some spiritual agency. In this sense, holy men may perform miracles, as may demons or spirits of various sorts, if they exist. In a rather narrower sense, a miracle is such an event which is caused by God, the one and only creater of all things. Many such miracles are recorded in the Bible; and even if some of these records are legendary, or contain elements of legend, the overwhelming testimony of the Bible is that God has acted in such ways at various times.

There seems no reason at all why, if he exists, God should not act in such ways, and arguments against the very possibility of miracles seem wholly unconvincing. The real questions, therefore, are why God should perform miracles; and why, if he does, he performs them so rarely. I have suggested that if there is a God with a purpose for this world, he will continually be modifying the operation of physical laws in order to realise his purposes. Such actions will normally be undetectible, since we have no way of observing God's actions. However, a good reason for performing a miracle would be to reveal at least the general divine purpose for the world. Thus the resurrection of Jesus reveals God's purpose to raise us from death and give us eternal life. We could hardly have known that otherwise, or have had good reason for thinking it was true, without some sort of divine confirmation. Nevertheless, in so acting, the biblical records suggest that God is both responding to a faith which opens the world, at a particular point, to the power of his Spirit; and he is speaking to a faith which will allow itself to be conformed to the purpose so revealed.

Miracles are neither arbitrary nor are they proofs of God's existence or decisions to eliminate suffering. When the way is prepared they reveal God's purpose to those who desire to conform their lives to it. The miracle of the resurrection was prepared by a long history of faith and hope in Israel, culminating in the willing response of Mary to the birth of Jesus and the perfected life of Jesus himself. It showed the purpose of God to redeem humanity through the community of the church. And it is not only rare but unrepeatable precisely because what it shows is the uniqueness of God's saving activity in Jesus. I conclude that at least the outlines of an intelligible account of miracles can be given. Christians may reasonably claim that the miracle of the resurrection, though wholly extraordinary and inexplicable in terms of physical laws as we know them, is a wholly natural manifestation of the power and purpose of God. It shows God's purpose for the whole human race and is the reasonable foundation of a life committed to God, whose will is that we shall all be raised with Christ in glory.

MIRACLES: SCEPTICISM, CREDULITY OR REALITY?

R. J. Berry

A few years ago I was one of fourteen signatories of a letter to *The Times* (13 July 1984) about miracles. All of us were professors of science in British universities; six were Fellows of the Royal Society. We asserted:

> It is not logically valid to use science as an argument against miracles. To believe that miracles cannot happen is as much an act of faith as to believe that they can happen. We gladly accept the virgin birth, the Gospel miracles, and the resurrection of Christ as historical events . . . Miracles are unprecedented events. Whatever the current fashions in philosophy or the revelations of opinion polls may suggest, it is important to affirm that science (based as it is upon the observation of precedents) can have nothing to say on the subject. Its 'laws' are only generalisations of our experience.

An article in the leading science periodical *Nature* (19 July 1984, p. 171), although accepting our statements on the nature of scientific laws, dissented from our conclusion about miracles on the grounds that they are 'inexplicable and irreproducible phenomena [which] do not occur – a definition by exclusion of the concept . . . the publication of Berry *et al.* provides a licence not merely for religious belief (which, on other grounds, is unexceptionable) but for mischievous reports of all things paranormal, from ghosts to flying saucers'.

Subsequent correspondents disagreed. For example, P. G. H. Clarke (*Nature*, 11 October 1984, p. 502) objected that 'your concerns not to license "mischievous reports of all things paranormal" is no doubt motivated in the interest of scientific truth, but your strategy of defining away what you find unpalatable is the antithesis of scientific'; Donald MacKay in the same issue emphasised that

> for the Christian believer, baseless credulity is a sin – a disservice to the God of truth. His belief in the resurrection does not stem from a softness in his standards for evidence, but rather from the coherence with which (as he sees it) that particular unprecedented event fits into and makes sense of a great mass of data . . . There is clearly no inconsistency in believing (with astonishment) in a unique event so well attested, while remaining unconvinced by spectacular stories of 'paranormal' occurrences that lack any comparable support.

The credibility of belief in miracles has resurfaced in *The Nature of Christian Belief*, a report of the Church of England bishops produced in response to the controversy about statements made by one of their number, David Jenkins, the Bishop of Durham (General Synod 1986). *The Times* (6 June 1986) commented on it: 'Did the two key miracles at the centre of the Christian faith, the Virgin Birth and the Resurrection, really happen? . . . The exercise has established one thing clearly: that belief in miracles, at least where they are central to the faith, is thoroughly intellectually respectable . . .'

It would be easy to decry the criteria or standards of truth accepted by the bishops, but their integrity is presumably not in doubt. It is more profitable to enquire whether miracles are really credible, and, if so, what are the circumstances where they might be expected.

The basis and breakability of natural law

A distinguished physicist turned clergyman has written:

> In an earlier age, miracles would have been one of the strongest weapons in the armoury of apologetic. A man who did such things must at the very least have the power of God with him. Jesus himself is represented as using this argument when he said, 'If it is by the finger of God that I cast out demons then the kingdom of God has come upon you' (Luke 11:20). For us today, by one of those twists that make up intellectual history, miracles are rather an embarrassment. We are so impressed by the regularity of the world that any story which is full of strange happenings acquires an air of fairytale and invention. (Polkinghorne 1983: 54).

The historical twist referred to by John Polkinghorne was an inevitable consequence of the separation of observation (or test) from interpretation, which is the essential feature of what we call science. Before the sixteenth century 'how' and 'why' questions were answered in much the same way: acorns fell to the ground so that new oaks might grow; rain came so crops might flourish and people feed; and so on. The realisation that the same event could be interpreted in more than one way led to an emphasis on mechanism, and therefore on the uniformity and predictability of natural events, with a consequent restricting of divine activity to the ever-decreasing gaps in knowledge. God became unnecessary, except as a rationalisation for the unexplainable (Coulson 1955).

By the seventeenth century scientists were using the 'laws of nature' in the modern sense, and the physical and (increasingly) the biological worlds were regarded as self-regulating causal *nexi*. God was merely the 'First Cause', and could intervene in the world only by breaking or suspending the 'natural laws'. Locke and Hume used the determinism of Newtonian physics to argue that natural laws were inviolable, and therefore that miracles could not happen (Brown 1984:

42–46, 80–86). Their conclusion seemed to be vindicated in the nineteenth century when the Darwinian revolution purged from biological systems the simple notion of purpose and created pattern. And as Don Cupitt says, 'religion was more badly shaken when the universe went historical in the nineteenth century than it had been when it went mechanical in the seventeenth century' (Cupitt 1984: 58). The futility of believing in a god unable to do anything exposed the problem that spurred the English bishops to reaffirm that miracles could happen (Harris 1985).

Miracles and mechanisms

Defenders of miracles have tended to descend into an unconvincing mysticism or an assault on determinism. A few decades ago, it was fashionable to claim that physical indeterminacy gave God enough freedom to control events. Biological indeterminacy is a live debate now, particularly in sociobiology (Berry 1984: 102–106). For example, R. C. Lewontin (an American geneticist who would be unlikely to argue that miracles are common or important) strongly attacked the reality of biological laws beyond

> very special rules of comportment or particular physical entities . . . If we are to find biological laws that can be models for social laws, they will surely be at the level of laws of population, laws of evolution, laws of organisation. But it is precisely such laws that are absent in biology, although many attempts have been made to erect them. (Lewontin 1985: 21).

However, the case for miracles does not depend on indeterminancy, since the intellectual orthodoxy stemming from Hume's underlying thesis is not as strong as it is usually made out to be. C. S. Lewis pointed this out succinctly:

> of course we must agree with Hume that if there is absolutely

'uniform experience' against miracles, if in other words they have never happened, why then they never have. Unfortunately we know the experience against them to be uniform only if we know that all the reports of them are false. And we can know all the reports to be false only if we know already that miracles have never occurred. In fact, we are arguing in a circle. (Lewis 1947: 106)

Exposing the fallacy of Hume's attack on miracles also reveals that it is based on an unjustified assumption, that events have only a single cause and can be fully explained if that cause is known. This is logically wrong. For example, an oil painting can be 'explained' in terms either of the distribution of pigments or the intention and design of the artist; both explanations refer to the same physical object but they complement rather than conflict. In the same way, a miracle may be the work of (say) a divine upholder of the physical world rather than a false observation or unknown cause. Such an interpretation does not depend on any irruption into a causal network, since the determinism of the machine is only one of the levels of the phenomenon (*sensu* Polanyi 1969).

'Complementary' explanations of causation are excluded only by making the reductionist assumption that a single identifiable cause is the sole effect operating in a particular situation. This assumption is common, but unnecessary and restrictive. The Nobel laureate Peter Medawar has dissected this clearly:

That there is indeed a limit upon science is made very likely by the existence of questions that science cannot answer and that no conceivable advances of science would empower it to answer. These are the questions that children ask – the 'ultimate questions' of Karl Popper. I have in mind such questions as: How did everything begin? What are we all here for? What is the point of living? Doctrinaire positivism – now something of a period piece – dismissed all such questions as nonquestions or pseudoquestions such as only simpletons ask and only charlatans of one kind or another profess to be able to answer. This peremptory dismissal leaves one empty and dissatisfied because the questions make sense to those who ask them, and the answers to those who try to give them; but whatever else may be in dispute, it would be universally agreed that it is not to science that we should look for answers. There is then a prima facie case for the existence of a limit to scientific understanding. (Medawar 1984: 66)

As far as miracles are concerned, this means that they are impossible to prove or disprove on normal scientific criteria; we accept the possibility of their occurrence by faith, and equally deny them by faith. Even if we know or deduce the mechanism behind a miracle, this does not necessarily remove the miraculous element. For example, the Bible tells us that the Israelites crossed the Red Sea dry-shod because 'all that night the Lord drove the sea back with a strong east wind and turned it into dry land' (Exod 14:21); the significance of the miracle lies in its timing and place rather than its actual occurrence.

Implications

The act of faith that denies the possibility of miracles is a straightforward reductionist judgement. Miracles by themselves are always susceptible to an explanation other than the miraculous (even if they have physical manifestations, such as 'spontaneous' healing or the empty tomb), so the value of the reductionist assumption can be best tested by its implications. These were spelt out with depressing clarity in the nihilism of Jacques Monod (1971), and comprehensively answered by W. H. Thorpe (1978), who expounded a version of the dualism of Sherrington, Eccles and Popper, which is kin to the complementarity espoused above (MacKay 1979a; MacKay 1979b).

There are implications of embracing a reductionist determinism which impinge on two recent controversies; creationism and the definition of human life.

Creationism is largely an insistence that God made the world in a particular way, without using a 'normal' evolutionary mechanisms. Part of this claim stems from a restricted interpretation of the Bible, but it has the effect of prescribing that God acted in an interventionist fashion. Notwithstanding, it is entirely consistent with both evolutionary biology and Bible texts to maintain that God worked 'complementarily' with genetic processes so that the world is both a causal outcome of mutation, selection, and so on, but *also* a divine creation. The creationist position is at odds with both scientific and theistic understanding (Midgley 1985; Berry 1988).

Individual human life has a physiological and genetic continuity with that of other humans (and indeed other animals); the *value* of individual life lies not in genetic uniqueness (cancers and hydatidiform moles are also genetically unique) but in being (in Christian language) 'made in the image of God'. This *imago* is not a physical entity, and it is a category mistake to confuse it with genetic coding or mental function. Notwithstanding, defenders of the inviolability of the early embryo make this precise mistake. The *imago* is a non-biological attribute, and there is no logical or scriptural reason for assuming that it is present from conception (Rogerson 1985: 85). If this simple point was realised, the ethical debate over developments in human reproduction could proceed more sensibly.

The conventional view of miracles is that they depend on supernatural intervention in, or suspension of, the natural order. Some theologians have been overimpressed with scientific determinism, and have attempted a demythologised (miracle-free) religion. This endeavour is now unfashionable, but it is worse than that; H. R. Nebelsick has characterised it as a speculative device imposed on unsuspecting persons 'based . . . on false presuppositions about both science and the "scientific world-view"' (Nebelsick 1984: 239). This is no help to scientists, and an interventionalist God will always be an embarrassment to us.

I believe that the interpretation that miracles are a necessary but unpredictable consequence of a God who holds the world in being is more plausible and more scriptural than deist interventionism. This does not mean that apparent miracles should be approached with any less objectivity than we would employ for any scientific observation; our standards of evidence should be just as rigorous. Those who deny the possibility of miracles are exercising their own brand of faith; but it is based on a questionable assumption, and one which creates problems with its implications, never mind historical problems with the empty tomb and such like. Miracles in the New Testament are described as unusual events which are wonders due to God's power, intended as signs. Confining oneself wholly to this category (leaving aside the question of whether other sorts of miracles occur), this makes at least some miracles expectable and non-capricious, and independent of any knowledge of their mechanism.

In his exposition of the 'Two Cultures', C. P. Snow described the scorn of the one for the other as intellectual Ludditism (Snow 1975: 21). Miracles are examples of events which may easily be denied by an illegitimate reductionist Ludditism; scientific reality will be hindered in the process. A doctrinaire disbelief in miracle is not 'more scientific' than a willingness to accept that they may occur. Some years ago Sir George Porter, currently President of the Royal Society, London, wrote:

> Most of our anxieties, problems and unhappiness today stem from a lack of purpose which was rare a century ago and which can fairly be blamed on the consequences of scientific inquiry . . . There is one great purpose for man and for us today, and that is to try to discover man's purpose by every means in our power. That is the ultimate relevance of science. (*The Times*, 21 June 1975)

He was not writing specifically about miracles, but his argument applies. Miracles are not inherently impossible or unbelievable, and acceptance of their existence does not necessarily involve credulity, but does involve recognising that science has limits.

WHAT IS WRONG WITH BIBLICAL EXEGESIS?
Reflections upon C. S. Lewis' criticisms

Alasdair I. C. Heron

C. S. Lewis was well known for his regular attacks on the use of the Bible by academic biblical scholarship, which he regarded as all too often tiresome, trivial and blinkered, overladen by historicism, short-sighted in its understanding of the message of the Bible, and therefore incapable of unfolding that message in a way that could catch and set afire the imagination of people in the twentieth century.

As a Christian working in the field of literature, Lewis was convinced of the power of the Christian message to shape and inform thought, imagination and life today and tomorrow as well as yesterday. His more academic publications were less coloured by this concern, for he was careful to distinguish between his personal and theological interests and his responsibilities as an Oxford don and, later, a Cambridge professor of English Literature. But it was his implicitly or explicitly theological writing that won him his place as a major advocate of Christian faith in the twentieth century. The liveliness of his style, the incisiveness of his analysis and the imaginative resources on which he so powerfully drew combined to make him one of the most influential Christian writers of his day.

What did Lewis have against his contemporary world of biblical exegesis? His complaint was that it all too often tended to reduce the Bible and its message to a dead letter. It had learnt, and learnt well, to treat the biblical texts as objects of scientific, archaeological, historical and literary analysis – and in the process rendered itself incapable of listening to them with awe, astonishment and appreciation. The world of the biblical exegetes had become cold and empty – empty of miracle, empty of revelation, empty of imagination. It was a world in which no 'distant strains of triumph' could be heard, a world in which it was no longer seriously believed that the church was on the march against the gates of hell, 'terrible as an army with banners' – whereby Lewis saw this army quite simply as made up of perfectly decent, normal and ordinary people who do not accept, refuse to believe in, and therefore constitute the most serious threat to Satan's drive for world-domination.

In Lewis' eyes, it was this very world of the everyday which is ever and again 'surprised by joy', illumined by transcendent light, a world of pilgrims looking forward 'till we have faces', a world of 'ordinary' people who precisely in their ordinariness are surrounded by intimations of grace, who are (or ought to be) on the way 'higher up and further in', but who are threatened and sometimes overcome by selfishness, meanness, arrogance and despair – a world, as he described it in *The Great Divorce* (1946), in which we are on the road either to the solidity and substance of heaven or to the last gnawing emptiness, the self-consuming insubstantiality of hell.

Lewis was above all a student of *literature*, though his early studies had been in philosophy. Unlike some other literary critics, however (most notably his Cambridge counterpart, F. R. Leavis), his interest in literature was not primarily *historical*, *social* or *political*. Literature presented itself to him as the art which at its best and highest is concerned with the profoundest depths and highest calling of human nature itself. He was and remained to the end of his days a Romantic, radically opposed to the reduction of literary criticism – or theology – to mere historicism or to a political or ideological programme. His thought was fed and his imagination nourished by the medieval allegories of love, by Milton, Bunyan and George Macdonald – and by the Bible.

Lewis' opposition to what he took to be the programme of contemporary biblical exegesis was especially sharply formulated in reaction to the influence of Karl Barth and, even more, Rudolf Bultmann. In neither case, certainly, does it seem that Lewis was very well informed at first hand on their concerns; Barth in particular had much more in common with Lewis (or vice versa) than Lewis ever realised. (Dorothy Sayers could have taught him better!) But Lewis' especial *bête noire* was Bultmann's 'demythologisation' of the New Testament (Bultmann 1960).

Lewis' own view of the issue can perhaps best be understood in the light of his own personal history as illustrated by a conversation some sixty years ago with his friend J. R. R. Tolkien, a convinced Roman Catholic and, like Lewis, an enthusiastic student of the old Norse sagas. (Lewis and Tolkien were later to found the 'Inklings', a group of dons and their friends who met regularly in the Thirties in Oxford to hear papers, among them some of Tolkien's preliminary studies for *The Hobbit* and *The Lord of the Rings*.) At the time of this conversation Lewis was an atheistically-inclined agnostic, having abandoned his Ulster Protestant faith some years before. Tolkien tried with all the argumentative power at his command to persuade Lewis that the Christian faith was true precisely because it answered all the longings incorporated in the innumerable myths giving expression to the strivings of humanity after a profounder destiny than the world as it exists appears to promise. Lewis' answer then was: 'Myths are lies, even though breathed through silver.' When, not very much later, Lewis was reconverted to Christian faith, this brought a turn of 180 degrees in his attitude to 'myth'. From then on 'myth' signified for him a literary and imaginative category and form deliberately designed and intended by divine purpose to engage our human imagination in willing response to the message of the gospel.

Paradoxically enough, this contributed to Lewis' estrangement from Tolkien in later years. Tolkien was deeply committed to what he called 'subcreation', the imaginative construction of a literary world which might indeed reflect the reality of the actual world as seen through the double prism of Nordic mythology and Roman Catholic dogma, but at the same time constituted a fresh 'subcreative' achievement. He demanded that others too should be as serious as he in the work of 'subcreation', and found Lewis' *Narnia* stories deficient by this standard. Lewis, by contrast, sought to rearticulate the classical themes of Christian faith together with *motifs* from the sagas and classical mythology as speaking to people of every age and era. He was less interested in constructing fictional 'alternative worlds' than in drawing on the resources of ancient myth, the gospel and contemporary imagination to hammer home the message that everyday human life is besieged by God and the devil. His writing is in intention the reverse of escapist; even when he goes on to develop conceptions of 'other worlds', as in the *Narnia* series of children's books or the *Out of the Silent Planet* trilogy, it is always *this* world that he is concerned with, *this* world as illuminated in the light both of ancient myth and of the biblical message.

It is not surprising that Lewis reacted so negatively to Bultmann's attempt to demythologise the New Testament. Lewis himself was not best placed to appreciate Bultmann's motives in advancing this programme, which he first formulated in 1941 in an address to a meeting of representatives of the German Confessing Church. The Confessing Church was confronted at that time with the massive challenge of German National Socialism, with its mythological and ideological programme and its apparent success in breaking and reshaping the mould of national, political and military history. Lewis' reaction took no account of this; it bore less upon the original German context of the programme than upon its influence in English biblical and theological scholarship. The net result of the appropriation of Bultmann's ideas in academic theology in England after 1945 seemed to Lewis to run out into the sand of a total evacuation of biblical meaning, a dissolution of theological substance, an abdication of evangelical conviction, and a failure of Christian imagination.

Were Lewis' diagnosis and reaction justified? Or were they, as some would have it, simply those of a disappointed, cross-grained and bad-tempered outsider – albeit one possessing rare gifts of literary communication? Whatever might be said here about Lewis himself, it is hard to resist the conclusion that he had put his finger upon a weakness of *some* Anglo-Saxon theology and exegesis which has become even more apparent in the last twenty years. The kind of biblical scholar in mind here might be one who has picked up a smattering of German New Testament exegesis (usually at second hand), who is profoundly impressed by the fact of the Enlightenment (without necessarily knowing much about it), and who is therefore convinced that the New Testament has little or nothing to say to the people of the modern era. His (or her) primary convictions as Lewis understood them might be paraphrased as follows:

> The Bible is an ancient collection of documents which is to be studied in theological faculties because the churches require the same. This gives us something to do, and justifies the drawing of our salaries.

> Our chief responsibility is to make clear to theological students that the Bible possesses no authority, is a highly doubtful and arbitrary collection, and is in any case far remote from the concerns and interests of human life today. For the Bible was written before the Enlightenment and is therefore wholly *passé*, indeed meaningless, for the modern world.

> If, occasionally, we nevertheless find it appropriate to stress the authority of the Bible, it is only to make clear that the entire tradition of Christian dogmatic theology is not biblically secured. This enables us to use the Bible (in which we do not really believe, but in which others do) as a means to undermine their confidence in the faith of the church.

> We continue to engage in our learned study of the biblical writings because that is our job, because progress in research holds out the hope of academic and ecclesiastical advancement, and because we might otherwise become unemployable.

This is, of course, a caricature, though some pretty close approximations to it can be found alive and well in various corners of the British academic and ecclesiastical establishment. Nevertheless, it would be grossly unfair to apply this caricature to more than a minority of our present biblical scholars or to give the impression – as Lewis was not on occasion above doing – that the whole enterprise of critical biblical scholarship had gone to seed in this fashion.

In much the same way, Lewis' *The Abolition of Man* (1943) takes as its target a thoroughly insignificant book which few would ever have heard of if Lewis himself had not attacked it for its reduction of ethical and aesthetic appreciation and judgement to expressions of subjective feeling. Yet Lewis had rightly detected that what that book articulated was a much more widespread attitude, shared by many others; and it was the attitude, and the book as symptomatic of it, not the book in itself, that primarily concerned him. Similarly, Lewis was certainly less than fair to the majority of British biblical scholars in his strictures on their biblical scholarship, yet did at the same time point to real dangers deserving serious attention.

Bultmann's programme of demythologisation of the New Testament was not intended to empty the New Testament or the message of the gospel of meaning for the people of the twentieth century, but to open up that meaning afresh. To that end, Bultmann employed an *existentialist* interpretation: he sought to ask what meaning and implications *for human existence* are conveyed in mythical patterns of thinking and speaking, and to uncover these in their abiding relevance for his contemporaries. In this, however, his interest remained *theological*: the really important question was that of the challenge of human existence under the word of God, the gospel of the crucified Jesus of Nazareth.

Bultmann's immense appeal to younger German theologians in the generation following the Second World War stemmed in part from the fact that this programme offered a new beginning and a new orientation to those who had been caught up and swept along in the firestorm of Nazi ideology and the nightmare of the Third Reich, with its consequences of national collapse and crushing defeat. But it was also possible, as examples from both Germany and Britain show, for others to take up the call for demythologisation simply as showing the New Testament to be largely irrelevant today and to present their own 'existentialist' programmes, purged of any discernible theological or evangelical content or interest.

This is what Lewis seems chiefly to have had in mind in his attacks on Bultmann and New Testament scholarship generally. Certainly, there remained fundamental differences between Lewis and Bultmann, above all in their attitudes to 'myth'. For Bultmann, 'myth' was a form of pre-critical thinking which was no longer viable in the modern world; for Lewis it was an essential form of communication, belonging ineradicably to divinely created human nature as such. There are good grounds for holding that here Lewis came far closer to the truth of the matter than Bultmann; and Lewis' attacks on post-Bultmann New Testament work must be seen in this light. But the fact remains that Lewis was less concerned with Bultmann's own programme than with what he detected as its reception and application in the habits of thinking of some British biblical and theological work. And here he could be devastating in his criticism – devastating in a way reminiscent of the nineteenth-century Oxford theologian H. L. Mansel. Mansel's *Phrontisterion*, a satirical lampoon on contemporary trends in academic theology, included the following lines on the most prominent 'left-wing' Hegelians in Germany:

> Theologians we,
> Deep thinkers and free.
> From the land of the new Divinity;
> Where critics hunt for the sense sublime,
> Hidden in texts of the olden time,
>   Which none but the sage can see.
> Where Strauss shall teach you how Martyrs died
> For a moral ideal personified.
> A myth and a symbol, which vulgar sense
> Received for historic evidence.

Where Bauer can prove that true Theology
Is special and general Anthropology.
And the essence of worship is only to find
The realized God in the human mind.
Where Feuerbach shows how religion began
From the deified feelings and wants of man,
And the Deity owned by the mind reflective
Is Human Consciousness made objective.
    Presbyters, bend,
    Bishops, attend;
The Bible's a myth from beginning to end.
             (Reardon 1980:225)

Lewis' reservations on the same subject are most fully spelt out in the address 'Fern-Seed and Elephants' (originally delivered to theological students in Westcott House, Cambridge, and posthumously published in *Fern-Seed and Elephants and Other Essays on Christianity*. The following quotations are taken from the 1977 edition by Collins Fount; this essay is given there in pp. 104–125). The title is Lewis' own reminting of Jesus' remark about those who 'strain out a gnat but swallow a camel' (Matt 23:24), who are obsessed with minutiae and lose sight of all larger issues. He wanted to impress upon his hearers 'how a certain sort of theology strikes the outsider' (p. 104). The reason:

The minds you daily meet have been conditioned by the same studies and prevalent opinions as your own. That may mislead you. For of course as priests it is the outsiders you will have to cope with . . . The proper study of shepherds is sheep, not (save accidentally) other shepherds . . . I am a sheep, telling shepherds what only a sheep can tell them. And now I start my bleating. (pp. 104–5)

Lewis goes on to distinguish

two sorts of outsiders: the uneducated, and those who are educated in some way but not in your way. How you are to

deal with the first class, if you hold views like Loisy's or
Schweitzer's or Bultmann's or Tillich's . . . I simply don't
know . . . But that is your headache, not mine. (pp. 105–6)

Lewis himself claims 'to belong to the second group of
outsiders: educated, but not theologically educated' (p. 106).
The rest of the address is the attempt of one highly educated,
erudite and informed literary scholar to convey to a group of
generally far less educated, erudite or informed theological
students four 'bleats' about the way in which 'the work of
divines engaged in New Testament criticism' is accepted as
'the authority in deference to whom we are asked to give up a
huge mass of beliefs shared in common by the early Church,
the Fathers, the Middle Ages, the Reformers, and even the
nineteenth century' (p. 106).

First, says Lewis,

whatever these men may be as Biblical critics, I distrust
them as critics. They seem to me to lack literary judgment,
to be imperceptive about the very quality of the texts they
are reading . . . A man who has spent his youth and
manhood in the minute study of New Testament texts and
of other people's studies of them, whose literary experience
of those texts lacks any standard of comparison such as can
only grow from a wide and deep and genial experience of
literature in general, is . . . very likely to miss the obvious
things about them. (pp. 106–7)

After giving some illustrations of what strikes him as wooden
literary insensitivity on the part of certain New Testament
critics, he concludes: 'These men ask me to believe they can
read between the lines of the old texts; the evidence is their
obvious inability to read (in any sense worth discussing) the
lines themselves. They claim to see fern-seed and can't see an
elephant ten yards away in broad daylight' (p. 111).

'Now for my second bleat. All theology of the liberal type
involves . . . the claim that the real behaviour and purpose

and teaching of Christ came very rapidly to be misunderstood and misrepresented by His followers, and has been recovered . . . only by modern scholars' (pp. 111–12). Lewis offers a parallel from the tradition of philosophy in which he himself had been trained: 'One was brought up to believe that the real meaning of Plato had been misunderstood by Aristotle and wildly travestied by the neo-Platonists, only to be recovered by the moderns. When recovered, it turned out (most fortunately) that Plato had really all along been an English Hegelian' (p. 112).

Another illustration of the same tendency is supplied from his own field of literary criticism: 'every week a clever under-graduate, every quarter a dull American don, discovers for the first time what some Shakespearian play really meant' (p. 112). But:

> I see – I feel it in my bones – I know beyond argument – that most of their interpretations are merely impossible; they involve a way of looking at things which was not known in 1914, much less in the Jacobean period. This daily confirms my suspicions of the same approach to Plato or the New Testament. (p. 112)

The third complaint is directed against the assumption that neither miracles nor genuine prophecy can have occurred in the fashion reported in the New Testament. This, Lewis insists,

> is a purely philosophical question. Scholars, as scholars, speak on it with no more authority than anyone else. The canon 'If miraculous, unhistorical' is one they bring to their study of the texts, not one they have learned from it. If one is speaking of authority, the united authority of all the Biblical critics in the world counts here for nothing. On this they speak simply as men; men obviously influenced by, and perhaps insufficiently critical of, the spirit of the age they grew up in. (p. 113)

Lewis' 'fourth bleat', however, is his 'loudest and longest' (p. 113). It is that all

> this sort of criticism attempts to reconstruct the genesis of the texts it studies; what vanished documents each author used, when and where he wrote, with what purposes, under what influences – the whole *Sitz im Leben* of the text. This is done with immense erudition and great ingenuity. And at first sight it is very convincing. (pp. 113–14)

But Lewis himself is not convinced. He instances the attempts of reviewers to reconstruct the genesis of his own books and those of others – attempts which according to his impression show 'a record of 100 per cent failure . . . And yet they would often sound – if you didn't know the truth – extremely convincing' (p. 115). 'The "assured results of modern scholarship", as to the way in which an old book was written, are "assured", we may conclude, only because the men who knew the facts are dead and can't blow the gaff' (p. 117).

Lewis recognises that it may seem absurd 'to compare every whipster who writes a review in a modern weekly with these great scholars who have devoted their whole lives to the detailed study of the New Testament' (p. 117). His riposte is, first, that respect for the *learning* of the great biblical critics does not necessarily entail the same respect for their *judgement*. Second, if the biblical scholars are more learned than the 'mere reviewers', the latter have the overwhelming advantage of dealing with works written in their own culture, their own day and their own language. In addition, the development of the study of English literature casts major doubt on some of the techniques – such as the extrapolation of hypothetical sources – used in biblical study. 'The huge essays in my own field which reconstruct the history of *Piers Plowman* or *The Faerie Queene* are most unlikely to be anything but sheer illusions' (p. 117). 'The confident treatment to which the New Testament is subjected is no longer applied to profane texts . . . Everywhere, except in theology, there has been a vigorous growth of scepticism about scepticism itself'

(p. 119). Indeed, 'I do not wish to reduce the sceptical element in your minds. I am only suggesting that it need not be reserved exclusively for the New Testament and the Creeds. Try doubting something else' (p. 122) – such as, he implies, 'the assured results of modern scholarship'.

This brief summary of Lewis' 'four bleats' could perhaps give the false impression that Lewis simply rejected the application of critical literary and historical scholarship to the New Testament. He did not do so, but believed he could distinguish between more and less appropriate methods and procedures:

> We are not fundamentalists. We think that different elements in this sort of theology have different degrees of strength. The nearer it sticks to mere textual criticism, of the old sort, Lachmann's sort,[1] the more we are disposed to believe in it. And of course we agree that passages almost verbally identical cannot be independent. It is as we glide away from this into reconstructions of a subtler and more ambitious kind that our faith in the method wavers; and our faith in Christianity is proportionately corroborated. The sort of statement that arouses our deepest scepticism is the statement that something in a Gospel cannot be historical because it shows a theology or an ecclesiology too developed for so early a date. For this implies that we know, first of all, that there was any development in the matter, and secondly, how quickly it proceeded . . . I could not speak with similar confidence about the circle I have chiefly lived in myself. I could not describe the history even of my own thought as confidently as these men describe the history of the early Church's mind. (p. 121)

[1] Karl Lachmann (1793–1851) was a pioneer in textual criticism of classical and Old German literature, notably the *Niebelungenlied*. He also published the first critical edition of the New Testament to be based primarily on ancient manuscripts rather than the received text of previous printed editions, with the aim of recovering the form of the text current in the late fourth century. His comparison of the contents of the three synoptic gospels, showing that Matthew and Luke agree on the order of events only where they share the material with Mark, paved the way for the hypothesis that Mark had been used as a source by the other two.

Or, as he remarks a little earlier:

> Dr Bultmann never wrote a gospel. Has the experience of his learned, specialized, and no doubt meritorious, life really given him any power of seeing into the minds of those long dead men who were caught up into what . . . must be regarded as the central religious experience of the whole human race? (p. 118)

Bultmann's answer to the challenge would doubtless have been that his existential interpretation was intended precisely to discern and broadcast what that 'central . . . experience' had been and remains even in the modern world. But the main focus of Lewis' attack as just outlined was the interest of Bultmann and other New Testament scholars in tracing 'the genesis of the texts', in the belief that this was the key to a proper understanding of them, along with such axioms as 'If miraculous, unhistorical' or 'The New Testament is the work of the primitive Church.'

Now that we have followed Lewis so far, however, it is perhaps time to consider how this attack is to be evaluated. It certainly requires a differentiated appreciation, one which distinguishes the strengths and weaknesses of different strands in his argument. It has already been indicated that Lewis was not well placed to understand or appreciate the special concerns of Bultmann (or Barth), though he had read and could quote them. It should also be sufficiently obvious that this writer is profoundly sympathetic to Lewis' contribution to presenting Christian faith and hope in terms adapted to catch and claim the imagination and commitment of people of the twentieth century. However, proper appreciation involves critical reception of ideas and arguments, albeit not of the kind that strains at gnats in order the better to swallow camels. But Lewis' paper does put a couple of camels – or elephants – on the menu.

1. Lewis seems to imply that source-analysis of the biblical texts is a useless diversion from proper engagement with

them, an exercise in hypotheses of a methodologically questionable sort.

2. Similarly, he puts a large question mark against all attempts to trace the development of thought and theology in the primitive church, as reflected in the New Testament.

Both reservations are buttressed mainly by appeal to Lewis' own experience of work in the field of English literature, not by appeal to work done in the field of biblical scholarship, on which Lewis comments only – and very selectively – as a critical outsider. There is a good deal to be said on the other side!

First, it was critical literary and historical study of the Bible that delivered some of the main impulses to the critical study of other literature as well. Biblical study has benefited from techniques and approaches developed in work on other literature – but the reverse has also been the case: biblical study has pioneered the field of historical literary criticism.

Second, the very character of the biblical documents – the existence of four different gospels, for instance, or the sheer quantity of the letters claiming to be by St Paul – is itself a challenge to analyse and consider how this complex body of literature came into being, how the different documents are related, what stages of development in early Christian teaching and witness they may reflect, how far and in what ways they can best be understood against that background of development and controversy.

Third, we do as a matter of fact possess far more witnesses to the New Testament tradition in the form of manuscripts and papyri than to any other body of literature from the ancient world. Yet these sources themselves provide a host of variant readings, parallel yet different accounts of incidents and sayings, diverse but related formulations which cry out for careful analysis and comparison in the attempt to recover, so far as may be possible, the reliable original wording or to trace what lost sources may underlie the texts transmitted to us.

In short, Lewis' strictures upon the historical-critical study of the biblical material do less than justice either to the integrity of the enterprise as seriously undertaken or to the insights it offers into the history of the emergence of the biblical documents. There is a qualitative difference between, for example, Wellhausen's detection of different strands in the Pentateuch – following such clues as the two accounts of the creation in Genesis 1:1–2:4a and 2:4b–25 – and the attempts of Shakespearian scholars 'to cut up *Henry VI* between half a dozen authors and assign his share to each' (p. 110). The former is serious literary, historical and theological scholarship, the latter may well be mere literary dilettantism. But the triviality and questionability of the latter is no proof of the inadmissibility of the former.

Or, to take another example from the field of New Testament study: we have no good reason today to reject the very considerable evidence that St Paul did not write either Ephesians or the Pastoral Epistles and that these represent two different appropriations and expressions of Paul's legacy, long years after his death, not his own writing. We can in fact learn far more about the dynamics of the emergence of the biblical documents if we accept such patterns of historical development and articulation than if we persist in insisting upon Moses' authorship of the Pentateuch or Paul's authorship of all the letters ascribed to him. And it is no service to the work of serious biblical scholarship to dismiss all such enquiries as if they were nothing more than pretentious guesswork, as Lewis seemed inclined to recommend.

Here, in fact, lies both the strength and the weakness of Lewis' argument. By temperament and training he was more philosopher and literary critic than historian. His desire was not, except incidentally, to understand the past 'as it was' or to track historical developments for the sake of their interest for the historian. He was therefore ill-equipped to appreciate the interest of historical-critical biblical study.

But if that was in one sense a weakness, it also enabled him to sense the difference between a purely historical approach to the Bible and the interest of Christian faith in reading the scriptures. And that difference is surely important. Why, for example, do Lewis' *Narnia* stories have the power to address and engage children who have never heard of theories of *Heilsgeschichte* and would not understand them if they had? Why does great literature in general have an appeal and an interest for the sensitive reader quite different from that of the scholar who is merely interested in analytical dissection of the same? Why, if not that God's word is also able and keen to use the powers of human imagination, baptised imagination, to discern and proclaim the gospel of mercy and of judgement? Why, if not that there are more avenues to confrontation with the sublime realities of which the Bible speaks than mere archaeological busyness with the history of the emergence of the biblical texts? The interest of historical-critical biblical scholarship is not invalid, but it is also not the be-all and the end-all. It can indeed become a distraction from the thing more important still.

Is there, then, something radically wrong with the approach and intention of contemporary biblical exegesis? Lewis is only one of many critics who have insisted that there is, though the critics are far from sharing the same views either as to diagnosis or as to remedy, as three other, rather different, examples can illustrate.

The profoundest theological thinker we have had in Britain in the last decades, Professor Thomas F. Torrance, is at least as critical of the reduction of biblical research and interpretation to a merely historical and archaeological discipline as Lewis was. His main line of counter-argument is, however, rather different from that of Lewis. Torrance (1969) maintains that the proper task of theological enquiry has to do with the objective probing of reality, that theology is itself in the proper sense of the word a *scientific* discipline – and one, moreover, which is called to subject its methods, forms of questioning and provisional conclusions, indeed its whole structure of thought and interpretation, to the same kind of rigorous objective control and testing as is expected in the natural sciences.

Taking his cue from Karl Barth, Torrance insists on the critical, scientific nature of theology; he goes beyond Barth, however, in tracing the interconnections in the history of thought between Christian dogmatic thinking and the development of the other modern sciences. This has led him to unfold a powerfully dynamic conception of the meaning of Jesus Christ as the central axis of the entire interaction between God and the created universe and, from that, a new perspective upon the history of the development of classical Christian dogma which is both critical and constructive, for example, in questioning traditions and habits of theological thought in the Eastern and Western churches to find how far they conform to the fundamental import of the gospel that God became man in the person of Jesus Christ in order to reconcile all things to himself.

Torrance's criticism of the enterprise of modern critical biblical scholarship is that it generally neither raises nor attempts to grapple with these methodological, theological and dogmatic issues, but remains largely set in a pattern of historical, literary and archaeological investigation which in its essentials was programmed by the flowering of historical scholarship in the nineteenth century. This is not to deny that these researches are *also* important; it is to question whether they exhaust the responsibility of biblical scholarship. Torrance challenges biblical researchers to think not merely *historically* or in terms of literary criticism or archaeological research, but *theologically* and *dogmatically* (*i.e.* scientifically), in the light of the real object of their work: the historical self-revelation of God in the person of Jesus Christ, incarnate, crucified and risen, who is the second person of the Trinity, the firstborn of all creation, the head of the church, the prototype of redeemed humanity and our future judge. In other words, he urges biblical scholars to take seriously the central message of the New Testament itself, and suspects that they do not always succeed in doing so, that in all too many cases, indeed, they have not even begun to try.

The second example is of a rather different sort. In recent years there has been a rising tide of conservative evangelical attacks on the entire undertaking of historical-critical biblical scholarship as at best misguided, at worst a betrayal of the

Bible itself. The beginnings of this movement lie in the nineteenth century with the movement known as fundamentalism. Its concern was to recall Christians to the 'fundamentals' of the biblical faith, as opposed to the corrosive acids of modern thinking, especially since the Enlightenment of the seventeenth and eighteenth centuries.

One especially vociferous offshoot of this movement in recent years has been the 'creationist' movement in the United States. Its programme is the introduction of a biblical conception of the process of creation, based on Genesis 1–2, as an alternative *scientific* model to the theory of evolution. That well illustrates the general approach of the attack on historical-critical study of the Bible more broadly characteristic of conservative evangelicalism, though most conservative evangelicals would not perhaps be prepared to go quite so far as the creationists. All nevertheless have in common a conviction that no approach to the Bible can be appropriate which treats it simply as a historical collection of documents, to be analysed, interpreted and explained simply by the application of the same methods by which other historical materials are analysed, interpreted and explained. This seems to them to put the truth of the biblical witness in question, and therefore to be a theological dead end.

The third example is very different again. One of the targets most frequently singled out for attack by some conservative evangelicals is the 'theology of liberation', represented chiefly (though not only) by theologians in the Third World. It is not possible here to sketch all the forms which this approach has taken in the last twenty years. Let me cite just one example of acute contemporary relevance: the approach of some theologians in South Africa. Their theological opposition to the policy and politics of apartheid may be summed up in the programme: 'We believe that the Bible is true; from the story of the Exodus onwards it is the message of God's liberation of his people, yesterday, today and tomorrow.' For theologians and church leaders such as Beyers Naudé, Desmond Tutu or Allan Boesak, the Bible and the gospel speak directly to the South African situation, a situation of structural injustice and oppression. They and other Third World theologians have little patience with what they see as the comfortable academic pursuit of literary and historical biblical study and dogmatic theological enquiry lacking in any kind of social or political resonance.

Liberation theology poses hard questions to theological and biblical work as conducted in the cloistered academe of First World libraries and seminars. In particular, it raises the question whether a purely literary and historical study of the Bible does not all too easily serve to blunt its challenge and promise, to make the ears of the scholars and of their hearers dull to the calling of the Lord and the promise of his grace, his judgement and mercy as bearing directly on the economic, social, political and racial ordering of society.

Each of these three critical attacks on current modes of biblical scholarship raises many different issues which cannot be adequately explored here. My own sympathies lie more with the first and third than with the second – but also with Lewis, whose strictures upon much contemporary biblical and exegetical work as lacking alike in imaginative power and theological and human seriousness are even today not without relevance. The trends he criticised are still alive and well; they may be illustrated from a paper by an English New Testament scholar which I recently read. The argument of the paper may be summed up as follows:

1. Loyalty to the principles of the Reformation requires that we affirm the authority of the Bible over all later theological and dogmatic development.

2. That means today that only those New Testament sayings which can reliably be traced back to Jesus himself possess authority.

3. Given the paucity of such sayings we are faced with the question whether we should continue to assert the authority of the Bible in general and the New Testament in particular, or cast around for some other basis for our theology.

4. It is questionable whether the patristic model – *i.e.* the doctrine of the Trinity – is the best or only one available to express the threeness of God to which the New Testament witnesses.

5. The patristic model drew upon the patterns of thought developed in Hellenistic philosophy. Since the Enlightenment, however, these patterns have become meaningless.

These theses might at first appear to be entirely reasonable; in their own way, indeed, they are just that: *reasonable*. The programme of the paper could equally well have been formulated in the eighteenth century, in the Age of the Enlightenment. Its appeal to the authority of the Bible reduces to an appeal to what historical study can tell us about the sayings of Jesus. In the process it irons out what most serious New Testament study of the twentieth century has been concerned to emphasise: that the witness of the New Testament is to the gospel of the crucified and risen Jesus Christ, not simply to 'the historically indisputable sayings of Jesus'. The last two theses reduce, it hardly needs to be said, to a provincial rejection of the greater part of the history of Christian thought.

Precisely here lies the weakness of *some* prominent recent British biblical and theological scholarship; it is insular, shallow and unaware of wider connections and responsibilities, theological, ecumenical, social and political. It is largely uninformed on all but a small segment of the history of Christian theology and exegesis. It goes its own way, concerned only with its own questions. That it does so is largely the product of structural and institutional conditioning; the development in particular of the English universities and the Anglican Church has not always been such as to encourage profounder theological enquiry. It has often been adapted rather to promote a kind of serene dilettantism in the field of theology.

Another factor also deserves to be mentioned: the rise and rise of the media-orientated theologian. At least in England it is possible to become prominent by presenting oneself as a theological *enfant terrible*, preferably by demolishing this or that biblical or dogmatic foundation or by 'taking leave of God'. By comparison with other recent escapades of this sort the paper presented by our English New Testament scholar is mild stuff. But in principle it is of the same weave. It is a confession of bankruptcy, exegetically and theologically.

As I was drafting this paper I happened to come upon an article by the President of the British Academy, Sir Randolph Quirk, in *The Independent* of 12 November 1986. After discussing the teaching of English grammar and the advantage of learning foreign languages, he concludes: 'After all, it is not only in the pages of Anthony Burgess that we are warned of "the monoglot Englishman, unworthy to enter any comity of nations, tied to one tongue as to one cuisine, and to one insular complex of myths".' This would seem to score a direct and devastating hit on the theological trends just mentioned.

In conclusion, however, I would emphasise that the trends singled out here for attack – which are very similar to those that Lewis held up to scorn a generation ago – are not typical of all biblical scholarship and exegesis, whether in Britain or elsewhere. But they have been prominently displayed in recent years, especially in certain quarters in England. And the extremes to which they lead can serve to highlight the dangers lurking in a purely historical-critical approach to the New Testament if unaccompanied by theological sensitivity, and prejudiced by a foreshortened view of the history of Christian thought. Our best theologians and our best biblical scholars are not guilty of this narrowness, but there are others, and they are not without influence.

The root cause of the problem lies in the branching-off of the various theological disciplines from each other in the last three centuries, so that exegetes, historians and dogmatic or practical theologians all too often work *alongside* but not *with* each other. The separation of the disciplines has been made necessary by the development of biblical and theological scholarship since the seventeenth century; no one today can hope to be comprehensively informed and expert in the technicalia of all the different fields, particularly so far as front-line research is concerned. But this makes it all the more needful that continuing dialogue should take place between the disciplines involved in the academic theological programme. We need historically and theologically informed exegetes just as we need exegetically and theologically informed historians and exegetically and historically informed theologians. All of these, individually and together, have their part to play. And all of them can perhaps gain by also paying sympathetic attention to a figure such as C. S. Lewis and his strictures upon the reduction of theology to a purely academic, *historical* discipline. Theology has more serious matters to attend to than mere academic games; not only biblical scholars need on occasion to be reminded of that.

THE NEW TESTAMENT AS HISTORY

James D. G. Dunn

Is the New Testament history? The question posed like that is obviously too compressed and needs to be restated more fully. Is the New Testament concerned with history? Does the New Testament consist of historical documents? Or better still, Were the writers of the New Testament documents concerned to record history? Does the New Testament provide good historical information?

The question, however, is still not clear. So much depends on this word 'history'. Indeed, the whole issue of the historical value of the New Testament hangs on this word. So we had better start by making clear what we do *not* mean by it.

The New Testament is *not* history

The New Testament is not 'history' if by that word we mean a wholly objective and literal account of 'what actually happened'. For one thing most of the New Testament writings do not actually fit into any such historical category. Twenty-one of the twenty-seven documents in the New Testament fall into the category of letters; they record the beliefs and counsel of the authors, not a dispassionate account of events with which they had to do.

The claim has often been made in the past that the last of the twenty-seven, the Apocalypse (= Revelation) of John, should be understood in some such literal sense. But that is certainly wrong. As is characteristic of the apocalyptic writings of that period, Revelation uses symbolism and often bizarre imagery to express its message. There is sometimes clear allusion to recognisable events and figures contemporary with the author, but never in a straightforward, literal sense. Apocalyptic is the clearest exception to the rule that the literal sense of a text is preferable to a symbolic or allegorical meaning. So with Revelation the history it contains is presented in heavily coded form, which we would be unable to decode (to the extent that we can do so) on its own.

So the issue revolves primarily around the other five New Testament documents – the four gospels and the Acts of the Apostles. Here too it quickly becomes apparent that if 'history' is defined too narrowly the answer to our opening question has to be a No. For the very fact of *four* gospels, with their innumerable differences of detail, order and emphasis, shows at once that the writers cannot have been concerned merely with 'what actually happened'. Had the evangelists conceived of themselves merely as archivists or been motivated by an archaeological concern to record every item of the tradition in the strictest possible chronological and geographical correlation, we would have had one, not four gospels, or at least gospels which could be integrated without difficulty. Even the gospels therefore cannot be assumed to provide 'straight' history. Which leaves only Acts among the twenty-seven New Testament documents. And that was written by one of the evangelists! In short, any attempt to argue that the New Testament is history in a narrow sense is bound to fail.

Another sense in which the New Testament is *not* history is that it is not *modern* history. For example, a modern historian would think it improper to attribute to a historical character a speech for which he or she lacked sound documentary evidence. And if only fragmentary or impressionistic 'ear-witness' testimony was available a responsible modern historian would so indicate. But in ancient historiography the dividing line between history on the one hand and poetry or rhetoric on the other was not at all so clear. Speeches were included to delight and impress the reader as much as to inform. The point can sometimes be exaggerated, as though all ancient historians felt wholly free to compose speeches as they liked and to attribute them to whom they liked. That is not borne out by the evidence and does not accord with what historians like Thucydides and Polybius claimed they were doing. Nevertheless it remains characteristic of ancient historical writing that a fair degree of what we may properly call 'artistic licence' was both accepted and expected as part of the historian's task and skill. In reading the speeches or sermons recorded by the first Christian history (Acts), therefore, this historical context, this understanding of what was proper and what could and would be expected, must be kept in mind.

We find another example of the danger of misreading the New Testament as modern history in the issue of whether the synoptic gospels can be called 'biographies' or not. The fact is that they are not biographies as we today define biographies. Although the gospels are set within a broad chronological framework, there is no real attempt to maintain a sustained chronological record: so many stories about Jesus are told without 'locating' them either temporally or geographically; frequently there are thematic rather than chronological groupings of teachings, parables and miracles. Above all there is no attempt made to trace out the development of the character of the hero (Jesus). But all that is simply to say that the gospels do not share the concerns of *modern* biographies.

They do however share many of the concerns of *ancient* biographies. At that time the conception of human character was much more fixed, so that the idea of development in character was not present to the thought. Rather the biographer's objective was to display the hero's character by recounting episodes relating to him and memorable things he had said. And this is just what we find in the synoptic gospels – Jesus portrayed in terms of event and word. To be precise, in terms of genre a gospel is distinctive; but the nearest parallel to a gospel is in fact the ancient *bios* or *vita* or biography.

All this means that if we come to the New Testament

documents with distinctively modern questions in mind we are likely to be disappointed. If we insist on trying to co-ordinate the four gospels into a single narrative we will almost certainly get it wrong, for the simple reason that we do not know what is correct. If we insist that different versions and sequences of events have to be harmonised in order to be counted historical we impose concerns on the gospels which the evangelists did not share, and may well miss the points which they wanted their readers to hear. If we insist that the speeches of Acts are not historical unless they were first spoken just as narrated, we impose limitations on Luke the historian which neither he nor those for whom he wrote would recognise.

In short, if we are to answer the question about the historical worth of the New Testament fairly we must avoid prejudging the issue by insisting on our own definition of 'history' and must beware of trying to squeeze the New Testament into a 'historical' mould which it was not intended to fit.

The New Testament *is* history

The New Testament is history, first of all, in the sense that those who wrote the documents which go to make it up were at one in their claim that Christianity was founded on events which actually happened. Actually it is not quite fair even to put it like that. For most of the New Testament writers the facticity of Jesus' life, ministry and death was not an issue. No one doubted or disputed it. So no elaborate defence of the claim had to be mounted. That tells us something right away: the historicity of Jesus was simply taken for granted both by the writers of the New Testament and by those for whom (and presumably also against whom) they wrote. Likewise it would seem ludicrous to ask about the historical fact of the beginnings and initial growth of Christianity. The New Testament writings are themselves witness to that fact: the people who wrote these documents and the people for whom they were written hardly needed to be convinced of the historicity of Christianity's beginnings; they were part of it!

But where the claims made by the first Christians were a matter of dispute it is also true that the New Testament writers made a point of asserting their historicity. This is clear from the earliest period in the case of the claim that 'God had raised Jesus from the dead'. One of the earliest formulations in all the New Testament is Paul's account in 1 Corinthians 15 of the confession which he himself had first received (that is, within two or three years of the event). There he lists the various appearances of Jesus after his resurrection and makes a point of stressing that many of the largest group of witnesses were still alive (1 Cor 15:6). In other words, any who might wish to question the confession could seek out the witnesses for themselves and hear their testimony first-hand. So too, later in the same chapter, he insists that the faith he proclaims is based on the firm fact of the resurrection of Jesus; without it both proclamation and faith would be empty and useless (1 Cor 15:14). No wonder contemporary theologians who wanted to maintain that faith must be based solely on the preached word and not be made to depend on any historical fact thought that Paul had lost his way at this point. An equivalent emphasis on the fact that the first disciples were 'witnesses' of Jesus as risen from the dead is also a consistent feature of the Acts of the Apostles (Acts 1:8,22; 2:32; 3:15; 5:32; etc.).

So too, when later on the reality of Jesus' life and death became an issue, we find a similar insistence on their historicity. John's gospel makes a point of stressing the real humanness of Jesus: to those who thought that material flesh was inferior and worthless, the evangelist states firmly, 'the Word became flesh' (John 1:14). To those who found it hard to believe that the divine could die, he asserts with equal firmness that he was an eye-witness of Jesus' death (John 19:35). Likewise the first letter of John insists on the concreteness of Jesus and dismisses any suggestion that he might not have been a real man (1 John 1:1–3; 4:2).

There can be little question then that the New Testament is

history at least in the sense that the New Testament writers were concerned with the historical reality of the events on which Christianity's distinctive claims were based.

Thus far the claim being made is modest enough – that the New Testament writers were concerned to maintain the historical fact of Jesus' life, death and resurrection. But we can say a good deal more. For once again the very fact of there being so many gospels in circulation among and cherished by the earliest Christians tells us something: that the first Christians wanted to remember and retell stories about Jesus and things he had said. Sometimes students of the gospels in effect make a very odd assumption: that the material which goes to make up the gospels (I am thinking here particularly of the first three gospels) was not in circulation before Matthew, Mark and Luke first wrote it down. As though the first disciples of Jesus, who had been with him during his ministry, did not speak at all of their time with Jesus, and after the first Easter spoke only of his death and resurrection! As though Mark (usually taken as the first gospel to be written), and then the others, had to go to the disciples and drag the information from them so that it could go into circulation for the first time in the latter decades of the first century! The idea is little short of ludicrous. Of course the traditions which appear in the gospels were in circulation, most of them at least, before the evangelists wrote them down. Which is simply to say that the earliest Christian communities among whom these traditions circulated were concerned to *remember* Jesus.

All the available evidence points firmly in this direction. Let me summarise it briefly.

1. Consider first what we might call 'the sociology of groups' – the recognition that groups naturally try to identify themselves and to mark themselves off from other groups by emphasising the distinctiveness of their beliefs, and that religious groups in particular tend to regard their founding traditions as especially important. Characteristic of such groups will be opportunities and rituals by which they will recall their members to these traditions and celebrate them together as part of 'group bonding' and demarcation. Clearly

the ritual occasions of baptism and the common meal (Lord's Supper, Eucharist) played an important part here, and there is no doubt that they were part of Christianity from the first. But so too would traditions about things Jesus had done and said. There must have been very few (if any) of all those early converted to the new movement who were content simply to celebrate the bare 'that' of Jesus' life, death and resurrection. Committed as they were to Jesus as 'Lord', they would inevitably want to know more about this Jesus. Who can doubt that the earliest material which now makes up our gospels served this purpose (among others) of giving new converts an informed understanding and picture of Jesus the Christ to whom they now belonged individually and together?

2. This 'in the nature of things' deduction is confirmed by the prominence given to teachers and tradition in the New Testament. As far back as our records go, wherever there is talk of recognised ministry among the Christian churches the teacher has an honoured position and the importance of teaching is stressed (*e.g.* Acts 2:42; 13:1; Rom 6:17; 1 Cor 12:28; Gal 6:6; Jas 3:1). Paul, writing within thirty years of Jesus' ministry, and often eager to stress his independence from the mother church in Jerusalem, is equally consistent in stressing the importance of tradition, of the continuity of the tradition he made a point of handing on to his newly founded churches (1 Cor 11:2,23; 15:1–3; Col 2:6; 1 Thess 4:1; 2 Thess 2:15; 3:6). Again, who can doubt that among the traditions Paul passed on to his new churches would be many of those we now have in the gospels? Christian congregations around the eastern end of the Mediterranean would have been odd indeed if they did not have a common stock of stories and sayings of Jesus which they shared and regularly celebrated for their mutual edification. Before the stories and sayings were written down, part of the teacher's function would be to serve as the oral repository of such tradition.

3. These deductions are also confirmed by the gospels themselves. As already noted, the synoptic gospels conform in large measure to the type of the ancient biography. That is to say, their purpose is to portray Jesus by telling stories about

him and relating his more memorable sayings and parables. But this biographical character was assuredly not stamped on the gospel material for the first time by the evangelists. There are forms and groupings of material behind the gospels which all New Testament scholars recognise, in principle at least. And the gospels all, in greater or less degree, attest the fascination which this Jesus exercised on those who rejoiced to be known by his name – Nazarenes, Christians. Nor is it coincidental that the most consistent and common title for Jesus in the gospels is 'teacher' and that they all stress how much of his ministry consisted in teaching. It would be ludicrously inconsistent if those who passed on these traditions from the first were not concerned to present their teaching precisely as the teaching of Jesus. The Cynic philosophers of the time are closest to the first Christian preachers in their missionary concern and practice. One of the ways in which they spread their message was precisely by telling stories about Diogenes, their honoured founder. Again, who can doubt that the gospel material served a similar function among the first Christians from the first?

The picture we must grasp with historical imagination, therefore, is of Christian communities scattered round the eastern end of the Mediterranean, each with its stock of traditions about Jesus. The churches in Palestine would retain most of these traditions in Aramaic, their everyday language. Most of the rest would already have them in Greek, the most widely used language of the eastern part of the Roman Empire. So when Mark wrote his gospel he would be drawing on traditions which were already widespread. And though he was (most probably) the first to put them together in such an extensive way, most of the churches would be familiar with many of these traditions. The versions might be different, but they would recognise many of the stories and sayings which they too cherished. So too when Mark's gospel reached the churches where Matthew and Luke worshipped it would hardly be the case that this was the first time they had heard all these traditions. Their congregations too would already include many of the same traditions among their own stock of stories about Jesus. And evidently they had more, which Mark either had not known or had chosen not to use. And so Matthew and Luke wrote their gospels to give a more complete portrayal of Jesus. In each case we are talking of communal memories of Jesus' ministry, most of which must have been part of different congregations' heritage from their earliest days. And however much they may have been interpreted and elaborated in the telling and retelling, they would go back to eyewitness testimony and reflect a basic concern to remember Jesus and to draw inspiration and instruction from that remembering. In short, what we have in the synoptic gospels is basically Jesus as he was remembered in the earliest Christian congregations of Palestine and beyond.

The point is harder to argue in the case of the Acts of the Apostles, since we have only the one record, and since we cannot make the same assumption that the stories and speeches used by Luke would have had the same foundational and authoritative significance for all the churches as the traditions about Jesus. But there are various indications that Luke was a careful historian who for much of his narrative at least was able to draw on good and accurate eyewitness accounts. For example, the well known 'we' passages, which are a feature of his narrative from Acts 16:10 onwards, are best understood in terms of the conventions of the time as a claim to have been personally present on the occasions recounted. And, where we can test the details of the narrative, the accuracy is impressive – as, for example, his awareness that the city authorities in Thessalonica had a distinctive title, 'politarch' (Acts 17:6,8).

Even with the speeches there are sufficient indications that Luke has sought out much earlier material and has incorporated it into the brief formalised expositions which he attributes to Peter, Stephen, Paul, *etc*. For example, the distinctive character of the speech in Acts 7 (Stephen's speech of defence), with its slanted review of Israel's history and its climactic attack on the temple (Acts 7:48 – 'made with hands' = idolatrous!), is best explained if Luke derived it from the group who made the break with the temple, before the law became an issue – that is, from the Hellenists, of whom Stephen was the most prominent. And the primitive presentation of Jesus in such passages as Acts 3:19–21 (where uniquely 'the Lord' is God and not Christ) and Acts 10:36–38 ('God anointed Jesus of Nazareth . . .') is likewise best explained if Luke was indeed drawing on material which had been preserved from the earliest days of the new movement, when Peter was in fact the chief spokesman.

This means that in terms of ancient historiography Luke has taken greater pains than many of his first readers would expect in order to present his material with as much authentic detail as he could. Like all historians, his presentation is slanted: he is a Christian and his portrayal is selective, as we might expect; he chooses to draw a veil over some of the strong disagreements in which Paul, his hero, was involved; his account of Paul's preaching does not always wholly match what Paul himself says; in describing the ministries of the first Pauline churches he probably uses terms which reflected his own time more than Paul's; and like all historians he most probably gets one or two details wrong (Acts 5:36). But even so, when all has been said and done, Luke comes across as one of the most reliable historians of his age, whose account can be credited with a high degree of trustworthiness.

In short, the New Testament *is* history, because the letter-writers were dealing with real historical situations, which are often reflected in their letters, and because Matthew, Mark and Luke were concerned to tell the story of Jesus and of Christianity's beginnings as these were actually remembered in traditions (oral and written) cherished within the first Christian communities.

The New Testament is *living* history

In stressing the positive historical value of the New Testament, however, we must not think of the New Testament writers as always looking back to what was past, as though they were simply purveyors of *dead* history. On the contrary, what was so important about their remembering was the continuing vitality and relevance, particularly of their traditions about Jesus.

This is a further deduction which can be drawn from the diversity of the four gospels. Again and again, in the first three gospels especially, we have different versions of the same episode or saying of Jesus. In most cases there are some significant differences of detail, but the overlap is so extensive that the most probable conclusion is that they stem from memories of the same event or piece of teaching (*e.g.* Matt 13:53–58//Mark 6:1–6; Mark 3:27–29//Luke 11:21–22 and 12:10; Matt 6:9–13//Luke 11:2–4). The point is that such differences emerged because the material remembered was being used – used in teaching, preaching, apologetic, polemic, worship and evangelism. And as it was being used, so it was being adapted to that use – translated, differently grouped, explained to bring out a particular point, and so on. Hence the differences. There was nothing underhand or devious in this – simply a concern that what Jesus had said and done might speak with greater force to the situation addressed. This is not to undermine what was said in the previous section, simply to note that as the tradition of Jesus was reflected on and heard afresh in new contexts that hearing inevitably reflected something of those contexts.

We see other indications of this in the way Paul uses the tradition of Jesus' teaching. The fact that Paul refers to Jesus' teaching explicitly in only a small handful of cases is one of the most notorious features of the New Testament. If the point was pursued with severe logic it might be taken to support the conclusion that Paul knew only a small handful of sayings. But, as we have already noted, the thought that Paul set up a whole series of churches without passing on to them a solid core of traditions about Jesus is hardly credible and runs counter to our other evidence. The better explanation lies in recognising a whole sequence of allusions to the teaching of Jesus in the sections of his letters where he turns to ethical exhortation. This is where we might expect the traditions of Jesus' teaching to make their influence felt, rather than in the more heavily doctrinal sections. And so we find – for example, in Romans 12:14,18,20; 13:8–10; 14:13–14,17,19–20; 15:1–2,8. Some of these are closer to traditions preserved in the gospels, others less so. But they all express the attitude which Jesus inculcated by his teaching (and by his life – the example of Jesus is explicitly cited in Rom 15:3,5,8). The reason why Paul does not cite them as 'words of Jesus' is presumably because he did not think of them as sayings spoken twenty-five years earlier, but as 'the word of the Lord' there and then. Presumably he also expected his readers to appreciate the authority of his counsel by recognising most of these same allusions. The same point is evident in one of the cases where Paul actually does cite Jesus explicitly, but adapts the teaching to the situation addressed (*cf.* 1 Cor 7:15 with Mark 10:11 and Matt 19:9). The point is, Paul did not merely remember the tradition of Jesus' teaching, he lived in it.

John's gospel is the most extensive example of tradition remembered and elaborated. The points of overlap with the other three gospels are sufficiently numerous for us to be confident that the Johannine version of the Jesus tradition is rooted in the same earliest memories of Jesus' ministry. But in John's case the whole process has moved into a higher gear, as the extent of the differences from the synoptic gospels makes clear. What we seem to have in the fourth gospel is an extended process of reflection on typical events in Jesus' ministry and on characteristic sayings which likewise go back to Jesus (*e.g.*, *cf.* John 3:3ff. with Matt 18:3, and John 10:1–18 with Luke 15:4–6). But the extended meditations are the work of the author or of the tradition which he used. In this case we most probably have to recognise a good deal less of historical information than in the other gospels. But that too should not be taken to undermine our earlier conclusions. For John was probably less concerned to write history than the others. It was no doubt his intention to present his gospel as what it seems to be – meditations designed to bring out the full truth of Jesus as that was now seen to be in the light of all that had happened. And had he been pressed on the historical character of his narrative he would probably have been the first to point out that it was not his intention to provide such narrative. Here too Jesus is not merely remembered but experienced in all his significance, with various typical episodes and characteristic sayings from his ministry allowed to unfold the full sweep of their meaning for faith. In this case the history as such is largely hidden within the brightness of the living history.

To sum up: the New Testament *is* history – not mere history, and not history as opposed to theology, but history which provides a firm foundation for Christian beliefs about Jesus and a living history which can still speak with its original authority and power.

MEDITATING UPON SACRED SCRIPTURE

Peter Toon and Graham Leonard

Meditation in the Bible

The importance of meditating upon the works and words of the Lord is clearly stated in Psalm 1. This short psalm was written as an introduction to the whole Psalter, which was the prayer book of the Jews (and thus of Jesus himself). It summarises the true, internal happiness of the person who is counted worthy before God:

> Happy is the man
>> who does not take the wicked for his guide
>> nor walk the road that sinners tread
>> nor take his seat among the scornful;
>> the law of the Lord is his delight,
> the law his meditation night and day.
>> He is like a tree
>> planted beside a watercourse,
>> which yields its fruit in season
>> and its leaf never withers:
>> in all that he does he prospers. (Ps 1:1–3, NEB)

The psalms are both prayers and meditations: they are sometimes meditative prayers and at other times prayers resulting from meditation.

What, then, is this meditation? In the first place, let us be clear that it is not that 'meditation' much in vogue at the present time which has its roots in Hinduism and Buddhism. In the second place, it is not an escape from reason, but the right use of the mind in the presence of God. Meditation is an activity of the mind employing memory, imagination and intellect: however, it is prayerful activity, undertaken in order to draw closer to God, to have communion with him and to be strengthened and guided to do what is pleasing to him. So it involves recalling, remembering, seeing (with the mind's eye), considering, reflecting and resolving. That which is recalled and considered is the 'law of the Lord', the record of the words and deeds of the living God, who has revealed himself and continues to reveal himself as Lord.

The psalmist recalled the covenant which the Lord made with Moses and Israel; he pictured the scene of the giving of the law at Mt Sinai; he considered what this revelation 'said' to him and required of him as a member of the covenant people. Thus meditation led to prayer and to faithful service of the God of the covenant. So meditation is not to be confused with study, although it involves a form of study: it is better seen as a kind of prayer – the activity of the mind working upon the word of God in the presence of God and assisted by the Spirit of God.

Jesus himself did what the psalmist described. Through meditation upon the sacred scriptures as he lived in obedience to and trust in the Father, he came to see his unique vocation as Messiah in terms of the Son of Man who must suffer and be vindicated by the Father. As a boy of twelve he had begun his deepening reflection upon the written word of God (*cf.* his conversation with the experts in Jerusalem), and after his baptism (some eighteen years later) he went into the wilderness of Judea, there to reflect upon God's revelation to Israel, Israel's response and his own vocation to be the new Israel, the anointed Messiah. Then throughout his ministry he was often engaged in meditation and prayer as he lived in communion with the Father.

Meditation has always been regarded as a fundamental activity for each Christian, linked as it is with reading/hearing the Bible and prayer. In particular, Christians leaders have always been expected by the church to spend much time in Bible reading, meditation and prayer. The apostles of Jesus followed his example and meditated upon both the Old Testament (as we call it) and the tradition of teaching, which, when written and collected, became the New Testament. The letters of the apostle Paul reflect his own meditation: they exhibit the results of his prayerful consideration and reflection upon a variety of aspects of God's revelation to mankind in and through Jesus, Messiah and Lord, who 'captured' him on the Damascus road. Take, for example, his treatment of God's righteousness in the letter to the Romans. Here we have the result of his consideration of how, under the new covenant, God gives his salvation freely through Jesus Christ to the Gentiles, without those Gentiles having to become members of Israel, the people of the old covenant. It is his teaching on race relations in the light of Jesus, Messiah and Lord.

Meditation through the ages

Augustine, bishop of Hippo in the early part of the fifth century, has left us many examples of his meditation upon God's written word of scripture. His great treatise *On the Trinity* is not only a theological book, it is also a theological meditation, produced both by a powerful intellect and also by a mind whose greatest delight was to contemplate God through his word and words. In contrast, his much-read *Confessions* is a meditation upon his own life seen in the light of his knowledge of God through Jesus Christ.

Like all the leading church fathers before him, Augustine viewed the sacred scriptures as holy books which contained several layers of meaning: and the deepest of these was spiritual truth concerning the God of grace and glory. 'The New Testament lies hidden in the Old', he said, 'and the Old is enlightened through the New.' This approach is well illustrated in his *Discourses on the Psalms* (*Enarrationes in Psalmos*), preached between AD 390 and 420. Only the person of humility and faith could truly appreciate and receive the deepest layer of meaning. Intellect was not enough; indeed, without humility, it was a hindrance to saving knowledge of God. Such faith and humility lead to the willingness to obey God which is essential if he is to be truly known. As St Paul says in Romans 12:1-2, it is through the mercies of God we present ourselves as a living sacrifice, our minds are renewed and we are able to know what is the good, acceptable and perfect will of God.

In the monasteries and convents of Europe in the Middle Ages men and women sought to draw close to God in lives centred upon prayer. All that they did in the common round and daily task was a part of and a preparation for true prayer – *oratio* – communion with God. But it was not prayer in isolation from the tradition and liturgy: rather it was prayer set in the context of the regular, daily worship and arising from *lectio* and *meditatio*. The reading of the sacred scripture and comments upon it (collected in *catenae*) was followed by meditation, which prepared for prayer: when prayer became difficult then the method was to go back to reading and meditation in order once more to feel and exercise the spirit of prayer.

At this stage there were no treatises on methods of meditation, although advice was given to novices, and there were examples of meditation, written down by various spiritual leaders. Outside the monastic life, pious laity used similar methods of reading, prayer and meditation: or where they could not read, they used the word of God stored in memory as the basis for meditation/prayer.

Books on the purpose and methods of meditation began to appear in the sixteenth century, after the invention of printing and the beginnings of that religious revival which we call the Protestant Reformation and the Catholic Counter-Reformation. They were produced to meet a growing demand from educated laity to know about the spiritual life – a life now freely available for all (religious or laity) to follow inside or outside the cloister. Some of these books have become spiritual classics. What they all sought to do was to present methods of meditation/prayer which were within the reach of the serious-minded and which were based on the distilled experience of the religious houses of the medieval period. Further, and this is important, they were produced in a period of revival and thus partake of a vibrant spirit and commitment.

What is of great interest to both the historian and ecumenist is that the purpose and basic method of meditation as presented on the one side by Roman Catholics and on the other by Protestants are virtually identical. This is hardly surprising, since they learnt from the same medieval experience, looked to the same scriptures, longed for communion with the same God, and employed the same Aristotelian psychology. Of course, it is possible to find differences – for example, Protestants have little or nothing to say about meditation upon the person, role and example of Mary, the mother of Jesus – but the similarities are so obvious that they must not and cannot be ignored.

The basic similarity may be seen if we take examples from Catholic Spain and Puritan England. One Spanish book which was translated into English in 1590 and was very influential in seventeenth-century England was *Libro de la Oración y meditación* (*Book on Prayer and Meditation*), first published in 1554 but known best through the revised edition of 1567. The author was Luis of Granada (1504–1588). Another, which used Luis' ideas, was *Tratado de la oración y meditación* (1556; English translation, 1632). This was attributed to Peter of Alcántara (1499–1562) and has been translated into English twice this century.

The obvious book to cite from an English writer is that by Bishop Joseph Hall (1574–1656) entitled *The Art of Divine Meditation: profitable for all Christians to know and practise* (1607). To this pioneering work we may add any one of numerous books produced by English Puritans between the 1620s and 1670s. For example, Richard Sibbes (1577–1635) wrote *Divine Meditation and Holy Contemplation* (1638) and Edmund Calamy (1600–1666) produced *The Art of Meditation* (1667). The Puritans saw meditation upon the gospel and scripture as a necessary part of the response of believing sinners to the grace of God in Jesus Christ, and thus they often spoke of it and wrote about it. John Bunyan's *Pilgrim's Progress* (1678) is a fine example of the result of such meditation.

The purpose of meditation is to prepare the heart for prayer and the will for action. It begins in the mind, then inflames and warms the heart, and energises the will. Thus it is different from intellectual study. In meditation what is called the discursive intellect is certainly used: all this means is that the mind is busy running about, as it were, within the themes and teaching of scripture, and using memory and imagination in order to bring fresh light upon the text or subject under consideration. So by this exercise greater understanding and insight emerges of how the Lord relates to his children and, particularly, to the meditator. Various techniques were suggested to help in this exercise, and it was emphasised that meditation is what the devout soul will do both in a general and in a formal sense each day.

As the mind is given new insight, so the heart (the centre of desires, aspirations and hopes) is touched: when meditation goes well it is set aglow with hatred of sin and love of God and thus prayer is a natural outcome. Prayer from the heart was called affective prayer, for the affections (hope, love, joy, gratitude, zeal) were being drawn to God as metal objects are drawn towards a magnet. And, sometimes, following meditation and affective prayer, the soul would be brought to an inner quiet and stillness, lost in wonder, love and praise before God in contemplation.

While Catholics emphasised that meditation (= mental prayer) is a beginning of the divine route to contemplation (the simple, loving gaze upon God), Puritans saw meditation as being of different types, of which the highest was meditating upon the glory of Christ in heaven. The end result of two different verbal explanations was the same – being filled with the Spirit and in mind, heart and will being united to God through Jesus in intimate communion. The deeper form of prayer as contemplation was described in detail by St Teresa of Avila, a friend of Peter of Alcántara: and the higher form of meditation, contemplating Christ in heaven, was described by Richard Baxter in *The Saints' Everlasting Rest* (1650).

Those who are called by God to a life of contemplative prayer usually experience a moment when they become aware of the fact that they cannot think and pray at the same time. This moment is called the 'ligature' by the 'masters' of the spiritual life. Those who experience such a moment know that they can and must think about God and meditate upon the revelation which he has given us of himself, but that when they turn to prayer this must exercise their whole attention – in a single act of adoration of God for his own sake. The elements of prayer such as penitence, thanksgiving and intercession are united in one act of loving obedience and humble attention to God. Those who are called to such prayer must nevertheless continue to practise meditation, for it is essential as providing the substance of their understanding of God which leads to contemplative prayer. If it is abandoned, simple contemplative prayer can lose its Christian content, and there is the danger that it can degenerate into little more than the contemplation of self.

In both Catholic and Protestant teaching, meditation was seen as the first step of Jacob's ladder, which stretched from earth to heaven. And, of course, it was recognised that techniques were merely means to an end and could be discarded or modified according to individual circumstances. The main task was to illuminate the mind, warm the heart and energise the will so that the whole soul, in all its faculties, desired to know, love and serve the Lord God. In this aim Catholics and Protestants were in full agreement, even though they had major disagreement in dogmatic theology: adoring God in and through Jesus united them.

Towards a way of meditation for today

There is a desire among Christians today to recapture the practice of meditation upon the scriptures (especially, it seems, upon the gospels): and the type taught by the Spanish Catholics – for example, Ignatius of Loyola and Peter of Alcántara – is the method most commonly encountered on retreats. Regrettably Protestants do not seem to be aware of the rich emphasis upon meditation in their own tradition (though Peter Toon has tried to begin to rectify this in two recent books – see Toon 1986 and Toon 1987).

What we have to recognise is that within the church today there is a very different approach to the Bible than that held by Catholics and Protestants in the sixteenth century. Today, to a greater or lesser extent, we open the Bible and read it influenced by the modern 'scientific' approach, with its commitment to the ascertaining of literal sense – that is, what the original author intended in his writing. This way of reading the text can be very interesting and fruitful in many ways, but it does not easily lend itself to meditation, which is the first step into prayer. We need to be able to open the Bible, meditate upon it and experience what our foreparents experienced – the enlarging of the mind, the warming of the heart and the motivating of the will. Regrettably, few of our biblical scholars are directing their attention to meeting this important spiritual need.

One book which does go some way to meet this need is *On Prayer* (1986) by the Jesuit, Hans Urs von Balthasar. However, it is written for people of high intellectual ability and so cannot speak to the majority of those who want help and guidance. Thus there remains a great need for a variety of semi-popular books on the purpose and method of meditation against the background of the scholarly search for the literal sense. Until we have these we run the danger of asking people to work with two different views of scripture in their minds – one for the classroom and one for prayer.

What now follows is an attempt to make some suggestions concerning the possibility of *fruitful* meditation upon sacred scripture by those who have been schooled in the modern, 'scientific' and 'critical' approach to the Bible – which these days includes both Catholics and Protestants. We are all aware that modern biblical scholarship seeks to ascertain what is usually called the literal sense – *viz.*, what the original author(s) intended. And to this end a variety of scholarly disciplines are used, including philology, archaeology, history, and source, form, literary, and redaction criticism. In this context it does not seem to matter whether or not the professor or student is a believing Christian: what is all-important is that she/he uses the right academic tools. The results of this 'objective' study have been of immense value to our knowledge of the background to, and contents of, the Bible.

Alongside this scientific approach there exists the further 'science' of hermeneutics, whose task is that of interpreting ancient documents so that they bear some kind of meaning today. It would be true to say that this task of interpretation has achieved only minimal success, and debate continues as to what principles should guide it. Further, it has generally lacked what we may call spiritual sensitivity – a virtue which older approaches certainly did not lack. In fact, while the ascertaining of the literal sense and the exploring of how to interpret this as a viable message or truth for today requires scholarship, the receiving of a word from the exalted Lord Jesus through the sacred text of scripture requires faith, humility, obedience and purity of heart. The latter can exist, of course, in a scholar. In meditation there are not professors and pupils, teachers and disciples, academics and non-academics: there are only forgiven sinners humbly waiting upon God to hear his word and to enjoy communion with him.

To meditate fruitfully upon scripture today requires of us no less than was required of our sisters and brothers in Christ of earlier times: we must be in a right relationship with God. What the Lord has to reveal to us through scripture as a word to our souls will remain behind locked doors unless our approach to him and to the sacred text is that of sinners seeking salvation, children wanting love and help, servants awaiting instruction and pilgrims desiring direction for their journey.

It may be claimed that to meditate upon scripture with a

view to definite spiritual benefits (which always lie in the gift of the sovereign Lord) requires the following of an individual:

1. That I suspend but do not abandon the use of the scientific method of biblical study; that I subordinate it to the high calling of waiting upon God, my judge and saviour, and that I recall such information from it as helps me in the consideration and reflection upon the text, as I use my memory, imagination and intellect.

2. That I am convinced that Jesus is risen from the dead and is in heaven as Lord of the church, freely bestowing the Holy Spirit and spiritual gifts upon his believing people.

3. That I believe that the scriptures of the Old and New Testaments exist because God willed that they should be written down and collected: and that they form a reliable record of his revelation in word, deed and through Jesus, the Messiah.

4. That I accept that the true, essential meaning of this revelation from the Lord was fully received in mind, heart and will by Jesus in his human consciousness, and that he (as exalted man) retains everlastingly this fullness. That in turn, in union with Jesus through the Holy Spirit, I am able (as a member of his body) to receive (as I meditate and pray) that meaning of God's revelation which he desires to share with me.

5. That through the words of the sacred text, as my mind is illuminated by the Spirit of the exalted Lord Jesus, I encounter the Word made flesh (or rather he encounters me), who speaks to me, sometimes powerfully and more often quietly.

6. That I am always a repentant, believing sinner, who truly desires to love, trust and serve God: thus I come to him and to the sacred text wanting to draw nearer to him as my Lord.

7. That I am conscious of my membership of the one, holy, catholic and apostolic church of God, and I meditate and pray not as an isolated individual but as a part of this communion of 'saints'.

Working on these principles, we find that we can use the methods of meditation recommended by experienced teachers of the past: and we see that we can incorporate into these methods the positive results of the scientific approach to scripture.

This 'updating' of method is probably most obvious when we consider what is involved in meditating upon a part of the gospels. We all know that the text of the four gospels has been subjected to more critical study than any other ancient text. And what we have come to recognise is that these four gospels are not simply biographies but are, rather, four related but different accounts of how the apostolic church *remembered* Jesus as God's Messiah and herald of the kingdom of God. Thus the four gospels are declarations of good news from God, the Lord, who in Jesus entered into our space and time to reveal himself and bring his salvation to us. Thus, today, in meditating upon the gospels, we share in the remembering by the apostolic church of Jesus: but we do so as those who are united in faith and love to the same Jesus, now alive and exalted in heaven, as Lord. We who do so believe that the Holy Spirit inspired the church to produce the holy scriptures and recognise their authority, and that they provide the material through which the Holy Spirit guides Christians of successive generations. They also provide the touchstone by which we are enabled to test our inspiration and discern whether it be of God.

We recall (with our sisters and brothers in Christ of the apostolic era) Christ Jesus as he proclaimed the kingdom, adopted the role of the suffering servant, and died as a sacrifice for sin, before being vindicated and exalted by God, the Father, in resurrection/ascension. We remember not a dead master but a living Lord, and in this remembering we use to the full our imagination and intellect as they are informed by the results of scientific biblical study. Therefore, through the activity of the Spirit of Christ, we come to see meaning in and through the sacred text which all the modern scholarship in the world could never find: it is meaning from Christ's mind to our minds, and it is meaning which is spiritual in content and which like a magnet draws us closer to God.

The key to meditation upon the Old Testament is to read its

books through the eyes and mind of Christ (according to Augustine's dictum cited earlier). This means that we should not use the Old Testament for meditation until we are well steeped in the contents of the New Testament. To consider the text of the Old Testament in this way is not to deny the literal sense but, again, it is to subordinate the literal sense to the spiritual sense. This means that it is considered with reference to Jesus, the fulfilment of the hopes and prophecies of the old covenant of grace. So in meditation we are not interested in a comparison of Israelite with Canaanite or Egyptian religion or with the precise historical circumstances behind the prophetical books or the wisdom literature or even of the psalms. We want to pray the psalms as Jesus prayed them, to read of the Exodus and Exile as Jesus read them, and hear the prophecies as he heard them.

The important point about Christian meditation (as Calvin made abundantly clear in the sixteenth century and as Balthasar has done in the twentieth) is that we contemplate Christ, crucified, risen, ascended and glorified, and see ourselves in the light of our union with him. All scripture points to him, directly or indirectly, and thus because of his Spirit within our hearts and illuminating the sacred text we are able to contemplate him through meditation upon any part of the Bible.

Part Three

CONTEMPORARY ISSUES FACING THE CHURCH AND SOCIETY

THE SPIRIT AS LORD:
Christianity, modernity and freedom

Colin E. Gunton

Two successive television programmes broadcast in the autumn of 1986 provide the theme for this paper. The first was a performance of Beethoven's ninth symphony: a monument, as the announcer reminded us, to the great achievements of the human spirit. The second took us to the English landscape, and its incomparable beauties. And yet what were the images which remained in the mind? The rape of peatlands by automatic excavator in the interests of quick profit; and a litter of plastic bags. On the one hand, the glories of modern achievement, set free by the great movement of European humanism; on the other, some of its by-products, the sheer tawdriness and destructiveness of which surround us on every side.

Modern civilisation is a mass of such contradictions. Juxtaposed are a naive belief in progress and a deep pessimism, sometimes in the same person; or the technological achievements and wealth which would civilise, but which seem incapable, sometimes, of building an attractive block of offices. The contradictions are in large part anthropological, as the illustrations from the autumn's television reveal only too well, for they are a function of the anthropocentrism of the age. On the one hand, we have claimed a kind of divinity for the human race – like the psalmist, but in a very different way, elevating ourselves to be near the angels. On the other, we have turned ourselves into mere consumers, knowing the price of everything and the value of very little. On the one hand, we are humanists; and, on the other, have lived in a century that is the most destructive of human life there has ever been, and bids fair to destroy even more. It can also be said that an age dedicated to the advance of human freedom has produced, indeed, democracies, but at the same time a clutch of tyrannies of scarcely paralleled viciousness.

The purpose of these introductory remarks is not to belittle our times – to remind us of our ethical infancy – so much as to ask whence such an astonishing turn of affairs could come to be, in which contradictions which make Christianity's deepest paradoxes a model of rationality are comfortably assimilated (by Christians as well as by others) with scarce an awareness of their absurdity. The answer – and it gives a reason why Christians should beware of claiming innocence or superiority in the matter – is to be found in large part in our own theological history. Modern humanism is to a great extent a reaction against the form Christianity took during its apparently most flourishing phase. Because the Christian church has for much of its history behaved in contradiction of both the words and manner of life of its Lord, our era has come to believe that to glorify God can only be at the cost of our humanity. And so the contradictions of the age have developed: by glorifying ourselves instead, we attempt to become what we are not. But that is to anticipate a fuller telling of the story.

The problem is set out in Dostoyevsky's story of the Grand Inquisitor in *The Brothers Karamazov* (1880). Those who know the story will remember that it tells of a return of Christ, not in glory but in a humanity that is yet recognisable, at the height of the Inquisition. He is hauled before the Grand Inquisitor, who tells him that he was wrong. The church knew better, and has therefore found it necessary to improve upon his work. Jesus brought freedom, but in view of the fact that people were not ready for this freedom, it has been replaced by miracle, mystery and authority. The underlying suggestion of this part of Dostoyevsky's tale is that the church transformed the faith of free believers into an oppression. The point is hardly a new one, and can be (and frequently has been) made too much of. But there is enough truth in the complaint to account for the development of the modern reaction against Christendom. Against a God who is the personification of power and imposed authority, the modern movement, represented especially by the Enlightenment, asserted, and to a large extent justifiably asserted, the necessity of human freedom.

The problem is that the freedom which was demanded was not always the freedom of the gospel, and for a number of reasons. First, it was regarded not as a gift to be received but as a possession to be grasped. That which had been usurped by an authoritarian institution was, hardly surprisingly, demanded as a right by those from whom it had been taken. Second, the freedom that was demanded tended to be conceived individualistically, of the claim of my rights against yours, my freedom to do what I want with my own life and the world. Third, it tended to be a freedom of dominion, of control, in marked contrast to the dominion of Genesis 1–2, where the human race is called to cultivate a garden in partnership with the beasts, not as their absolute disposer. Put the three features together, and you gain a picture of humankind as absolute lord, arrogating divine powers in an abstract way, grasping at divinity. The root of the contradictions of modernity is thus a contradiction of life: the attempt to be what we are not.

It was Søren Kierkegaard who, in intellectual engagement with Hegel, isolated the theological heart of the matter. Hegel's response to the crisis of the modern world was a work of genius. He realised only too well that the collapse of the once unified medieval civilisation would bring in its train a fragmentation of culture and society. Unlike some nineteenth-century theologians, notably in England, however, he did not view the Middle Ages nostalgically, as a model to be imitated, but saw in them and in some features of post-Reformation thought alike an unacceptable authoritarianism. In that respect, whatever the totalitarian outcome of aspects of his thought, Hegel was a philosopher of freedom, a thoroughly modern man. His daring response to the crisis brought on by the Enlightenment was to attempt to reshape Western culture by the use of central Christian categories, particularly those of spirit and incarnation. But the Christian categories were at the same time transformed in such a way that instead of moving away from the modern tendency to divinise humankind, Hegel brought it to a kind of apotheosis.

He did this in two ways. The first was a transformation of the concept of God. In place of a transcendent creator – thought to be the enemy of freedom by virtue of his otherness – Hegel developed the notion of a God who realised himself within the world of space and time: an immanent deity, coming to be in the dialectical movement of history. The second was to draw the corresponding christological conclusions from the revamped theology. What had Christianity traditionally thought? That Jesus of Nazareth was God made man for our salvation. Hegel fought to retain what he saw to be the elements of truth in that doctrine, but he was more interested in its general possibilities for a philosophy of culture. The God-man becomes a symbol of a possibility inherent in humanity – a freedom to be realised by ourselves – and therefore a call to all to realise their divinity. To put it the other way round, God is to come to be as the result of humankind's realisation of its inherent divinity.

Kierkegaard realised that Hegel and his successors – the 'relevant' and modernising churchmen of liberal Denmark – were simply using Christianity as the means by which to 'baptise' the emerging liberal society. By the fact that he called the phenomenon 'Christendom' he showed that he was aware of the pedigree of the programme: it was precisely what had been done with Christianity before, and so was continuous, for all its appeal to freedom, with the programme of the Grand Inquisitor. Looking forward, he showed that its consequences were ultimately authoritarian and totalitarian. Equally importantly, however, he penetrated, particularly perhaps in *Training in Christianity* (1850), to the theological question underlying the new theology. To teach the divinity of the lowly, suffering Jesus is one thing – and authentic

Christianity; to teach the inherent or even potential divinity of us all is paganism, and the opposite of Christianity.

Kierkegaard is not always fair to Hegel, but he is basically right, especially in view of what some of Hegel's successors on both the left and the right have since made of him. For it is our grasped divinity that is the problem, and leads directly to the contradictions of modernity. It must also be remembered that Hegel is not alone, and that the company he keeps is equally influential. Before Hegel, Kant's moral philosophy had moved towards a position in which human moral decision was given a function which in effect placed it in the place of God ('knowing good and evil'). Similarly, Hegel's great contemporary, the theologian Schleiermacher, though in many ways different, developed a Christology whose outcome is in effect the same as that of Hegel. Jesus is the man whose religious experience represents a virtual existence of God in him, and is as such the possibility and example of our incipient divinising. The shared danger is that to seek the divine too soon and too immanent to the present human condition is to lose the human. By another path, accordingly, we return to the place where we began: the contradiction of our essential reality in the attempt of the finite to exercise the prerogatives of the infinite.

II

What has come to be called 'modernist' theology takes its assumptions, essentially, from the combined influence of Kant, Schleiermacher and Hegel. It is not, of course, all of a piece; nor should it be possible for anyone writing after the Enlightenment to be unaffected by the movements of truth in the modern rejection of authoritarian forms of Christianity and of political order. The complaint is not against the aim of the modernity, but against the fact that its outcome has been the opposite of that intended. The old authoritarianism has not been driven out, but has been replaced with a new one. If, therefore, there is to be opposition to modernity, it must be made not in the name of some obscurantist authority, but because its end product has not been liberation but a deeper slavery. If this is so, the appropriate response is not a return to the past, but a quest for the possibility of freedom: in this case, the freedom which is the promise of the gospel and the gift of the Spirit. The devil can be driven out only by putting something better in its place. To be sure, theological papers do not often drive out devils, but they can do the preliminary work of questioning assumptions. Certain of the working assumptions of much modern theology militate against the freedom that is the gift of God the Spirit. What are they?

The first is the assumption that 'modern man' is a different kind of person from all who went before. Here, if the divinity of the human mind is not always asserted or supposed, something like it is often near to the surface: that we *necessarily* see things more clearly (for example) than did they who wrote the Bible and most theology up to the modern era. The chief objection to such an assumption is that it does justice neither to the achievements of the ancients nor to the fallibility and finitude of the moderns. It makes the modern age an idol, and blinds us to the continuity of our humanity with that of other times. Equally seriously, it introduces a savage rent in the tradition. One of the positive lessons we have learnt from modern thought is to appreciate the movement of thought and culture from one generation to another. To know our place in the tradition is possible only if there are no artificial breaches. Modernity must be rooted in its past if it is not to be treated as something above criticism.

The second assumption that is often made is that any God about whom we may speak must be discernible as a feature of the general structure of our world: he must be conceived immanently. The obverse of this dogma – and it is a marked feature of Mr Cupitt's writings – is that any God conceived to be other than the world as its creator and redeemer is necessarily the foe of human freedom: if we are to be free, we must be free from the authority of the *other*. There are, to be sure, various versions of this dogma which relate us closely to the problem of the Grand Inquisitor. Some would hold that we may speak of God only as a symbol of certain possibilities inherent within us; others would allow speech of a divinity who qualifies or works within the general (evolutionary) order of things, as for example G. W. H. Lampe in *God as Spirit* (1971). The general direction, however, is held in common. The otherness of God is a positive menace to human flourishing, and the more we involve him in the processes of history and evolution the better. Hell is not only other people, but the otherness of God.

Closely linked with that second assumption is a third, this time about the nature of human freedom. To be human is, on this account, to be an autonomous individual, the creator of one's destiny and the decider of one's ethics. The authentic human person is the one whose decisions are made on the basis of no 'external' authority, certainly not that of tradition or church (even though some moderns are willing to concede to the state – as in some way incorporating individual freedom – an authority beyond that ever claimed by the church). The way this emerges in modern theology is to be observed in its Christology. Modernist Christology has ceased to see Jesus as the incarnate Word, the human agent of a divine redemption, coming from the Father and dying for us. In that respect, it has followed the lead of Kant, Schleiermacher and Hegel. In its place, we have Jesus the example of autonomous humanity, an autonomy expressed in various ways: existentialist, moralistic, political. The underlying assumption is that for Jesus to be divine is the same thing as for him to express a divinity which is inherent in our humanity. The ambiguity intrinsic to this dogma was well expressed by the words placed by *Private Eye* on the lips of one of the essayists of *The Myth of God Incarnate*: 'Jesus was no more divine than I am.'

As has already been hinted, the greatest danger presented by the uncritical adoption of the assumptions of the age is of a collapse into new forms of authoritarianism. They are about us all the time: religious fundamentalisms of Bible, experience or tradition; political fundamentalisms of left and right. One welcome refuge from the storms of a life lived in contradiction is the safe haven of some apparently secure and tested 'orthodoxy'. But that is to return to the equal and opposite contradiction, to place one's faith equally in a divinity which can be identified with some finite institution or form of words. If theology can do no better than that, it had better leave the battle to more determined combatants. It seems to me, however, that the problem, like all real problems, is at root theological, so that the challenge must not be evaded.

III

We have so far observed two features of the intellectual landscape of our time. The first is that the modern age, in its justified rebellion against authoritarian religion and politics, has generated a nest of contradictions. I have argued that the source of the contradictions is a failure to distinguish between finite and infinite. For the finite to behave as if it were infinite is to live a contradiction. Our modern world is living out that contradiction today. The second is that the theology known as modernist – that which accepts the main assumptions of the dogma of modernity – is unable to find a way out of the contradictions because it operates on essentially the same assumptions. To question questionable assumptions, how-ever, requires a viewpoint from which the landscape can be surveyed. Is there one?

Because we cannot jump out of our conceptual skins to a place where we can operate with a total freedom from presup-position, we must be grateful that there is no absolute division between modernism and some supposedly pure orthodox standpoint from which *ex cathedra* pronouncements can be made. In most of us there is a continuing conversation between two sides – that which would accept the good things of the modern world and that which is wary of all who bring gifts. Moreover, it is possible to see the history of theological thought since the dawn of the modern era as a continuing conversation in which elements of a tradition stretching deeper into the past continually make their presence felt. (After all, one of the contentions of this paper is that it is

wrong to accept at face value modernism's claim that there
can be a completely new start.)

The crucial move is to show that even on the ground
marked out by modern ideology there are questions to be
asked and distinctions to be drawn which are not always
brought to the surface. Let us therefore take as our paradigm
the question that has already occupied us as the central one
for modern humanism: freedom and autonomy. Modernism
is right to hold that the two are inextricably related. To be free
is to live according to the law of one's being. It is to be and to
do, freely, that which belongs to us rather than that which is
the alien behest of another. Where, then, is to be found the
difference between the freedom which is grasped at, and
which draws ineluctably to contradiction, and what is here
being claimed to be the freedom of the gospel?

'Where the Spirit of the Lord is, there is freedom' (2 Cor
3:17). The dispute within theology about freedom is at bottom a dispute about who the Spirit is and how he operates. All
Western theology, pre- and post-modern alike, has tended to
conceive the Spirit as a force operating within a person and
qualifying in a right direction that person's life and activity.
Pre-modern thought, particularly in what we now call the
Catholic tradition, tended to channel that Spirit through
ecclesiastical institutions, calling down upon itself in the
process often justified accusations of attempting to control
and limit the free activity of God. In rebelling against such a
conception, modernity secularised the action of the Spirit,
which in the process became not so much a distinct divine
hypostasis as a possession inherent within the life of the
individual or of modern culture. That which had been claimed
as the possession of the institution became the equally con-
fidently grasped qualification of the individual or of modernity as a whole. It is no accident that *spirit* was so central a
category for the immanentist thought of Hegel.

The mistake of both these tendencies (for they are only
tendencies, whose extremes have been outlined here) was to
identify the Spirit too closely with immanent human realities.
Here, too, we must discern a failure to maintain the essential

distinctness of finite and infinite. The Spirit is not the automatic qualification of anything finite, whether church or
individual. He is the Spirit of the Lord, the distinct but
inseparable person of the Trinity. First of all he is the other,
who proceeds in eternity from the Father: in Irenaeus' terms,
one of the two hands of God. The sin of the West, church and
modernity alike, has been against the true otherness of the
Spirit, against his true infinity and freedom, in an attempt to
institutionalise or assimilate his work to some finite reality or
work.

It was Kierkegaard who, following in the steps of Tertul-
lian, stressed (especially in the early works written under the
pseudonym of the sceptic Johannes Climacus) the essential
paradox of Christianity: that in Jesus Christ time and eternity,
man and God, are given together in a way that baffles reason.
Kierkegaard stressed the paradox to the point of contradiction, but his contention remains that this makes for greater
truth, greater respect for the way things are, than the logical
and immanentist blandness which characterises the work of so
much recent Christian apologetic. In this paper, however, I
have tried to isolate and expound another paradox of time
and eternity, the pneumatological. It is only the otherness,
the eschatological transcendence of the Holy Spirit, his irre-
ducibility to anything human, which sets us free. Such a claim
is paradoxical for a number of reasons, but largely because it
appears to take away our autonomy, our apparent need to
realise our own humanity. (On modernist assumptions, it
appears to be not a paradox but a contradiction, because any
autonomy that is *given* rather than *taken* will contradict
assumptions about what it is to be human.)

But 'where the Spirit of the Lord is, there is freedom'.
Why? It is a fact of our being that we are truly ourselves when
we are constituted by our relation to the other. There are
many levels at which this must be understood. The first is the
most obvious. It is no surprise that the chief casualty of the
rationalism of the Age of Reason was the Christian doctrine
of salvation and its associated doctrine of sin. If there is
already a divine Spirit within me, if to be human is to be at

least potentially divine, salvation consists in realising my reality on my own. Against this, classic Christian teaching (as it is to be found in Paul and in representatives of both East and West such as Athanasius and Augustine) is that apart from redemption in Christ and its realisation through the Spirit there is no true humanity. It is only by the agency of God's two hands, Son and Spirit, that what is fallen, stained and alienated from its true being may be lifted up and restored. We need the other in order to be redeemed.

That first level, however, cannot stand on its own, if only because to assert it is simply to produce a counter-assertion to the modern claim that such a redemption is simply not needed. One positivism cannot be vanquished by the naked assertion of another. Rather, we must penetrate deeper, to show that it is not simply a question of fallenness, but that our being as human people is adequately encompassed neither by modern individualism nor by its *alter ego* collectivism. We begin, however, with the development of the point about the need for redemption. It is only an apparent paradox to say that to be myself I must be freed from myself. To set myself up as the centre of the world – as we all attempt in different ways and at different times – is to place myself out of the reach of my fellows and therefore to deny the possibility of human community. In particular, it is to attempt to live as if I do not need my neighbour in order to be as I really am. Hell, therefore, is other people only because it is first of all myself.

In what sense does such a way of being deny our human reality? John Macmurray in his important *Persons in Relation* (1961) demonstrates that human persons are what they are only by virtue of what they receive from and give to each other. Children are constituted by their relations first with their mothers, then with a wider and ever-growing circle. Such relatedness is not accidental, but the centre of what it is to be human. There are no persons who 'happen to have' relationships with others, although that is the way in which moderns frequently talk. Persons are what they are in their relations. In that sense, both heaven and hell are other people. We unmake as well as make each other's personhood. Common to both sides of that matter – the making and unmaking of each other as persons – is a denial of naive doctrines of individualism and autonomy. We cannot extricate our being from that of others. If there is to be a genuine doctrine of autonomy, of living according to the law of our being, then it must embrace what Daniel Hardy has called our sociality: our being in relation as determinative of our created reality.

Macmurray's insights are profound because they derive ultimately from theological sources. It is an element of the Christian doctrine of the Trinity, recently spelt out in John Zizioulas' *Being as Communion* (1985), that God is what he is as a communion of persons. The three persons constitute each other as persons, receive from and give to each other what they are, and only as such are one God. It is, in the terms of this paper, only through their otherness to and distinctness from each other that they are able to be mutually constitutive. Their being consists in their free communion of giving and receiving: that is the *autonomy* of God, his inner orderedness in free relations.

To seek a genuine alternative to the inadequacy of Western theology, both ancient and modernistic alike, we must attend to the implications of such a trinitarianism. If God *is* only in the free communion of distinct persons, how is our own freedom to be conceived? Two points should be made. The first follows from the more recent argument of the paper: we are free not when we extricate ourselves from each other as individuals or when as in totalitarianism we compel each other to be free – for there lies the way of treating others as things – but when, in analogy with the trinitarian *hypostases*, we freely share in the constituting of each other as *particular* persons. The tragedy of the historical Christian church is that this dimension of its life has been reduced to a minimum. Particularly since the developments consequent on Constantine's legislation, it has often operated as an institution to which otherwise unrelated individuals come for salvation. The effective community has too often been, despite the rhetoric of service, a male caste, devoted to maintaining its privileges rather than to the creation of genuine community of women and men. There have been whole classes whose function has been to give rather than to receive, and vice versa.

Here once again we see the moment of truth in the modern rebellion that is characterised by the story of the Grand Inquisitor. The outbreak of feminist protest (merely secularising though it must sometimes appear) is only one manifestation of a historical series of revolts against a system which has effectively denied community, particularly in rendering some – lay as well as women – largely passive rather than actively free. We shall finally overcome the modernist threat to Christianity not by berating its follies, manifold as they are, but by the practical faithfulness of building communities in which the free otherness-in-relationship of all particular persons may be given leave to grow.

The second point follows from the wider theological framework of the paper. Human community is the community of finite and fallen human beings: therefore the freedom to be with and for each other has to be received ever and again as gift. It is only as God is our other that this can take place. Here we must take leave of one of the dogmas of modernity. The modern tendency to conceive God as immanent is not our liberation but our enslavement. The closer the world is tied up with the immanence of God, the more it loses its otherness and therefore its autonomy and freedom to be itself. The doctrine of the incarnation is not the principle of a general immanence but of a particular immanence realised and set free by the Spirit. It was only by virtue of his relation to this other that Jesus realised his divine and human calling.

The Spirit's activity in freeing Jesus to be himself – as is instanced in the temptation narratives – provides a model for human liberation in general. Jesus' particular calling was to be one kind of Messiah rather than another: to be in a certain definite relationship to the people of Israel, and so ultimately to the whole of humanity. Human freedom, so far as we can speak of it in general, is that which enables people to be

constituted as *particular* persons in free and social relationships. This is not expected to happen only in the church,
for the Spirit is the free Lord; but the church is there to
embody the kind of freedom in community which is God's will
for human life everywhere. That is why we must say that only
where the Spirit of the Lord is, is there freedom. The Spirit is
the Father's liberating otherness, realising in our present the
life of the age to come. Without that, there is no freedom,
only enslavement to the finite. That is the paradox of
freedom.

The argument of this paper is not a plea for paradox for its
own sake, but for an acceptance of the nature of human
finitude and the limits of human achievement and control.
The 'paradoxes' of Christianity are truer to what we are than
the manifest existential contradictions of modern ideology.
Freedom is freedom when it is received as a gift, from God
and from each other, not when it is grasped as an inherent
divinity. This freedom takes shape at the human level in
mutually constitutive relations with the other. The shame of
the church is its failure in so much of its own life to realise this
freedom. Its glory is not its institutional success, but its calling
to reflect the divine light that shines in the face of Jesus Christ.
That is the work of the Spirit who is Lord.

THE THEOLOGY OF LIBERATION IN LATIN AMERICA

Alan J. Torrance

Introduction

All Paul's letters were written in the context of problems, and out of his concern to interpret Christ in those contexts – the problems of a divided church in Corinth, the legalism of the Judaisers at Galatia, the fears and misunderstandings of the Christians in Thessalonika. Indeed, his passionate concern for people with their problems helped him to see the meaning of the person and work of Christ, as he expounds it in his letters. So in his concern for the poor Christians in Judea, he writes to the Corinthian church, 'Consider the grace of our Lord Jesus Christ, who though he was rich, yet for our sakes became poor that we through his poverty might be made rich' (2 Cor 8:9). In other words, 'If you know who Christ is, and what he has done for you, how then do you respond to the needs of your poor brothers and sisters in Judea?' And it soon becomes plain that, for Paul, thinking in the light of Christ should lead us to desire an equal sharing and distribution of wealth (2 Cor 8:13–15).

Liberation theology arises out of a concern to interpret the gospel in the context of the sufferings of the poor, and their cry for justice and freedom, their cry for humanity and dignity. The task of the theologian is not only to listen to the word of God, but to listen to the cry of the poor, the powerless and oppressed and interpret the word in that context. He or she must therefore interpret both the social context of his or her prophetic proclamation and holy scripture, and thereby gain a better understanding of the relevance of the gospel, and of God's concern to give to all people their humanity in Christ.

What *is* liberation theology?

> To understand liberation theology, we must grasp one basic claim: suffering and its quest for freedom is the fundamental reality of human experience as well as the location of God, Christ and the church in history. Liberation theology urges action, strategy, and change in human existence; it demands justice, equality, and freedom in Christian witness. Consequently, liberation theology is a new language of God, seeking, in the present historical situation, to be the voice of those who suffer. (Chopp 1986:3).

This is how Rebecca Chopp, in her excellent analysis of liberation theology, expresses its main concerns as she seeks to interpret the 'paradigm shift' – the shift in thinking and perspective – which distinguishes liberation theology from other forms of modern theology. This paradigm shift involves nothing less than a radically new perception of the nature and character of theology, offering a revision of the methods, content and domain of the enterprise as it has been traditionally conceived. Justice and freedom become central themes, while social and political categories of analysis become essential tools of interpretation. This, it is argued, is demanded by the brutal reality of the large-scale suffering of the oppressed, impoverished and marginalised in Latin America. The fact of this suffering requires us to break with the more traditional approaches to the theological task – because the reality of this suffering 'ruptures' our academic theological systems.

The theology of liberation seeks to ask, out of the context of poverty and the human degradation which accompanies it, (a) how we conceive of the liberating message of the gospel in relation to this situation, (b) where God is to be found in such contexts, (c) what the implications of the crucified Christ are for our perception of the oppressed and our relation to them and (d) how we are to conceive of the New Testament message of *hope* in situations characterised by the passive despair of a people who are so oppressed to the extent that their attitude or mentality is conditioned into being dominated by those who would exploit their poverty for profit. The theology which emerges may be described as the faith of the Christian community of the oppressed of South America seeking understanding.

Its background and context

Liberation theology is not an academic system of theology. It does not engage in the abstract ordering of theological concepts. Rather, it seeks to reflect a concrete form of Christian perception, the perception of faith. It is a practical, theological apperception or 'way of perceiving' the world and its suffering, grounded in what the Latin American church has become in and through its engagement within the context of South America. As José Miguez Bonino points out, it emerges

> *after the fact*, as the reflection about facts and experiences which have already evoked a response from Christians. This response, undertaken as Christian obedience, is not the mere result of theological deduction, or of political theory. It is a total, synthetic act, often going far beyond what one can at the moment justify theologically. Then, as one is called to explain, to understand the full meaning or to invite other Christians to follow the same path, a theology is slowly born. (Miguez Bonino 1975:61)

Because this theology sees itself as irreducibly rooted in the concrete existence of the poor in South America we cannot expound or indeed evaluate it without looking at it in its context – to seek to lift this kind of theology out of its particular setting and then evaluate it in abstraction from the cruel poverty and oppression which has given rise to it would involve a radical distortion of what it itself perceives to be its nature and function.

Latin America is characterised by desperate poverty on the one hand and extremes of wealth on the other. A United Nations report in the 1950s describes the situation out of which the theology of liberation emerged as one where 'Two-thirds, if not more, of the Latin American population are physically undernourished to the point of starvation in some regions', 'Three-fourths of the population in several of the Latin American countries are illiterate', 'One-half of the Latin American population are suffering from infectious or deficiency diseases', 'An overwhelming majority of the Latin American agricultural population is landless. Two-thirds, if not more, of the agricultural, forest, and livestock resources of Latin America are owned or controlled by a handful of native landlords and foreign corporations'.

José Miguez Bonino describes in the mid-1970s how scenes of appalling poverty are almost universal, with children combing garbage dumps around the cities and, in the rural areas, chewing cocoa leaves and even mud to dull hunger pains. Unemployment is high and wages are low, creating a context of widespread exploitation by multinational corporations. Medical services are meagre and disease rife. Governments are unstable, oppressive and undemocratic, stifling protest movements and attempts to introduce reform.

The immediate historical context of Latin American liberation theology is the period since the early 1950s. This has been characterised by the 'First World' engaging, on the one hand, in the exploitation of Latin America through the medium of its multinational corporations while, on the other, operating various programmes of development in the optimistic belief that technological expertise and financial aid would soon produce 'developed' First World countries in Latin America. While the former interests flourished the latter failed, and the term 'developmentalism' is now used pejoratively, conjuring up images of feeble attempts by the First World to lessen the offence of its primary role as exploiter. In the 1960s, following ten years of development programmes, the gap between the rich and the poor was wider than ever and the political regimes of the countries in question more unstable than ever. Dictatorships emerged, and these were supported by the increasingly extensive (and sometimes undercover) involvement in South America by the government of the United States, motivated by the desire to protect American business interests and to oppose communism in all its forms in the name of freedom and democracy.

The failure of developmentalism, which was to become the symbol for liberation theology of all that was wrong with the First World (and its churches) in relation to the poor and the oppressed, was due to the fact that, as Gustavo Gutiérrez argues, 'the supporters of development did not attack the roots of the evil'. Consequently, they not only failed but they 'caused instead confusion and frustration'. He continues,

Development must attack the root causes of the problems, and among them the deepest is the economic, social, political and cultural dependence of some countries upon others – an expression of the domination of some social classes over others . . . Only a radical break from the status quo, that is, a profound transformation of the private property system, access to power of the exploited class, and a social revolution that would break this dependence would allow for the change to a new society, a socialist society – or at least allow that such a society might be possible.

For this reason, he concludes, 'to speak about the process of *liberation* begins to appear more appropriate and richer in human content. Liberation in fact expresses the inescapable moment of radical change which is foreign to the ordinary use of the term *development*' (Gutiérrez 1973:26–27).

It was the failure of developmentalism, therefore, in the midst of appalling oppression, exploitation and suffering, which occasioned the cry for liberation – a cry which reverberated throughout the church of Latin America and which was to question and, in many contexts, to redefine its structures, its understanding of its role and function, its socio-political worldview and its theology. And it was the vacuum left by the failure of 'First World charity' which was to lead the theologians of liberation to look to Marxism for what they hoped would be more adequate answers.

The church and *aggiornamento*

The failure of the developmentalist approach in addressing the problems of a continent characterised by encroaching poverty and oppression and the ever starker contrasts between the rich and poor compelled the church to break with the dualism between the spiritual and the temporal realms which traditionally characterised its message and restricted its utterances to expressing concern for the *spiritual* and *moral* (rather than social) welfare of its people. Following the attempts of Pope John XXIII through the Second Vatican Council 'to open the windows of the church to let in fresh air from the outside world', a new awareness of the relevance of the Christian faith and the obligations of the church in situations of poverty emerged. By a natural progression the concern in the Roman Catholic Church for renewal ('*aggiornamento*') quickly became a call for the transformation of oppressive social and political structures.

Two documents proved to be of immense importance and significance here. *First*, there was the response of fifteen bishops speaking on behalf of Third World nations to the encyclical *Populorum progressio*. The encyclical had spoken unambiguously of 'building a world where every man, no matter what his race, religion or nationality, can live a fully human life, freed from servitude imposed on him by other men or by natural forces over which he has no sufficient control' and denouncing elsewhere the 'international imperialism of money', and the growing gap between rich and poor countries. The open document which the fifteen bishops produced in response to this went much further, affirming that the 'peoples of the Third World are the proletariat of today's humanity' and that the church had a duty not to find itself 'attached to financial imperialisms'. The role of the church was to identify with those who are exploited in the attempt to help them recover their rights. This document played an important role in forming the conclusions deriving from the Second General Conference of Latin American bishops held in Medellín, Colombia, in 1968. *Second*, there were the documents that emerged from this which (together with the statement from the fifteen bishops) were to become the foundation documents of Latin American liberation theology and which were to lead to the formation and proliferation of grassroot 'basic Christian communities' which characterised the movement of liberation as it took place within the context of the solidarity of the oppressed.

In dealing with the themes of justice and peace, evangelisation and spiritual growth, and the nature of ecclesiological structures, a dominant concern at the Medellín conference was to find ways of involving the masses in the decision-making processes as they affected their lives. Two concepts came to the fore here which were to denote central themes in liberation theology, namely *participation* and *conscientisation*. '*Concientización*' was a word coined by Paulo Freire to denote the process of the 'making aware' of the people so that they might come to 'own' their own futures (Freire 1972). This meant liberating the oppressed from their 'dominated-conditioned attitudes', and involved, as Freire describes in his *Pedagogy of the Oppressed*, a movement on their part from 'naive awareness' to an enlightened 'critical awareness' where they themselves actively begin to analyse their problems, replacing magical explanations with real causes, and boldly and freely come to engage in genuine dialogue with their circumstances. 'In this process . . . the oppressed person rejects the oppressive consciousness which dwells in him, becomes aware of his situation, and finds his own language' (Gutiérrez 1973: 91). *Participation*, on the other hand, denoted the need to identify with the oppressed and dispossessed, to engage in their struggle for liberation from the chains of their exploited circumstances, and to participate in their attempt to realise their humanity and dignity. It spoke, therefore, of loving the exploited 'concretely', that is, refusing to 'abstract' the exploited from their social setting in the act of loving them, and this meant in practice to stand in solidarity with the oppressed in their class struggle. 'To participate in class struggle not only is not opposed to universal love; this commitment is today the necessary and inescapable means of making this love concrete. For this participation is what leads to a classless society without owners and dispossessed, without oppressors and oppressed' (Gutiérrez 1973: 276).

Accordingly, the church's concern for 'renewal' was to find expression in its working for the renewal of the humanity of the oppressed. *Aggiornamento* meant, in the context of Latin America, the renewal of society by following Christ and working in faith and *within history* for the new creation, for the kingdom and for the renewal of humankind. This required nothing less than the decisive action of the church in faith, and the rupture of the traditional social structures as they sustained the status quo – a conclusion which could only savour strongly of Marxism.

Liberation theology and Marxism

The influence of Marxism is explicit in the writings which characterise the development of liberation theology, and not least in the Medellín documents themselves. This influence led some church leaders and theologians to criticise the theology of liberation as a thinly veiled baptism of Marxism by an uncritical translation of it into theological categories. Even Jürgen Moltmann, a theologian profoundly sympathetic to their concerns, would later criticise the liberation theologians for their 'school-book Marxism'.

What was the appeal of Marxism, and is this criticism justified? The appeal lay not so much in the detail of its economic and social analysis, nor indeed in its claims as a philosophical system, but rather in its ability to provide, on the one hand, some form of analysis of the problems of Latin American society and, on the other, a new and dynamic conception of the human being in society and of his/her role in working for a future free from polarisation and the vicious cycle of poverty and hopelessness. In other words, if the gospel was effectively and realistically to address the suffering of the vast majority of the people of Latin America it required specific tools of social analysis, new political options, and a new understanding of history and the rôle of the human being – and this was precisely what Marxism seemed to have to offer.

In his very useful book on liberation theology, Andrew Kirk outlines five areas of Marxist influence. First, it emphasised praxis as the epistemological reference for all theoretical thought. Second, it contributed socio-political tools of analysis to inform and structure the interpretation of 'the signs of the times'. Third, it offered an objective means of detecting and liberating false ideologies which underlay and gave support to systems of oppression. Fourth, it focused on the freedom of the human being as an agent in control of his/her future destiny in seeking to realise truly human community. And finally, it encouraged the interpretation of the Christian faith by the liberation theologians in essentially prophetic terms (Kirk 1979: 41).

Perhaps the most important general area of Marxist influence, however, is reflected in what has been described as the central theological 'base point' of liberation theology, namely its emphasis on history as the primary arena for God and human action, where 'history' denotes the social, political and economic realities of daily existence. As Gutiérrez himself admits, 'it is to a large extent due to Marxism's influence that theological thought . . . has begun to reflect on the meaning of the transformation of this world and the action of man in history' (Gutiérrez 1973: 9).

It is also in this area, however, that one realises that the dialogue with Marxism was not an *uncritical* one. At the heart of Marx's analysis of the problems of society lies 'alienation'. This alienation concerns, on the one hand, the estrangement

between human subjects and their products and, on the other,
the related estrangement of human beings in their social
relationships. These are the key factors which lead to the
failure of human beings to fulfil their nature as social beings
(what Marx called their 'species-being'). However, in terms
of his deterministic view of history, he sees the movement of
history as irreversibly progressing towards the manifestation
of the new society where alienation will be no more and there
will be manifest the social equivalent of the 'synthesis of
opposites', of which Hegel spoke, in the form of the classless
society. The liberation theologians, however, could have no
such commitment to the natural outworking of any social
principle, because they understood *sin* as an irreducible
dimension of alienation. The fact of sin meant that the
manifestation of 'Utopia' was ultimately contingent upon the
redemption of society by divine engagement within history
through the medium of the church. The Christian conceptions
of creation, sin and redemption significantly conditioned,
therefore, the use of the Marxist conception of the nature of
humanity and the outworkings of history. This is made clear
when Gutiérrez outlines three levels of meaning in the notion
of 'liberation': (a) political liberation, (b) the liberation of
man through history, and (c) liberation from sin and admis-
sion to communion with God. He writes, 'These three levels
mutually effect each other, but they are not the same. One is
not present without the others . . . they are all part of a
single, all-encompassing salvific process.' The means, first,
that the growth of the kingdom cannot be 'reduced to temporal progress'. Second, we discover through 'the Word
accepted in faith' that it is sin which is 'the fundamental
obstacle to the Kingdom' and 'the root of all misery and
injustice'. And third, 'the ultimate precondition for a just
society and a new man' is the growth of the kingdom into
which we are introduced by Christ and by the gift of his Spirit
(Gutiérrez 1973: 176).

In response to those who see the liberation theologians as
uncritically echoing the theme tunes of a foreign ideology,
one would also have to point out the extent to which the

liberation theologians saw their theological perspective as being in a position to provide a constructive perception of issues and problems inherent in historical praxis, such as 'fellowship', 'death' and 'sacrifice', which Marxist ideologies 'ignored or refused to face' because, as Bonino argues, 'they lack categories to grapple with them' (Miguez Bonino 1975: 73).

This brings us to the question: What were the distinctive themes and emphases in liberation theology which, although emerging in dialogue with Marxism, succeeded in distinguishing it from Marxism?

Three basic themes in liberation theology

Although there are a number of themes (biblical and otherwise), categories and characteristics which occur and recur throughout the writings of the Latin American theologians of liberation, following Rebecca Chopp I shall focus on three of these which are of universal and elemental importance. These are: (a) the preferential option for the poor, (b) the conception of God as liberator, and (c) the need for the liberation of theology and for its grounding in praxis (Chopp 1986: 22–27).

The preferential option for the poor

The failure of the developmentalist approach to poverty in South America engraved on the minds of the theologians of liberation the fact that the church's obligations towards the poor cannot take the form of charity, which is itself a feature of, as well as a consequence of, class division and the polarisation between rich and poor. The church is called to a bias towards the poor, to express a preferential option for the poor, to strive for their rights to speak, to eat, to work and to be engaged in the decision-making process as it affects their future. This 'bias' or 'preference' must seek therefore to redress the imbalance obtaining in contexts of opposing extremes of wealth and poverty which, in a sinful world, can lead to a vicious downward spiral of oppression and 'dispossession'. This preferential option does not simply derive from the influence of Marxism and the desire for the 'revolution' of the social order; it emerges clearly from the Bible when it is read with eyes which are not blinded by foreign 'Western' ideologies.

This perception is reflected clearly in Gutiérrez's analysis of the ambiguities in the meaning of the word 'poverty' in the Bible. In one sense of the term, poverty is seen as a scandalous condition and is expressed in the Old Testament with words which reflect the extent to which it degrades the human condition – '*indigent*, *weak*, *bent over*, *wretched* are terms which well express a degrading human situation', terms which in themselves 'insinuate a protest'. But this kind of poverty is not simply denounced, the Bible advocates 'positive and concrete measures to prevent it becoming established' with, in Deuteronomy and Leviticus, 'very detailed legislation designed to prevent the accumulation of wealth and the consequent exploitation' (Gutiérrez 1973: 292–293). But there is another use of the term, to denote 'spiritual childhood' where the poor person is the 'client of Yahweh', someone who has no other sustenance than the will of God.

In the person of Christ, however, in his act of voluntary impoverishment (2 Cor 8:9) and *kenosis* – self-humbling or self-emptying (Phil 2:6–11) – a synthesis of the two different forms of poverty is to be found. Poverty applies to him in both senses, and these are integrated in his mission of salvation. His physical poverty and self-emptying is not a taking on of humankind's condition in order to idealise it, but rather it is done in

> love for and solidarity with those who suffer in it. It is to redeem them from their sin and to enrich them with his poverty. It is to struggle against human selfishness and everything that divides men and enables there to be rich and poor, possessors and dispossessed, oppressors and oppressed. Poverty is an act of love and liberation. It has a redemptive value . . .

The Christian commitment to poverty, therefore, serves to 'witness to the evil which has resulted from sin and is a breach of communion' (Gutiérrez 1973: 300).

The Christian act of becoming poor in solidarity with the oppressed and to participate with them in the struggle for justice is what the liberation theologians refer to as 'liberation praxis'. This is not the result of a romantic asceticism, but is an act which derives from faith in and communion with God as the One who is the liberator and the power of liberation within history.

God as liberator

Liberating praxis is grounded in and flows from God as the liberating God. This is reflected in the continual reference to the Exodus, which becomes a recurring allegorical *motif*, symbolising and signifying the redemptive engagement of God in the history of his people. The Exodus manifests a 'politics of God':

> Israel is not merely conscious of having liberated itself, but of having been liberated; a future which was objectively and subjectively closed (because of Egypt's oppressive power and its own 'slave consciousness') is broken by a God who reveals himself as free from history (namely, from the determinations of history) and for history . . . God as the future of freedom and freedom for the future makes the liberating project possible even in the most oppressive circumstances. (Miguez Bonino 1975: 77, expounding the thought of Rubem Alves.)

The activity of God in the Exodus is paralleled in the redemptive work of his incarnate Son. Gutiérrez writes,

> In the Bible, Christ is presented as the one who brings us liberation. Christ the Saviour liberates man from sin, which is the ultimate root of all disruption of friendship and of all

injustice and oppression. Christ makes man truly free, that
is to say, he enables man to live in communion with him;
and this is the basis for all human brotherhood. (Gutiérrez
1973: 37)

Elsewhere he writes, 'In Christ the all-comprehensiveness of
the liberating process reaches its fullest sense . . . In him and
through him salvation is present at the heart of man's history,
and there is no human act which, in the last instance, is not
defined in terms of it' (Gutiérrez 1973: 178).

God's liberating purposes are further 'incarnated' in the
church as the sacrament of God, the visible presentation of
God's invisible liberating grace. Here the 'base-level Christian communities' are interpreted as liberating society by
'living the values of the Kingdom' (Gutiérrez), liberating the
poor from the chains of poverty and the wealthy from the
bondage of their wealth, such that all humanity can be
liberated to receive the 'gratuitous gift of the Kingdom'.

The notion of God as liberator testifies, therefore, both to
the unity of history and also to its open-ended character, in
that it witnesses to the continuity between divine creation and
redemption understood in terms of God's creative and liberating engagement in and through history.

The need for the liberation of theology and for its grounding in praxis

The theology of liberation offers us not so much a new
theme for reflection as a *new way* of making theology.
Theology as critical reflection on historical praxis is thus a
liberating theology, a theology of the liberating transformation of the history of mankind and, therefore, also of
that portion of it – gathered as *ecclesia* – which openly
confesses Christ. (Gutiérrez 1973: 15)

There has been strong criticism of this theology from some
quarters for attaching too much weight (by way of insisting on

the relevance of praxis and the sociological context for the task of theology) to *historical circumstances*, when the primary concern of theology should be 'the timeless and objective study of God'. Assmann (1973) has responded to this by arguing that attaching a determinative weight to historical circumstance is and has to be of the very essence of the task. Indeed, the very supposition that one can start from 'purely' abstract and objective sources could be seen as testimony itself to the compromised idealism of the 'rich world'. The West idealises the detachment, the isolation and the abstraction of Christian truth – and its theology exemplifies this! Truth is interpreted in terms of transcendent formulations belonging to a remote (lit. removed) realm of ideas. God is defined as an abstract, transcendent being who is 'isolated' and 'above' historical reality. But those who advocate this fail to realise the extent to which they are projecting on to God their own individualistic self-understanding as beings who are self-contained, removed and detached from the real world. Underlying this conception of God, it is suggested, we find the self-understanding of the wealthy, those who are in a position to 'transcend' and isolate themselves from the reality of suffering in the world. And this they can do only by belonging to the world of the oppressor and self-possessed rather than that of the oppressed and dispossessed.

No theology, however, can be done in abstraction, and it is the convenient myth of the First World to think that it can be. The conviction that 'objective' theology is detached in this way is a presupposition which cannot be true to the God who refuses to be 'detached from the world'. Accordingly, for the liberation theologians, one of the central tasks of theology must be the unmasking of those subtle ideologies hidden in the pseudo-objective theologies of the past, so that we can begin from the standpoint of faith grounded in the concrete realities of history and not be seduced by elements and systems foreign to the historical reality of the kingdom.

Theology is 'in reality' act-ual in that it has its 'beginning from concreteness', from 'particular realities'. Accordingly, all theology conceived in abstract, metaphysical terms is ruptured by the reality of the historical person who is 'the way and the truth and the life', the incarnate Son, the crucified God. Christ determines that 'truth is at the level of history, not in the realm of ideas'. Christian truth cannot be 'truth', therefore, while being abstracted from reality. Torn from reality it can only cease to be truth. The love of God as it is conceived in and through the truth of Christ, and him crucified, necessitates the fact that knowledge of God *in truth* can occur only in the context of union and communion with God as the one 'given' and engaged in history. Accordingly, 'just as the criteria for an effective love of God belong to the historical and human order of the neighbour' (Miguez Bonino 1975: 73; *cf*. Assmann 1973: 123), the context of historical solidarity and identification with one's neighbour is the only possible ground for the *knowledge* of God, since knowledge of God can only derive from communion with God, that is, by our being redeemed and reconciled into the kingdom of God 'real-ised' in space and time in the church as the sacrament of God and the *place* of theology (*locus theologicus*). This redemption is actualised just as Christian truth is 'veri-fied' (lit. 'made true'), as Gutiérrez argues, in praxis, that is, in active and engaged solidarity with the oppressed and suffering. Accordingly, *orthopraxis* (right practice), rather than *orthodoxy* (right belief), becomes the criterion for theology. This is not, however, to deny the importance of true belief, it is rather to see the place of Christian belief in proper perspective: 'the goal is to balance and even to reject the primacy and almost exclusiveness which doctrine has enjoyed in Christian life' (Gutiérrez 1973: 10).

This has profound implications for our conception of the nature and function of theological language and, concretely, for our choice of terms in theology. Marx believed that philosophy should stop explaining the world and start transforming it. For the liberation theologians this applies to an even greater degree to theology, and has profound consequences for our understanding of theological language. We must leave behind the belief that words and meanings have access to a theological reality outside history. We must, in the words of one theologian, 'resign reference to a metaphysical realm, a world of ideas in which theological categories have their referents'. Consequently, 'the only possibility is to relate a language to forms of conduct, to action, to a praxis'. Theological language as the language of the church should be seen to be 'performative', since the meaning of the expressions used must be inseparable from what they actually *do*. (An example of a 'performative utterance' would be, 'I baptise this child, Mary Anne.' This sentence is meaningless independently of the *act* of baptising the child! When a minister makes this statement he or she is not simply describing what he or she is doing but is actually doing something in and through the uttering of these words.) Theological expressions and statements, if they are to have meaning, must actually transform the way things are rather than merely describe abstract entities.

This Copernican revolution in theology, relating both to the function of its terms and the nature of interpretation, means that theology is no longer 'an effort to give a correct understanding of God's attributes or actions, but an effort to articulate the action of faith, the shape of praxis conceived and realised in obedience' (Bonino 1975: 81). In the words of Gutiérrez, 'the understanding of the faith appears as the understanding not of the simple affirmation – almost memorisation – of truths, but of a commitment, an overall attitude, a particular posture toward life' (Gutiérrez 1973: 7). And its function is therefore 'evangelical', that is, it concerns the spread of this faith, this commitment.

In terms of this total transformation of the traditional conception of the language and function of theology, there ceases to be any 'possibility of invoking or availing oneself of a norm outside praxis itself'. 'This does not involve a rejection of the scriptural text or of tradition, but the recognition of the simple fact that we always read a text which is always incorporated in a praxis, whether our own or somebody else's' (Bonino 1975: 81). Engagement with the text is the engagement not of praxis with theory but of praxis with praxis, and the correction of the one in the light of the other. This includes the freeing of contemporary praxis from (Western) ideologies which distort the form and therefore the content of Christian truth by making it 'abstract'. Such abstracting (lit. 'dragging away') of the faith from the real world leads to our 'spiritualising', 'privatising' and 'individualising' the Christian faith – and this process culminates ultimately in the destruction of faith as we discover it in the Bible, rooted as it is in the everyday life and practice of the people.

Theology for the theologians of liberation, therefore,

> does not stop with reflecting on the world, but rather tries to be part of the process through which the world is transformed. It is a theology which is open – in the protest against trampled human dignity, in the struggle against the plunder of the vast majority of people, in liberating love, and in the building of a new, just and fraternal society – to the gift of the Kingdom of God. (Gutiérrez 1973: 15)

Critical evaluation

We have sought to present liberation theology not as a new or modernistic system of theology but as a form or way of theology which has grown up in response to the brutal realities of suffering in Latin American society. For this reason we have chosen to present it *historically* rather than *systematically*. In accordance with its own claims, it should not be seen as 'another' theology in the traditional mould but as attempting to bring about in us a 'paradigm shift' – a radical change in our whole approach and way of thinking – in relation to the very nature of the theological enterprise. This is something which one dare not forget when one engages in critical evaluation. Indeed, its exponents may argue that any criticism lodged at the purely intellectual or theoretical level has necessarily missed the mark!

However it is precisely this 'paradigm shift', defined over and against traditional European theology, which points to an area of weakness arising from the negative side of liberation theology, where it can be seen as a reaction against certain tendencies in the 'First World'. This is best discussed if we look for a moment at the weakness of European theology and its disjunction between theory and practice – what is seen by the liberation theologians to be the abstraction of theology. This can be traced, at least in part, to the influence on European thought of the seventeenth-century French philosopher René Descartes, who can properly be described as one of the founders of modern thought.

For Descartes (1641) the self was defined as essentially a 'thinking thing' (*res cogitans*). The fact that 'I think' is the most fundamental and indubitable truth about my own being and, as such, must be seen as defining the very essence of the self. Due, however, to Descartes' failure to realise that thought is a form of physical activity, he established an absolute dualism between the *mind*, as the independent domain of thought, and the *body*. That is, he introduced a dichotomy between the spiritual or mental on the one hand and the physical or material on the other.

On the basis of this dichotomy he went on to assert the superiority of the realm of thought on the one hand and the secondary and derivative nature of mere activity or practice on the other. The effect of this on European thought, not least on theology, has been inestimable. Theology was interpreted as the product of the realm of thought or reason, such that the influence of any extraneous concerns, be they physical, emotional or practical, was deemed to undermine the intellectual purity of the discipline. Accordingly, there tended to be a divorce between, on the one hand, the task of theological investigation and, on the other, the realm of ethical or political concern and practice. The former was regarded as 'theoretical', whereas the latter was interpreted as belonging to the realm of 'applied' or 'practical' theology – where the 'outworkings' of theories which emerged in abstraction from the historical realm were simply *applied*. The direction of influence between the two sides of this split – between the doctrinal, theological realm on the one hand and the ethical, political and practical realm of application on the other –

tended to run in one direction: from the higher realm of contemplation of the divine to the lower realm of pragmatic concern; from a realm of primary and inherent value to a lesser one of secondary and derivative 'application'. The effect of this was that the harsh realities of real life were effectively prohibited from calling in question or challenging both the content of the faith of the Christian church and therefore its practice, since these were decided upon by academic theologians who, in order to do good theology, withdrew to live lives in isolation from the everyday world of ordinary people. In other words, the dialogue between the problems of the everyday life of the people and the content of the Christian faith which was so fundamental in Paul could not take place.

For the theologians of liberation, however, the brute fact of suffering ruptured this order. In the face of the human tragedy of suffering and exploitation we can no longer do theology or interpret the Christian faith in abstraction from the real world, from the realm of practice. Consequently, we witness in liberation theology a swerving to the opposite extreme, whereby it finds itself compelled to assert the primacy of the practical while giving theological belief a position of derivative and secondary importance. In this total reversal of the relationship, orthopraxis comes to take pride of place over orthodoxy – the 'I act' over the 'I think' of Descartes. The emphasis shifts from saving *belief* to saving *work*, and we find Miranda suggesting, 'The human disposition to do "good works" or not to do them . . . is the only criterion for who is to be saved and who is to be condemned that we find in the New Testament' (Miranda 1977: 192). Likewise the emphasis shifts from who God is to how God acts, where the tendency is to identify the action of God with *our* action to the extent that we *are* the church, the sacrament of God. Simultaneously, there is a tendency to interpret the role of the Holy Spirit, who retreats in significance, simply in terms of our spirituality, the 'spirituality of liberation'. It is in Christology, however, that the most noticeable shift in emphasis takes place. The person of Christ tends to be displaced by an emphasis on the value of his salvific *work* – interpreted in terms of its *effect* in the world. Knowledge of the person of Christ is effectively reduced to a mere knowledge of his benefits. All this culminates in a subtle move away from the incarnation conceived as the once-and-for-all, gracious self-gift of God in Christ to a reinterpretation of 'incarnation' in much more general (and less concrete?) terms as the somewhat amorphous and impersonal presence and engagement of God in the world in the form of the church as the sacrament of God. Paradoxically, this has tended to lead to a characteristically European weakness of 'translating' the message of the kingdom of God into a human programme and set of human ideals such that the kingdom of God stands in danger of being conceived of as a human ideological construct. In sum, the concern to emphasise the 'praxis' side of the theory–practice dualism (which has been characteristic of European theology since Descartes) has led to the fusion of, and confusion between, the act of God and human praxis.

A key contribution of the theologians of liberation has been their revelation of the extent to which the traditional dualism inherent in the church's theology has led to the transformation of the gospel into something which is in many ways quite alien to the New Testament. However, the weakness in liberation theology has been to operate in terms of the *same* dualism by simply emphasising the other side of the disjunction, focusing now too exclusively on praxis and on our work and action – and hence leading to the transformation of the gospel into *another* alien form. In this way liberation theologians have tended simply to import and impose on the Latin American people European categories (as are those of Marxism, as Jürgen Moltmann (1976; Anderson & Stransky 1979: 57–70) points out in his open letter to José Miguez Bonino) and, contained within them, European dichotomies and polarisations which serve only to undermine the express concern of the liberation theologians to do theology and interpret the Christian faith *with*, *for* and *from* the people of South America.

What was really demanded by the situation was that they

seek to work for new and more adequate forms of understanding which did not condition the gospel but allowed it to
interpret itself in a manner true to itself (rather than to foreign
philosophies and ideologies) in the Latin American context.
In this way the person of Christ as the focus of the faith would
be interpreted, not in terms of prior categories which create a
divorce between his person and his work, but as he gives
himself to be known by reinterpreting and redeeming all our
prior categories in an *act* of reconciling us to himself and
transforming our *whole* being through bringing us into communion with his *person* in and through the church. This would
allow for a conception of the self – unpolluted by Western
dualisms deriving from Descartes and closer to that of the
early church – where the self is conceived neither simply as the
'thinking subject' nor as the 'agent of work' but in terms of
another unitary and holistic category of 'personhood' where
the essence of the person is conceived in interpersonal terms
as constituted by communion. In this way a person would be
defined as having his or her being in loving, where this love is
reduced neither to a form of social praxis nor (by way of
individualistic categories) to a form of private, subjective
perception, but is rather conceived as a way of being which
unites all our capacities and capabilities, our thought and our
agency, as we are drawn to participate cognitively and actively in that communion which flows from the being of the
triune God, made manifest uniquely in Christ and known in
union and communion with him through the Spirit. This is a
communion which at one and the same time transcends the
world and history while at the same time sending us into the
world in radical solidarity with those who are suffering, in
manifestation, by the Holy Spirit, of the reality of Christian
hope as it transforms this world and yet is neither confined to
this world nor limited by it.

In these terms the kingdom of God is conceived as transcending and judging all our human, social and political
systems in such a way that it can never be identified with any
of these since it is defined in terms of communion with the
God whose reign is conceived solely in terms of divine grace.

This is not to 'spiritualise' or 'privatise' the kingdom, since it is 'humanised' by the active presence of the person of Christ in this world as the one who 'realises' the kingdom in human history by the activity of the Holy Spirit. The kingdom, conceived in this way, is *neither* realised by being 'given up' to human history (that is, by being naively identified with some social or political programme, as some of the liberation theologians tend to do), *nor* by being 'evacuated from' human history into some spiritualised realm (as the First World has tended to do), but is realised rather by its being 'opened up' to human history in such a way that we can glimpse in space and time, in and through the body of the crucified Christ as it exists *in* and *for* the world, God's eternal purposes for this world defined in terms of total, personal communion and characterised by peace, justice and liberation of the most radical kind.

AGAINST RELIGIOUS PLURALISM

Gavin D'Costa

Introduction

There was a time when Eastern religions were accessible only to those who spoke Sanskrit or Pali and had travelled to distant continents. Today most public libraries will contain English translations of the Hindu *Bhagavad Gita* or the Buddhist collection of teachings *The Dhammapada*. To meet Hindus one need not travel to the banks of the sacred river Ganges – the Thames or the Mississippi will suffice. There was a time when Muslims were viewed as 'infidels' and 'religious wars' were waged against them by popes and barons. Today the pope visits Muslim countries as a friend and fellow worshipper of the transcendent God, and the barons have been replaced by terrorists on both sides! The twentieth century has inescapably witnessed the meeting of the major world religions. This meeting has produced racism, intolerance, bloodshed, co-operation, hope, love, and equal doses of sympathy and misunderstanding. Religious pluralism raises many practical questions, personally, socially and politically. It also raises profound theological questions for Christians.

   In this essay I want to examine an increasingly popular response by some Christians to the questions posed by non-Christian religions. Very often these theologians are children of modernism and their whole approach is dictated by highly questionable assumptions. I want to draw out these assumptions and show that central Christian concerns have been slowly abandoned and covertly replaced by a post-Enlightenment rationalism, with an emphasis on experience and a historical relativisation of truth claims. This position is often presented as the *only* viable and tolerant Christian approach to a pluralist society. I want to suggest an alternative. Here my purpose is twofold: to expose and criticise what I shall call 'Christian pluralists'; and to suggest an approach that I shall call 'Christian inclusivism'.

Theological pluralists

What is the stance of 'Christian pluralists', and what are the claims that they make for their approach? The most apt analogy to encapsulate their view is the Buddhist parable of the blind men and the elephant. Pluralists often employ this story. Saxe's poem humorously tells the parable:

> It was six men of Hindostan,
> To learning much inclined,
> Who went to see the Elephant,
> (Though all of them were blind):
> That each by observation
> Might satisfy his mind.

> The first approached the Elephant,
> And happening to fall
> Against his broad and sturdy side,
> At once began to brawl:
> 'Bless me, it seems the Elephant,
> Is very like a wall.'

> The second, feeling of his tusk,
> Cried, 'Ho! what have we here
> So very round and smooth and sharp?
> This wonder of an Elephant
> Is very like a spear.'

> The third approached the animal,
> And happening to take

The squirming trunk within his hands,
Then boldly up and spake:
'I see,' quoth he, 'the Elephant
Is very like a snake.'

. . . .

And so these men of Hindostan
Disputed loud and long,
Each in his own opinion
Exceeding stiff and strong,
Though each was partly in the right
And all were in the wrong.

Pluralists argue that in relation to other religions Christianity has often acted like one of the blind men in the parable. A Christian claiming that Christ is the way to salvation and that other religions are not as adequate is like a blind man claiming that only his perception of the elephant is correct and all others false. Pluralists advocate that Christians should regard Christ as just one among many revelations of the infinite God. Each of the revelations and the religious tradition that has formed around it may consequently be viewed as an alternative and equally valid path to one divine reality. Hence, Hindus will call this divine reality *Brahman*, mediated through the sacred scriptures; Buddhists, *Nirvana*, the path to which is taught by the Buddha; Muslims, *Allah*, whose final and authoritative messenger is Muhammad; Jews, *Yahweh*, whose will is definitively revealed in the Torah; Christians, *God*, who is revealed in Jesus Christ. This list can be extended of course to include Zoroastrianism, Sikhism, Jainism, and Chinese, Japanese and African religions – to name just a few.

This pluralist approach, according to its exponents, has the virtue of abandoning theological arrogance and fostering harmonious and fruitful relations between the religions of the world. Christians need not defend untenable claims that only in their religion is the single saving revelation found, nor need they defend the idea of 'mission to the heathens' which too often has been a covert form of Western imperialism. And pluralists insist that Christians need not abandon the belief that through the person of Jesus they have encountered the God who saves, heals and restores. But, they argue, while this is a perfectly reasonable claim, it should not be taken negatively and unreasonably to imply that only through Christ can God be savingly encountered.

One can appreciate the attraction of this position, but like the music of the sirens it also lures us into dangerous waters.

As a way of dismantling this approach and inspecting its various presuppositions, I will list below some of the basic tenets held by pluralists and then deal with each by turn. I have numbered each supposition for clarity and cross reference.

Pluralist presuppositions

1. The Christian God is a God of love and would not exclude non-Christians from salvation simply because they are non-Christians.

2. This means that Jesus cannot be seen as the special revelation of God, but is one among many equal revelations – all adequate for salvation.

Number two will usually be deduced from number one.

3. If we actually look at the religions around the world in their various forms it is difficult to deny that all religions seem to produce a history marked by both saintly and demonic behaviour. If 'by their fruits ye shall know them', then Christianity cannot win (or lose) when its history is compared.

Number three supports the contention of number two.

4. We can also see that for the majority of men and women throughout history the religion to which they belong is determined by birth – and for many this means that they would never have even heard of Christianity.

Number four is closely allied to number one.

5. Christians cannot ground their claims concerning the uniqueness of salvation brought by Christ on the basis of their experience. The golden rule is to grant to others what one deems reasonable for oneself. Hence, if Christians base their claims on their own experience, then equally the *experience* of people in other religions must be granted equal status. If the Hindu, Muslim or another claims to experience salvation through his or her own religion then, as our claims are based on experience, so must his or her claims be respected.

Number five supports numbers two and three.

6. One difficulty for Christians is that their view of truth has been determined by an *either-or* model. Either *x* is true or *y* is true: either it is raining outside or it is not; either this table is square or it is round – either Christianity is true and other religions false or all religions are equally true. But when we deal with the infinite God then the logic of finites is not appropriate. With a finite object (tables, or rain outside my window) we can say that an either-or notion is appropriate. However, with the infinite God we need not adopt a view that if one revelation is true, all others are false. The logic of the infinite allows for the plurality of a *both-and* model of truth – 'Yes, both this revelation is true and so is that one. God cannot be captured and limited by a single revelation.'

Number six provides a theoretical framework to facilitate number two.

7. Christians with this pluralist approach can now be released from imperialist and sometimes racist attitudes towards adherents of other religions. This new-found respect will provide the environment in which interreligious co-operation can tackle the global problems of famine, wars, suffering and hatred. Otherwise, religions will always be locked in a combative embrace.

Number seven provides a practical benefit for the acceptance of number two.

8. Pluralism calls for a new form of 'mission'. Clearly traditional missions will be redundant, except perhaps to the atheist/secular world. Towards each other the religions can now learn and grow through the mutual sharing of the riches

of their respective traditions. Mission now concerns serving one's neighbour in an international sense: aid work, medical supplies and the fostering of human development in under-developed and deprived countries. Furthermore, without the dangerous justification of saving souls at all costs, many misdeeds of previous missionaries need not be repeated.

Number eight points towards future developments within this pluralist approach.

I should stress that individual pluralists may hold all or only some of the eight propositions above. Clearly they develop and express these points in a variety of ways and in different styles. All eight points are, however, based on pluralist writings, and I have carefully documented my sources else-where (D'Costa 1986b). As I have tried to indicate, all of the points are interrelated, so that the weakening of one may result in the weakening of others. (The domino theory is applicable to a certain extent.) What can we say in the face of such arguments?

The pluralist case examined

The most important of the pluralist suppositions are con-tained in the first two points: 1. that a God of love would not allow the perdition of millions of people simply because they are not Christians; 2. that consequently Jesus must be seen as one among many equal salvific revelations if all religions are equal paths to the one God.

Point two is crucial, and represents the influence of post-Enlightenment rationalism, which leads increasingly to the utilisation of humanistic criteria to judge and dictate religious truth and revelation. Christianity is dictated to by these alien criteria, rather than dictates the terms in which it conducts the debate on religious pluralism.

Let me develop these remarks in more detail.

If the first pluralist presupposition were true, then the force of the second could carry conviction; but we need to qualify it to a considerable extent if we are to be true to strands present in the Christian tradition. Christians from different denominations have tried to tackle this first point while remaining thoroughly Christocentric (Christ-centred), rather than jettison its central affirmation of God's love. If it can be shown that God does not simply abandon millions of people who have never had a chance to encounter Christ, then we will see that the pluralist programme has been set up incorrectly from the start. In this essay, however, I can point in only a limited number of directions rather than develop a systematic argument (see also D'Costa 1986a for fuller discussion).

From the very beginning of Christianity's history, Christians were troubled by the question of the just men and women in the Old Testament. As sons of Abraham, Isaac and Joseph, and so aware of their sacred heritage, they faced precisely the question faced by Christians today: What of those men and women who persistently followed the promptings of the Spirit in their heart before the time of Christ? Are they lost through no fault of their own? Clearly there are men and women in non-Christian religions who are in an analagous situation inasmuch as, historically and existentially, they have not been confronted with the gospel. The answer evident in some of the New Testament material and non-canonical literature explored the solution of the descent into hell by Christ to preach to the just souls and redeem them. While most of these early Christians considered only the Jewish saints of old, some, like Clement of Alexandria, also considered the just of the pagan world.

A number of modern Protestant and Roman Catholic theologies have developed this idea to allow for some sort of confrontation with Christ by the non-Christian either at the last judgement or immediately after death and before the general judgement. While there are a number of significant differences among theologians here, what they have in common (with each other and with the early Christians) is their insistence on the centrality of Christ for salvation.

It is this same insistence that has marked the work of some Roman Catholic theologians who argue that the saving grace of Christ can be present and effective even when a person has not been confronted by Christ. In a sense, the God who revealed himself to Israel as a holy, merciful, just and jealous God – for all the imperfections of his people – was nevertheless the Father of Jesus, and hence a trinitarian God. Hebrews 11, among other New Testament passages, testifies to Christ's hidden presence before the incarnation, as does John's '*Logos*'/'Word' theology. A number of the early fathers such as Justin, Clement and Irenaeus took up this idea of the Logos as fragmentarily and obscurely present throughout the world – and now finally revealed and unobscured through the incarnation. This view, too, demands that Christ is the mediator of all salvation – always and everywhere.

What is important to note about these different solutions is that they attempt to answer the question set up by pluralists in their first point. If God is not a despot who consigns people to perdition for no fault of their own, then this indicates that one need not necessarily follow the pluralist path in reflecting upon religious pluralism.

But, before proceeding, a few other points need to be noted. Pluralists are often in danger of trying to force salvation upon everyone! It is one thing to say with 1 Timothy 2:4 that a loving God *desires* the salvation of all men and women; it is another to insist that this amounts to universalism – that is, that all men and women *are* saved. If freedom is real freedom to accept or reject God, then it would surely be presumptuous to claim that all people will be saved. We may hope that this will be the case, but we also have a graphic and devastating picture of the extent and depth of human sinfulness – in the cross. The cross is a constant reminder of the painful inadequacy of human striving, and a warning against liberal humanistic optimism. However, the cross and resurrection must be balanced dialectically together: despite the resurrection, humanity has not collectively experienced the salvation won by Christ. The kingdom of God is a present and future reality.

One last point. It must be made clear that the above points do not sanction other religions as a way to God *per se* – but only inasmuch as the adherents from those religions have not been confronted by the gospel. If a person is truly confronted by and rejects the God revealed in Jesus, then this must amount to a sinful rejection of God. Whether the gospel is always confronted when historical Christianity is presented – given the sinfulness of Christians and their sometimes disgraceful methods of proselytising – is an issue that must be left open.

'The Christian God is a God of love and would not exclude non-Christians from salvation simply because they are non-Christians.' Given the comments above, it is possible to subscribe to this point *without* being a pluralist. Clearly, point two does not logically follow – but it is to point two that I now turn to pursue my investigation further. It is at this juncture that the slippery slope of relativism is encountered.

Pluralists answer point one by (unnecessarily) suggesting that if it is true (which it is), it must mean that 'Jesus cannot be seen as the special revelation of God, but is one among many equal revelations – all adequate for salvation.' The most decisive difficulty in adopting this solution is that it is self-defeating! Why is this?

God is not an idea or theory. Our understanding of God is based on revelation and the gratuitous self-disclosure of God. The doctrines of the incarnation and Trinity provide the grammatical safeguards and regulative stipulation that when we speak of God – as Christians – we cannot but also speak of Christ and the Spirit, while at the same time saying they are distinct and in unity. Christianity from its earliest days has maintained this linking between Jesus and God. Not only are the pluralist suggestions in danger of severing this link (which they deny), but in asserting point two they actually cut the link while maintaining it! This is because the assertion of a 'God of love' who cares for all men and women (point one) requires grounding. If the Buddhist or humanist, for example, were (understandably) to question this notion of God, then the Christian could only point to Christ as the basis for such talk of God. And this is precisely why point two is self-defeating. The pluralist grants equal validity to different views, some of which by definition cut across the *raison d'être* of the pluralist case. For example, could a Christian pluralist justify his or her assertion that 'God is love' to a Buddhist whose beliefs he or she claims are equally true if that Buddhist does not believe in a God – and even thinks that the question about God is unnecessary for 'salvation'? ('Salvation' thereby has very different implications within these two traditions, a point to which I shall return later.)

There are many examples of the way in which point two leads to self-refutation. The example above concerns the basic theistic underpinning of the pluralist case being contradicted by non-theistic religions. The oddness of the pluralist case is that it legitimises and defends such contradiction by granting equal validity to all religions. It is difficult to see how the pluralist case can get off the ground when its basic point concerning an all-loving God cannot rationally be substantiated or defended as the revelatory event it depends on is relativised.

If the above issue is a fundamental problem, there are many other difficulties with the pluralist suggestion. Again, I will give only one example. Muslims faithfully hold in accordance with the Qur'ān that Jesus did *not* die on the cross, although the Qur'ān holds that Jesus ascended into heaven and was born of a virgin. If the Qur'ān is to be taken as an equally valid revelation as the New Testament revelation, we are then confronted with a dilemma that can bear only an *either-or* answer. Either Jesus did or did not die on the cross. Upon this fact Christianity depends, and upon the opposite depends the authority of the Qur'ān. A 'both-and' solution is inadmissible, particularly since many Western theistic religions tend to place a strong emphasis on the historical and particular. How can we decide or adjudicate? We have seen that the pluralist option leads into a cul-de-sac. The one other alternative, which some pluralists adopt (thereby implicitly acknowledging their standing outside the Christian circle of discourse), is that we have to judge the truth or falsity of the revelations by criteria outside of any one revelation. That this option is adopted is indicative that all christologically centred thinking (and therefore Christian thinking) seems to be abandoned. It leads to non-Christocentric criteria such as Jungian notions of wholeness defining 'salvation', or to equally problematic and sometimes vacuous criteria which would often be more satis-fying to humanists than to many adherents of the world religions.

The pluralist refuge in non-christological criteria indicates both its 'strength' and its weakness. (Depending on where one stands, they are actually the same thing!) Its apparent 'strength' is that it produces a non-controversial and watered-down version of Christianity: a Christianity that does not gain its meaning, its challenge and its promise from the person of Christ. It produces a Christianity that is not a salt to the earth or a light to the Gentiles, but is rather a Christianity that will accommodate all claims to truth – even when they are contra-dictory. If this is the price of 'harmony' then it is a 'harmony' based on principles alien to the gospel. Such principles are probably equally alien to many adherents of world religions – who would also refuse to surrender their truth claims. If Christianity has anything to offer a troubled world, then it is Christ – the source and criterion (although it may appear folly to many) of true harmony, justice and peace.

The pluralists relinquish the central teaching of the Christ-ian tradition that ultimately our only criterion for talk of God, goodness, grace, truth and light derives from Christ. Christ judges the entire world, and that includes the religions of the world, one of which is of course Christianity. It is by subject-ing ourselves and all things to the judgement and mercy of God in Christ that Christians have something really signi-ficant to offer in a religiously pluralist world. Not in terms of a triumphalist self-glorification, but in accepting and pointing to the scandal of particularity that culminates in the cross. It is by the criterion of the crucified Christ that Christians can evaluate and provide the framework for assessing the truth claims made by the various religions. The scandal of particu-larity also implies that it is more likely that, rather than assuming multiple and equally valid revelations, God has chosen to reveal himself in a definitive and normative fashion once and for all – and irreversibly. This particularity does not deny that God has acted elsewhere in history (Israel is testimony to this), but it requires that God's action and nature can be discerned only through a primary focus that then allows all history to appear in its proper perspective. The Christian confronted by religious pluralism – as with any other question – must wear christological spectacles, so to speak, or is in danger of losing sight and vision.

It is nearly time to develop these comments further in order to indicate a positive alternative to pluralism and its relativistic tendencies by working through the remaining points of the pluralist programme. But first, let me summarise my argument so far.

The pluralist introduces a false solution to a badly posed question! To relativise the salvific revelation of Christ so as to facilitate that non-Christians may possibly be saved is self-refuting (from a Christian standpoint) and theologically destructive and unnecessary. Through this manoeuvre, pluralists relinquish all normative criteria for talk of God, grace and salvation, and thereby cannot even properly assert that God acts in all religions. One may ask, 'On whose God and from which revelation are such claims based?' They minimise historical, theological and philosophical truth claims, and by relativising such claims eventually abandon the notion of religious truth. Their both-and model of truth, as opposed to an either-or model, has limited application. While Christians claim that Christ was *totus dei* (totally divine), they do not claim that he was the divinity in its totality. Hence, insights and wisdom from the world religions can often be incorporated within a christological outlook, enriching and deepening the faith of the Christian. But this is a far cry from entertaining truth claims inimical to faith in Christ while at the same time confessing the Christian faith. It is a simple matter of rational coherence.

The pluralist case relies on its cumulative force. While I have tried to counter its main arguments, what of some of the remaining points?

Point three concerned the maxim 'by their fruit ye shall

know them' and argued that the history of religions would fail to vindicate any one religion as being better than another. Hence, all religions could and should be viewed equally. There are two fundamental flaws in this argument, which again highlights the humanist-rationalist outlook of pluralists.

First, Christians do not claim that they themselves are superior or better than the next person. In fact, a venerable doctrine within the Christian tradition affirms that the church is a church of saints *and* sinners. However, Christians do proclaim the crucified and risen Christ. Therein lies the truth of Christianity, a truth which judges the church and all religions and human life. To argue that Christianity bases its claims on having morally better adherents is absurd. Revelation is the issue at stake, not the history of religions.

Second, the pluralist view assumes a God-like vantage and a naive causal equation: where good works operate then there is God's grace. While this may certainly be the case, the genuine difficulty of seeing the deep and secret ways of the heart is neglected. Can we really tell by someone's outer actions alone where their heart is? Deception, jealousy, pride – these and many more factors operate in our motives, motives ultimately known only to us and God (and not always clearly at that for the former!). The saints will not always blaze the pages of history, and are often those who have silently and patiently accepted God's will in hope, faith and charity in their unglamorous and difficult lives.

There is a truth contained in this third point which should not be obscured. Where and when grace is responded to outside Christianity – and the history of Israel is evidence of this – this grace is always and everywhere the grace of the true God, disclosed in Christ and maintained through the Holy Spirit. There is no need to try and discredit or deny the existence of saintly figures in the world religions. Given the qualifications above, we can rejoice that the Spirit of God groans in creation and blows where it will. As in the analogous case of Cyrus in the Old Testament or the Samaritan woman in the New, persons from outside 'our group' may often have much to show and tell us.

The fourth point concerned the fact that the majority of people have had their religion determined by their birth. There is an element of truth and falsity present in this claim. Taken strictly, the argument would amount to a form of determination denying any real freedom to the human agent. While many people are born into a religion, through the process of maturation and adulthood they can come to radically criticise, change, and even leave the religion into which they were born! This happens all the time. Conversion, in whatever direction, is an important phenomenon that also requires explanation. In fact, most of the founders of the various world religions were born into a religious environment which they challenged and changed. Mohammad, Guru Nanak, the Buddha and Jesus are all examples. To suggest that all religions are true because people are born into them and often have no alternative is analogous to suggesting all beliefs are true because people hold them! In a logical sense one cannot reduce truth to a function of birth without incurring a lot of odd implications. For example, if one was born and brought up a Nazi in Hitler's Germany, can we say that Nazi beliefs are thereby true? It is an extreme example, but it underscores the logical point I am making. We can of course have sympathy for the person born into such a situation, but in an analysis of freedom and morality we must clarify the theoretical issues. Truth is surely not a function of birth.

The positive aspect of this fourth point is in reminding Christians that many people have never encountered the gospel and have often lived their lives without the chance to explicitly confess Christ. We have seen how non-pluralist theologians have attempted to reflect on this issue, suggesting a post-mortem confrontation with Jesus Christ or suggesting that Christ may be implicitly followed through the promptings of and openness to grace. These inclusivist theologians do not believe that all non-Christians are inevitably lost, and therefore do not require that one adopt the suspect 'truth is a function of birth' argument. This point, then, should be an inspiration for mission. The gospel must be proclaimed to the ends of the earth, and until the missionary imperative is carried out sensitively and respectfully, the catholicity of the church in its true sense – its universality – is only partial. This fourth point should also be a reminder to Christians that they should always be self-critical as to whether their own faith is based on mature and responsible free choice or simply on habit, upbringing and societal pressures. When Christianity becomes a matter of 'What I was born into' rather than 'What I am called to by the crucified and risen Christ', then Christians too are in danger of allowing birth – rather than revelation – to determine perceptions of truth.

The fifth point has similarities with the previous one: if Christians base *their* claims on *experience*, then equally other claims based on experience must be legitimate. Hence, other religious claims must also be considered true. But again, such a strategy is self-refuting and the basic assumption betrays post-Enlightenment humanist and rationalist influences. To take the latter issue first. Schleiermacher was instrumental – in the Kantian tradition – in putting experience rather than revelation centre-stage. Inevitably, such a move has exalted experience at the cost of the object of experience. Sociologists have been quick to point to the similarities of experience of the Nuremberg rallies and revivalist evangelical meetings. That this similarity tells us nothing of the motives, intentions and focal objects of such meetings is significant. We arrive at the same cul-de-sac in granting equal validity to claims based on experience. Contradictions abound. The self-refuting nature of the argument becomes clear. If the theist experiences a world infused with God's presence and the atheist does not, would it be appropriate to say both are correct? They may both base their claim on experience, but this tells us nothing of the truth or falsity of the object and interpretation of that experience.

Furthermore, this stress on experience removes attention from another vital issue. When a Buddhist or a Muslim or a Hindu claims to *experience* 'liberation' or 'salvation' they may actually mean very different things. On one level we have the difficulty of making adequate and appropriate translations from Pali, Arabic or Sanskrit words into English terms. During the process of translation, echoes from one tradition (the host translator) may falsely colour the original terms (the translated tradition). If I literally translated 'It's raining cats and dogs' into Chinese, my Chinese friend may well think I've been drinking when she looks for evidence in the street! Similarly, translating the (Zen) Buddhist notion of *Satori* into 'salvation' may detract from the issue that the Zen Buddhist does not believe in a God or in individual souls; similarly for the Advaitin Hindu notion of *moksha*. Can 'salvation' in Christ be said to be similar to the experience of 'salvation' in another religion in which the soul, God and often the reality of the world is denied or viewed quite differently?

The point I am making is that if we strongly emphasise *experience* (and even make it an argument for religious equality), we inevitably get further away from the real issue: the object of revelation and the type of 'salvation' being spoken of. If we take other religions seriously, we must also take seriously their specific claims about the nature of reality and our relation to that reality – not just their claim that in *experiencing* this they have gained what may loosely be termed 'salvation'.

The sixth point concerning either-or/both-and models to deal with truth claims has already been treated above, so I shall pass on to the seventh: that Christian pluralists can be freed from racist and imperialist attitudes towards those of other religions; that global problems can finally be tackled constructively; and, furthermore, that without a theological pluralism religions will always be locked in a combative embrace. While the sincere attitude of pluralists cannot be questioned, their extraordinary theological and political naivete can.

While Christians and Christian history cannot be immune to the charge of racism and imperialism, one may question whether these traits are intrinsic to the gospel. This is surely the point at issue. If Christ's message is taken seriously, then surely the critique of racism and imperialism is supplied by the gospel itself. To suffer with and care for the oppressed, outcast and lowly is central to the crucified founder of Christianity. And precisely to believe that the cross discloses the true face of God is also to believe that all forms of oppression are sinful. To hold to Christ, rather than relativise Christ, actually protects the values of human dignity so dear to pluralists. If Christ can be relativised, why not the ethical values that derive from the gospel? It can be argued that a Christian truly committed to Christ must also be committed to justice, peace and equality. To unpack these terms is a complex matter, but for my present purpose (and without being a pluralist) it would certainly mean that each person's dignity and freedom are paramount. There is to my knowledge no major Christian church that does not uphold the right to the freedom of religious belief (and that means *all* religions) within due limits, and also condemns coercion and other unlawful forms of proselytising. It is somewhat facile to think that equal rights for different religious practices and beliefs automatically entail equal validity.

Hence, the second part of this point is also misleading. A non-pluralist theology can be firmly committed to attacking global problems of famine, suffering and hatred. Such a programme is hardly the prerogative of pluralists. In the light of Christ, the Christian must try and sow the seeds of peace and hope wherever she or he can. When this means co-operation with people of other faiths there is no injunction from the gospel to desist. Clearly, in a pluralist society each person will bring the 'solutions' from their own perspective to bear upon common problems. In many cases, there will be substantial room for agreement and joint action. History is complex and one cannot lay down absolute guidelines, except to say that in all decisions the Christian is accountable to his or her community, to his or her own conscience and to God. Instances of religious inter-cooperation are found throughout history and thankfully are increasing today – without the requirement that participants relinquish their central beliefs.

Finally, it may be said that in a troubled world the abandon-

ment of the central tenets of Christian faith as a solution to the
clash of worldviews represents at best a liberal desire to please
everyone (and consequently no one) and at worst a policy that
enhances rather than relieves the crisis. If Christ is a light to
the nations, then it is odd to hide this light under a bushel in
embarrassment.

It is appropriate to finish this essay on the issue of mission.
By now, it will I hope be clear that the pluralist version of
mission amounts to a humanist version of social service! It is
of course absolutely right that the welfare of the whole person
be the centre of Christian concern. Poverty, disease and
famine all endanger the glory and beauty of God's creation.
But ultimately, if the salt is to keep its flavour, the source of
these values and the source of eternal salvation must also be
proclaimed. If the Christian truly wishes to share with and
love the non-Christian then, as with a close friend, one's most
treasured beliefs and commitment should also be shared.
Proclaiming the risen Christ through one's deeds, thoughts
and words is always, and has always been, the central
challenge of the gospel.

However, it should be added that any real dialogue and
friendship requires mutual trust and respect. In the same way
that the Christian would expect his or her right to mission, he
or she must equally be willing to listen to and be challenged by
his or her partner's faith. This openness does not imply a lack
of commitment, or a suspension of one's beliefs (a phenomenological *epoché*), but a genuine respect for the person as he
or she is.

Conclusion

I began this essay by outlining our situation of religious
pluralism in the twentieth century. The title 'Against Religious Pluralism' is directed at the pluralist theology that has
arisen in the light of this situation – and *not* as a comment
against non-Christian religions! Certainly, this new situation

challenges us to rethink our faith. My suggestion is that we do not rethink it along the lines of theological pluralism, as this avenue seems more of an abandonment than a rethinking.

Elsewhere I have developed what I have called 'Christian inclusivism', that is, a critical appreciation of the worth and limitation of non-Christian religions (D'Costa 1986a; D'Costa 1987). In this essay I have tried to show that Christian theology can be faithful to its central claims and beliefs about Christ without thereby implying the condemnation of most of non-Christian humanity. I have also tried to argue that for Christians a true evaluation and appreciation of non-Christian religions can arise only from a Christ-centred theology rather than a humanist-rationalist one. If this essay acts as a signpost towards new avenues in need of further exploration and as a warning against other paths of exploration its purpose will be achieved.

DIFFERENT GOSPELS:
The social sources of apostasy

Peter L. Berger

This is not a sermon. It is, as advertised, a lecture. A sermon is an act of proclamation of the gospel by an individual who has been ordained to preach. That is a very solemn business indeed, one to which I have neither claim nor aspiration. I am not a preacher; I am a social scientist. I exercise a vocation that deals, not in proclamation, but in empirical enquiry, which by its very nature is tentative, probabilistic and open to falsification. Most of what I have to say in this lecture is based on my observations as a sociologist with an interest in American religion. I see no reason, however, to limit myself to doing sociology of religion. I am also a Christian; as such I find myself constrained to relate my understanding of the world to my faith, and I will attempt to do this in the latter part of the lecture. It is with this intention, and definitely not to suggest a sermon, that I begin with a passage from the New Testament.

The apostle Paul wrote to the Galatians as follows:

I am astonished that you are so quickly deserting him who called you in the grace of Christ and turning to a different gospel – not that there is another gospel, but there are some who trouble you and want to pervert the gospel of Christ . . . As we have said before, so now I say again, If any one is preaching to you a gospel contrary to that which you received, let him be accursed. (Gal 1:6–7,9, RSV)

The theme of this passage is apostasy. People, especially those of a conservative bent, have the tendency to think that their own age has unique evils. To some extent, I suppose, this is a correct perception. Every age has a distinctive genius, for evil as well as good, and our age has produced evils that can safely be called unique. But apostasy – the substitution of different gospels for the gospel of Christ – has been a constant in the history of the church. It was there right from the beginning, as the letter to the Galatians (along with many other portions of the New Testament) serves to remind us. The essence of apostasy is always the same: seeking salvation, not in the grace of Christ 'heard with faith', but rather in what Paul calls 'the works of the law'. The specific contents of apostasy, the details of 'works-righteousness', vary from age to age. This lecture is a reflection about apostasy in our own age. As a social scientist I have certain analytic tools allowing an attempt to understand the mundane context of the 'different gospels' of the age. As a Christian I must also make some moral and theological assessments.

Let us do some sociology.

For historically well-known reasons (elaborated, among others, by H. Richard Niebuhr (1929) in the book whose title I have paraphrased here), there has always been a close linkage between religion and culture in America. This is a culture whose values and institutions, even whose aesthetic style, have been crucially affected by Protestantism. Thus there is a direct line from the Puritan covenant, through the 'half-way covenants' of a disintegrating Puritanism, to the various secularised notions of American exceptionalism – all having in common the idea that, somehow, American society has a unique and putatively sacred mission. To be sure, there have been dissenters from this vision (within Protestantism and from without) and some American groups have never shared it, but its pervasiveness in American history to this day is remarkable, especially in comparison with societies having a more sober conception of themselves. In due course Catholics, Jews and others have come to participate in this quasi-covenantal vision, but, not surprisingly, the major Protestant denominations have had the most intimate connection with the culture. American civilisation is a distinctively Protestant product; conversely, American Protestantism is a distinctively powerful case of so-called *Kulturprotestantismus*.

Sociologically, however, one can describe this religio-cultural unity more precisely. Here again H. Richard Niebuhr (building to some extent on Max Weber) is helpful: it is not culture in general that has been the partner in this marriage with religion; it is a specific *class* culture. The class, of course, is the bourgeoisie, lately called the middle class, that creator and carrier of capitalism which had to struggle against older classes in Europe, but which had hardly any serious competitors in America (except, though even that is debatable, in the *ante-bellum* South). America, from the beginning, was a bourgeois society – not, of course, in the sense that all Americans were middle-class, but because this society was shaped by middle-class values and institutions without having to overcome antecedent aristocratic or peasant cultures. As both Weber and Niebuhr showed, Protestant morality and Protestant social arrangements were highly instrumental in this construction of a bourgeois world. Not only did Protestantism inspire the culture of the great American middle class, but it served as the very effective mobility machine by which people from the lower reaches of society, generation after generation, were assisted in *moving into* the middle class. Religiously (and, of course, sincerely so) lower-class individuals were washed in the blood of the Lamb, in one great revival after another. But in the process they also learnt to wash their feet and to wash out their mouths – that is, to act and speak in accordance with middle-class norms, and *ipso facto* to acquire habits and attitudes conducive to upward mobility in a relatively open class system. Already John Wesley observed (and was troubled by) the fact that Methodists had a pronounced tendency to start out poor and end up rich; Weber and Niebuhr would have had no difficulty explaining to him why this was happening.

As recently as the 1950s this class-specific 'culture Protestantism' was very much alive and well. The so-called main-

line denominations existed in a by-and-large happy symbiosis
with middle-class culture; lower-class sects and churches were
continuing to grind away their time-honoured mobility
machinery; and (as Will Herberg astutely observed at the
time) Catholics and Jews had very largely joined this all-
American celebration. To be sure, there had been a good deal
of secularisation in the contents of this common American
faith, both in its social and its personal ethics (President
Eisenhower embodied the former modification, Norman
Vincent Peale the latter), and many of the harder theological
contents of the various traditions had been softened, relativised (or, as John Murray Cuddihy has put it, 'civilised'). The
main point, though, is that there was little tension between
the major religious groupings and the cultural milieu in which
they found themselves. They existed (if I may use a term I
employed in my first writings about American religion) in an
'okay world': America was okay; the middle-class way of life
was okay; indeed, it had become difficult to distinguish
between the religiously sanctioned virtues and the values
propagated by politicians, civics teachers and therapists. If I
am to recall one *locus classicus* in the portrayal of this
religio-cultural symbiosis (a critical one, of course), it would
be William Lee Miller's essay 'Piety Along the Potomac'
(published in *The Reporter* magazine in 1954); his 'The
Gospel of Norman Vincent Peale' (*Union Seminary Quarterly
Review*, 1955) would round out the picture in its more
personal aspect.

Looking back on this period thirty years later one can easily
say that the situation today is very different. So it is, in many
respects. It is all the more important to understand that, in
many respects, the situation hasn't changed that much.

I would argue that one of the most important developments
of the post-Second World War period in America (and incidentally in other Western societies) has been *a bifurcation
of the middle class*. This is the so-called 'New Class thesis', an
idea that, interestingly, has been held in common by observers on the right and the left of the political spectrum. Thus
Irving Kristol, the *doyen* of neo-conservatism, and Alvin

Gouldner, the late neo-Marxist sociologist, have both written about the 'New Class', pretty much agreeing on its empirical characteristics; Kristol thinks that this class is bad news, while Gouldner hoped that it would bring about very desirable changes in the society. When observers with diametrically opposed ideological views agree on an empirical assessment, this gives good grounds for surmising that the assessment is close to reality. What is the reality in this case?

The underlying process is technological and economic: in our type of advanced industrial society an ever-shrinking segment of the labour force is needed to keep material production going. This frees up, indeed compels, the growth of an occupational sector that is geared to miscellaneous services (economists call this the 'quaternary sector'). Within this sector there is what has been called the 'knowledge industry', and within *that* there is a very peculiar activity, devoted to the production and distribution of what may be called symbolic knowledge. The 'New Class' consists of the people who make their living from this activity. These are the educators (from pre-school to university), the 'communicators' (in the media, in public relations, in a miscellany of propagandistic lobbies), the therapists of all descriptions (from child analysts to geriatric sex counsellors), and, last but not least, substantial elements of the bureaucracy (those elements concerned with what has been called 'lifestyle engineering') and the legal profession. They are, of course, a minority of the working population, but, because of their power in key institutions that provide the symbols by which the society understands itself, their influence is much greater than would be supposed by their numbers. Whether one calls this group a 'class' or not is a matter of sociological conceptualisation; I use the term because I think it helps to clarify what is going on.

It is a class because it is a group with a distinctive relation to what Marx called the 'mode of production'. It is a *rising* class, and as such it finds itself in conflict with the class that previously controlled the societal areas into which it is moving. That class, of course, is the *old* middle class, still centred in the business community and the traditional professions. The conflict between the two middle classes, I believe, serves to explain many otherwise strange features of recent American politics – notably the fact that many economically and culturally privileged people have moved into strong, sometimes virulent opposition to key American institutions and values. The new knowledge class is generally left-of-centre. This fact, I think, can very largely be explained by the vested interests of this class, which, to put it very broadly, stands to gain from a shift of power from business to government. Thus this class has a vested interest in domestic policies that expand the welfare state and in foreign policies that de-emphasise military power. I regret that I cannot elaborate on this assertion here, but, be this as it may, the most relevant point to be made here is that the new class (like all classes, of course) has distinctive cultural characteristics. Again, I would argue that many of the socio-cultural conflicts today, from the environment to the sphere of sexual intimacy, must be understood as symbolic expressions of an underlying class conflict. Thus we know that class is the most reliable predictor of an individual's stand on such matters as nuclear energy, abortion or the gamut of items on the feminist agenda. By their bumper stickers you shall know them: it is not difficult to guess the class affiliation of individuals whose automobiles sport messages like 'US out of Central America', 'Save the Whales' or 'ERA Now', as against 'Nicaragua is Spanish for Afghanistan', 'Register Criminals not Guns', or 'Abortion is Murder'. The former, of course, is likely to be a fully accredited member of the new knowledge class; the latter may be an unrepentant bourgeois, or he or she may belong to that working class which (contrary to all Marxist theories) is now one of the staunchest carriers of traditional bourgeois culture.

The religious fall-out of this *Kulturkampf* is all too visible. The mainline Protestant denominations still contain (probably dwindling) numbers of old-middle-class and working-class individuals. But (and this is a decisively important fact) their clergy, officials and intellectuals have (understandably enough) identified almost completely with the culture and *ipso facto* the political agenda of the new middle class. A very similar process has been under way in the Roman Catholic community. Contrary to what was predicted by Jeffrey Hadden in his still-interesting book *The Gathering Storm in the Churches* (1969), lay people who dislike the new-class rhetoric assailing them in these churches have put up remarkably little resistance; instead, they have quietly moved out. Some have joined the ranks of the unchurched; others have helped to swell the impressive numbers making up the great evangelical upsurge. And the latter too makes much more sense in the light of class analysis: to a large extent it may be seen as part of the 'bourgeois insurgency' (the apt phrase is by Richard Neuhaus), which is the movement of resistance by the old middle class and much of the working class against the political and cultural power grab of the new class. In this perspective, the New Christian Right is the mirror image of the mainline leadership in the ongoing class conflict.

What I am saying here is that, appearances notwithstanding, there has been no basic change in the relations between religion and culture, and between religion and class, in America. What *has* changed is the class system and its cultures. But, as always, most of American religion (and especially Protestantism) faithfully reflects the class culture in which it finds itself. As before, there is very little consciousness of the class location of one's own cultural and ideological propensities. *Kulturprotestantismus* prevails, eagerly emulated by many non- (or should one say neo-) Protestants. American society continues to be pluralistic and broadly tolerant, and one should not overestimate the degree of polarisation. There are many people and entire groups who manage to live quite comfortably detached from all this political and cultural conflict. All the same, there are two class armies arrayed against each other on a sizable number of cultural battlefields. Increasingly, major religious organisations are serving the function of military chaplaincies in these armies, doing what chaplains have always done on battlefields – solemnly blessing the banners of their side and assuring the troops that their cause is God's.

Mainline Protestantism has suffered a good measure of decline. The future course of the aforementioned class conflict will largely determine whether this decline will continue, and I would not want to make predictions here. But one point should be made: if the mainline churches continue to decline, it will *not* be because of their alleged 'prophetic ministry'. It is hardly 'prophecy' if one says exactly what people in a particular social milieu want to hear. The decline will not be the result of 'speaking truth to power', but rather of backing the wrong horse in a game of power politics.

Needless to say, this sociological analysis could be greatly refined and elaborated. Of necessity, I have been exceedingly sketchy here. I would strongly emphasise, however, that the analysis is 'value-neutral'. *All* religious and moral affirmations occur in a social context; to point out what this context is by no means prejudges the validity of the affirmations. I, for one, find myself unable to identify fully with the agenda of either side in the current conflict. Still, *morally speaking* (and leaving aside both cultural tastes and theological convictions), I find the new-class agenda the more reprehensible of the two. It seems to me that the most pressing moral issues of the present age are the avoidance of nuclear war, the survival of freedom and the alleviation of misery. These goals, I believe, depend upon the maintenance of a balance of power based on American military strength and upon the institutions of democratic capitalism; I further believe that the much-maligned bourgeois culture, albeit modified, continues to be a better vehicle for sustaining a decent society than its current competitors. Therefore, if pushed to make a moral choice between the 'bourgeois insurgency' and the new-class agenda, I opt for the former (even if I have to dissent from some planks of the platform). Put simply, I fail to see the moral superiority of an ideology committed to unilateral disarmament, a vague socialism and an assault on the family. I have elsewhere written at length about my reasons for this moral position and for the right-of-centre politics that follow from it. That, however, is not my purpose here. I mention it for two reasons. First, I will in what follows maintain that, in making a theological assessment, one can say the same things about those who would make a 'gospel' of a right-wing agenda and those who do this with an agenda of the left; I am *not* suggesting a symmetrical *moral* equivalence. And second, I want to make my own political position clear, precisely because what I have to say theologically is meta-political; indeed, I would say *exactly the same*, speaking theologically, if I located myself on the other side of the political divide.

Let us now do some theology. (For those of us who are not theologians, the warrant for doing this lies in the priesthood of all believers. Or, to put it in more mundane terms, theology is too important to be left to the professional theologians, especially seeing what they have done with the business of theologising in recent years!)

Paul wrote to the Galatians: 'A man is not justified by works of the law but through faith in Jesus Christ. [Even] we have believed in Christ Jesus, in order to be justified by faith in Christ, and not by works of the law, because by works of the law shall no one be justified' (Gal 2:16, RSV).

Faith in the gospel of Christ is constitutive of the church. The church is the community that embodies this faith. Apostasy occurs when any other content is deemed to be constitutive of the Christian community. At that point, the community becomes something other than the church of Christ. Of all the so-called 'marks of the church', the central and indispensable one is that the church proclaims the gospel, and not any other message of salvation. Compared to the true gospel, all these other messages appear as 'works of the law', as manifestations of 'works-righteousness'. These allegedly salvific messages, of course, differ greatly in different periods of history. Thus it requires a considerable effort on our part to enter into the dispute over the status of Jewish law in the Galatian community; however important one may deem the dialogue between Judaism and Christianity in our own time, I think it is safe to say that it will have to be couched in very different language and that the specific problem of the Galatians is not our problem today. The underlying question, though, has not changed at all: Is it the gospel of Christ that constitutes the church, or is it a 'different gospel'?

It seems to me that we face precisely this question in American Christianity today – nothing less – and it is an awesome question. Compared to this question, the different moral and political options available to us pale, not into insignificance (because Christians are in the world and responsible for the world), but into what Dietrich Bonhoeffer called 'penultimacy': the ultimate question is the question of salvation. Thus the issue I want to address now is *not*, emphatically not, the substitution of one cultural or political agenda for another. Rather, it is the issue of placing *any* such agenda into the place that is reserved to the gospel in the faith and the life of the church.

Allow me to explicate this point in somewhat personal terms. My own politico-cultural positions have much to do with the insights I believe myself to have gained over the years of working as a social scientist. While, by definition, these insights have no inerrancy and are always open to revision as new empirical evidence comes up, I am reasonably certain that I understand some things about the modern world. Thus, when I go to church or read church publications, I am irritated when I am confronted with statements that I consider to be empirically flawed. I don't go to church in order to hear vulgarised, 'pop' versions of my own field. The irritation deepens when these terrible simplifications are proclaimed to me in tones of utter certitude and moral urgency. Bad analysis obviously makes for bad policy, and here I am not just intellectually irritated but morally offended. For example, when, in the name of the 'preferential option for the poor' (a phrase with which, in principle, I have no quarrel), policies are presented as moral imperatives which, in my understanding, are likely to increase rather than reduce poverty (such as all the socialist and quasi-socialist panaceas proposed for the Third World by liberation theologians – and Third World development has been my major concern for the better part of my career as a sociologist), then I am more than irritated: I am constrained to make the moral judgement that what goes on here is profoundly irresponsible. Being human, I am sure that I would be less irritated, and less offended, if what I heard in church were, in my understanding, more competent analysis and more responsible politics. *Nevertheless*, not for one moment am I advocating here that *my* analysis and *my* politics should be substituted for the left-of-centre rhetoric rampant in our churches today (I am speaking, of course, of the mainline Protestant and Catholic churches). *Neither* side's agenda belongs in the pulpit, in the liturgy or in any statements that claim to have the authority of the gospel. *Any* cultural or political agenda embellished with such authority is a manifestation of 'works-righteousness' and *ipso facto* an act of apostasy.

This theological proposition, over and beyond all prudential moral judgements or political options, 'hits' in all directions of the ideological spectrum; it 'hits' the centre as much as the left or the right. 'Different gospels' lurk all across the spectrum. No value or institutional system, past or present or future, is to be identified with the gospel. The mission of the church is not to legitimate any status quo *or* any putative alteration of the status quo. The 'okay world' of bourgeois America stands under judgement, in the light of the gospel, as does every other human society. Democracy or capitalism or the particular family arrangements of middle-class culture are not to be identified with the Christian life, and neither is any alternative political, economic or cultural system. The vocation of the church is to proclaim the gospel, not to defend the American way of life, not to 'build socialism', not even to 'build a just society' – because, quite apart from the fact that we don't really know what this is, all our notions of justice are fallible and finally marred by sin. The 'works-righteousness' in all these 'different gospels' lies precisely in the insinuation that, if only we do this or refrain from doing that, we will be saved, 'justified'. But, as Paul tells us, 'by works of the law shall no one be justified'.

In the face of all these 'different gospels', the true gospel is *liberating*. As Paul puts it: 'For freedom Christ has set us free; stand fast therefore, and do not submit again to a yoke of slavery' (Gal 5:1, rsv). It seems to me that this liberating power of the gospel has two aspects. The first, of course, is the liberation from sin and death that is Christ's work for us. This liberation is at the heart of the gospel, indeed *is* the gospel. While it affects everyone who believes it in a very singular way, its import is cosmic, transcending all the structures of this world. What is more, this liberation is available only to faith; it cannot be proved or demonstrated except by faith. I would contend, though, that there is, as it were, a lesser liberation brought about by the gospel – lesser only if compared with the world-shattering cataclysm of Christ's victory over sin and death – and this is the liberation from the bondage of mundaneness. This lesser liberation, unlike the first, can be perceived even short of faith; it is, if you will, an empirically available liberation. *The gospel liberates by relativising all the realities of this world and all our projects in this world.*

We know – not by faith but by reason – that everything in this world is bound to perish. All men are mortal, and so are all the societies they create, even the most attractive ones. It is foolishness to act as if any one of the social constructions of men possesses ultimate importance or even reality. We can also know – and this knowledge is one of the major if bitter fruits of the modern social sciences – that our projects in the world almost never yield the results we intend. Our actions regularly escape us, turn against us; all too often, they fail precisely in succeeding. This bitter truth is the common insight of allegedly successful conquerors and revolutionaries. History, which is the sum-total of all human projects in this world, has no rationally discernable direction – only faith can perceive in it the unfolding of God's hidden purpose. Empirically, history is an unending repetition of cruelty and madness: the gospel liberates because it opens up to the eyes of faith a reality *beyond* history. The currently fashionable politicalisation of the gospel, especially the one ironically called 'liberation theology', restores us to the yoke of slavery that is imprisonment in history and imprisonment in the typically tragic web of our own projects in history.

I can already hear the muttered responses to what I have just said – accusations of 'other-worldliness', more appropriate perhaps to Buddhism than to Christianity; instructions about the concrete, historical character of biblical revelation; a brief lesson on how Christians are supposed to be in the world, not escape from it. Need I say it? Believe me: *I know all these things*. I am always amused when clerical types, who only yesterday emerged from some pietistic underworld to discover politics and sex, take it upon themselves to lecture me on worldliness; *the world is my proper vocation* – I know it fairly well; I especially know it in its modern and modernising structures; I spend most of my days weltering in the affairs of this world – *I don't need you to tell me about worldliness!*

Of course Christian faith is 'worldly', in the sense that this world is believed to be God's creation, and history the arena of his redemptive actions. Of course the Christian is called upon to act in this world (or perhaps one should say, *most* Christians are so called upon; there is, I believe, the legitimate Christian vocation of the contemplative life). But the question is *how* we act in the world.

If we are liberated by faith, we act in the full knowledge of the precariousness and tragic unpredictability of all human projects. Most important: we act in this world, *not* to be saved, *not* to attain some perfect purity or justice (which goals are not attainable), but to be of specific and necessarily limited service to others. Again, Paul addresses himself to the Galatians on this issue, when he insists that the freedom of the Christian is to be used as an opportunity for service, in love of one's neighbour (Gal 5:13–14). Let me put this in as *worldly* terms as I can: we get no moral brownie points for good intentions or noble goals. The moral measure of actions is their probable consequences for others. This is especially so in the case of political actions, because this is a category of actions with particularly unpredictable and potentially disastrous consequences. Precisely because of this, we are most likely to be effective politically (effective, that is, in being of service to our neighbours) if we ground ourselves in a realm beyond politics, thus becoming free to deal with political reality soberly and pragmatically; we cannot do this if we look on politics as the realm of redemption.

But let me return to the central point of these observations, which point is the church as constituted by the gospel. This is a community liberated, in faith, from all the constraining contingencies of both nature and society: 'There is neither Jew nor Greek, there is neither slave nor free, there is neither male nor female' (Gal 3:28, RSV). We know, of course, that in this world no Christian group has ever lived up to this promise, but commitment to it is an essential part of what the church purports to be. For this reason, catholicity has been counted among the 'marks of the church'. That catholicity is denied if a Christian community excludes people on such grounds as race, class or gender. It seems very clear that catholicity is also denied if people are excluded on the ground of political affiliation or allegiance.

This is the final ecclesial implication of the politicalisation of the church: *wherever a political agenda is seen as constitutive of the church, all those who dissent from it are excluded from the church. In that very instant, the church is no longer catholic; indeed, it ceases to be the church.*

If I am told from the pulpit, or by the language employed in the liturgy, or in public pronouncements of church authorities, that a particular political agenda is mandatory for Christians, this has ecclesial as well as moral implications. If I cannot in good conscience subscribe to this agenda, I am implicitly (perhaps, of course, even explicitly) excluded from the Christian community. To take another ironic example, if the liturgy is translated into so-called 'inclusive language' (which is, in fact, an ideological jargon), then this very language excludes anyone who cannot in good conscience subscribe to the feminist agenda which the language represents. Empirically, of course, this is exactly what this linguistic strategy does in our churches today. But, *mutatis mutandis*, the same exclusion occurs when *any* political or cultural agenda is elevated to the status of 'gospel', no matter whether this agenda is of the right, the left or the centre. And here is the ultimate irony: *all such politicalisation is an act of*

implicit excommunication. But, in politicising its message, the church is in actuality excommunicating itself!

Finally, with some reluctance, I have to make some comments about one troubling phrase in the passage that I read at the beginning of this lecture – the phrase applied to one who preaches a 'different gospel' – *'let him be accursed'* (*anathema estō*). (Actually, Paul uses the phrase *twice* in the passage; perhaps out of embarrassment, I have read it only once.) Such a phrase jars the ears of most of us, who do not reside on the wilder shores of Protestant fundamentalism (or possibly in the secret chambers of the Roman Curia). And let me quickly reassure you that I am not about to conclude here by hurling anathemas: I am in the business of hypotheses, not curses. However, even if none of us is prepared to claim the apostolic *exousia* by which Paul felt authorised to utter this terrible phrase, we may usefully reflect on why the preaching of 'different gospels' in the church might merit a curse.

I can think of one very good reason indeed: *because this false preaching denies ministry to those who desperately need it.* Our congregations are full of individuals with a multitude of afflictions and sorrows, very few of which have anything to do with the allegedly great issues of history. These individuals come to receive the consolation and solace of the gospel, instead of which they get a lot of politics. I can think of no clearer case of one asking for bread and being given a stone. Some time ago a friend of mine went through a very difficult period when it was suspected that he might be suffering from cancer. It turned out later that this was not the case, but during this anxiety ridden period neither he nor his family were given any attention by the clergy and the active members of his congregation. This is a congregation famous for its social and political activism. No one was interested in what, compared with the allegedly great historic challenges of our age, was the trivial matter of one man's fear of pain and death. The people of this congregation had more important things to do – attacking the 'root causes' of hunger by lobbying in Washington, organising to 'show solidarity' with Nicaragua, going on record ('making a moral stand') against apartheid.

My friend says that, during this time, he felt like an invisible man in that congregation. Needless to say, this is a congregation that religiously employs 'inclusive language'. (Again, I can hear some mutterings: can one not lobby in Washington and *also* minister to the sick? Perhaps. In the event, the first activity precluded the second. And one may reflect that it is easier to love people in distant lands than people next door.)

And this case leads me on to a further reflection: perhaps no apostolic anathema is required to damn the gospels of works-righteousness. *The curse is built-in.* Put differently: *those who put their faith into these works in the end damn themselves.* And here, again, it seems to me that this process can be perceived empirically, even without faith; Paul describes the unredeemed condition as one of being 'slaves to the elemental spirits of the universe' (Gal 4:3, RSV). Yes, I too have read Bultmann; I too am a modern man who uses electric razors and antibiotic medication, and I am not sure (though I am not prepared to exclude the possibility) whether I believe in the sinister beings that Paul evidently had in mind. But I do think that the processes of history and politics, which I don't have to believe in, because I know them all too well, may safely be included among the powers to whom we are enslaved in this world. The gospel promises us liberation from *all* these powers, be they historical or meta-historical, natural or supernatural. What a terrible thing it is to turn away from this promise to the vain pseudo-salvations of social existence! Here indeed is a curse, but it is a self-activating one. Paul tells us as much: 'whatever a man sows, that he will also reap. For he who sows to his own flesh will from the flesh reap corruption' (Gal 6:7–8, RSV). That corruption too is 'empirically available': it is the harvest of unintended consequences, bitter disappointments and tormenting guilt that is reaped by those who seek justification by political acts.

There is a form of discourse much favoured by intellectuals such as myself that may be called 'crisis-speech'. It consists of portraying an awful crisis and then suggesting that this crisis is about to happen *unless* the author's recommendations are promptly adopted. I am tempted, but I cannot quite conform to this formula. Speaking sociologically, I don't really see any great crisis: American society is, overall, in fairly robust condition; its class conflicts are more likely to end in compromise than in conflagration; and the various religious groups will adapt or fail to adapt to change, and if some of them (especially the denominations of mainline Protestantism) end up as rather marginal sects, I, for one, would not see this as a major catastrophe. Speaking theologically, there is a crisis of ultimate seriousness – it is the crisis brought on by the gospel being proclaimed, or not proclaimed, in any moment of history – yet it is a crisis that has been with the church from its beginning.

We are justified by faith. This means that nothing depends on us: our personal destiny and that of the entire world rests in God's hands. It also means that everything depends on us: we are called, to the best of our ability, to serve both church and world. I have said very little in this lecture about serving the world; most of my professional work is devoted to worrying about this and, when I am active politically, to doing a few things in this department. Serving the church today, I believe, must begin with an understanding of the specific forms of apostasy that confront us today, to recall the true meaning of gospel, church and ministry, and then to put our ecclesial houses in better order. I see very little evidence of any of this happening in American Christianity today, but then, if we believe that the Holy Spirit is active in the church, we must also believe that its actions cannot be predicted. If and when the Spirit revitalises the church, this has the surprising quality of a summer thunderstorm. I wish for all of us that, in our lifetimes, we may yet be so surprised.

Bibliography

Sometimes it has been necessary to give the original date of a book in the text (*e.g.* Schleiermacher 1821; Lewis 1943) in order to make the necessary chronology clear. This detail is used in the left-hand column here. In the right-hand column that date precedes the more up-to-date publication detail. In the case of modern foreign theological works the date given (*e.g.* Jüngel 1983) is that of the English translation.

Altizer 1966	T. J. J. Altizer, *The Gospel of Christian Atheism* (London: Collins, 1966)
Altizer & Hamilton 1966	T. J. J. Altizer and W. Hamilton, *Radical Theology and the Death of God* (Harmondsworth: Penguin Books, 1966)
Anderson & Stransky 1979	G. H. Anderson and T. F. Stransky (eds), *Mission Trends No. 4: Liberation Theologies* (Grand Rapids: Wm B. Eerdmans, 1979)
Assmann 1973	H. Assmann, *Theology for a Nomad Church* (1973), trans. P. Burns (Maryknoll, NY: Orbis Books, 1976)
von Balthasar 1986	H. U. von Balthasar, *On Prayer* (San Francisco: Ignatius, 1986)
Berry 1984	R. J. Berry, 'Sex', in J. R. W. Stott (ed.), *Free to be Different* (Basingstoke: Marshall, Morgan & Scott, 1984), ch. 5.
Berry 1988	R. J. Berry, *God and Evolution* (London: Hodder & Stoughton, 1988)

Bloom 1988   A. Bloom, *The Closing of the
                      American Mind* (Harmondsworth:
                      Penguin Books, 1988)

Brown 1984   C. Brown, *Miracles and the Critical
                      Mind* (Grand Rapids, MI, and
                      Exeter: Wm B. Eerdmans/
                      Paternoster Press, 1984)

Bultmann 1960   R. Bultmann, 'New Testament and
                      Mythology', in H. W. Bartsch (ed.),
                      *Kerygma and Myth: A Theological
                      Debate* (London: SPCK, 1960)

Butler 1736   J. Butler, *The Analogy of Religion,
                      Natural and Revealed, to the
                      Constitution and Course of Nature*
                      (1736) in W. E. Gladstone (ed.),
                      The Works of Joseph Butler
                      (Oxford: Clarendon Press, 1896),
                      vol. 1

Chopp 1986   R. Chopp, *The Praxis of Suffering*
                      (Maryknoll, NY: Orbis Books,
                      1986)

Clapp 1987   R. Clapp, 'Democracy as Heresy',
                      Christianity Today, 20 February
                      1987, pp. 17–23

Coulson 1955   C. A. Coulson, *Science and Christian
                      Belief* (Oxford: Oxford University
                      Press, 1955)

Cupitt 1979   D. Cupitt, *The Debate About Christ*
                      (London: SCM Press, 1979)

Cupitt 1984   D. Cupitt, *The Sea of Faith* (London:
                      BBC Publications, 1984)

D'Costa 1986a   G. D'Costa, *Theology and Religious
                      Pluralism* (Oxford: Basil Blackwell,
                      1986)

D'Costa 1986b   G. D'Costa, 'The Pluralist Paradigm
                      in the Christian Theology of
                      Religions', *Scottish Journal of
                      Theology* 39 (1986), pp. 211–224

D'Costa 1987   G. D'Costa, *John Hick's Theology of
                      Religions* (New York: University
                      Press of America, 1987)

Descartes 1641

R. Descartes, *Meditations* (1641) in N. K. Smith (ed. and trans.), *Descartes' Philosophical Writings* (London: Macmillan, 1952)

Dostoyevsky 1880

F. Dostoyevsky, *The Brothers Karamazov* (1880) (Harmondsworth: Penguin Books, 1982)

Durkheim 1915

E. Durkheim, *The Elementary Forms of the Religious Life* (1915) (London: George Allen & Unwin, 1976)

Ferreira 1986

M. J. Ferreira, *Scepticism and Reasonable Doubt* (Oxford: Clarendon Press, 1986)

Frazer 1907

J. G. Frazer, *Adonis, Attis, Osiris: Studies in Oriental Religion* (London: Macmillan, 1907)

Freire 1972

P. Freire, *Pedagogy of the Oppressed* (Harmondsworth: Penguin Books, 1972)

General Synod 1986

The Nature of Christian Belief (London: Church House Publishing, 1986)

Goulder & Hick 1983

M. D. Goulder and J. Hick, *Why Believe in God?* (London: SCM Press, 1983)

Gutiérrez 1973

G. Gutiérrez, *A Theology of Liberation* (Maryknoll, NY: Orbis Books, 1973)

Hadden 1969

J. Hadden, *The Gathering Storm in the Churches* (Garden City, NY: Doubleday, 1969)

Harris 1985

M. J. Harris, *Easter in Durham* (Exeter: Paternoster Press, 1985)

Hartshorne 1941

C. Hartshorne, *Man's Vision of God and the Logic of Theism* (1941) (Chicago: Shoe String Press, 1983)

Hegel 1807

G. Hegel, *The Phenomenology of Mind* (1807) (New York: Macmillan, 1931)

Hick 1977   J. Hick (ed.), *The Myth of God Incarnate* (London: SCM Press, 1977)

Hooper 1979   W. Hooper (ed.), *They Stand Together: The Letters of C. S. Lewis to Arthur Greaves (1914–1963)* (London: Collins, 1979)

Hume 1748   D. Hume, *An Enquiry Concerning Human Understanding*, Section X, 'Of Miracles' (1748), in D. Hume, *Enquiries Concerning Human Understanding and Concerning the Principles of Morals*, ed. L. A. Selby-Bigge (Oxford: Clarendon Press, [2]1902)

Josipovichi 1971   G. Josipovichi, *The World and the Book* (London: Macmillan, 1971)

Jüngel 1983   E. Jüngel, *God as the Mystery of the World* (Edinburgh: T. & T. Clark, 1983)

Kant 1787   I. Kant, *Critique of Pure Reason* (1787), trans. N. K. Smith (London: Macmillan, 1933)

Kant 1788   I. Kant, *Critique of Practical Reason* (1788), trans. T. K. Abbott (London, 1879)

Kasper 1976   W. Kasper, *Jesus the Christ* (London: Burns & Oates, 1976)

Kierkegaard 1850   S. Kierkegaard, *Training in Christianity* (1850) (Princeton: Princeton University Press, 1944)

Kirk 1979   J. A. Kirk, *Liberation Theology: An Evangelical View from the Third World* (Basingstoke: Marshall, Morgan & Scott, 1979)

Künneth 1965   W. Künneth, *The Theology of the Resurrection* (London: SCM Press, 1965)

Lampe 1971   G. W. H. Lampe, *God as Spirit* (Oxford: Clarendon Press, 1971)

264 BETRAYING THE GOSPEL

Lawrence 1961	D. H. Lawrence, *Psychoanalysis & the Unconscious and Fantasia of the Unconscious* (London: Viking Press, 1961)
Lewis 1943	C. S. Lewis, *The Abolition of Man* (1943) (London: Collins Fount, 1977)
Lewis 1946	C. S. Lewis, *The Great Divorce* (1946) (London: Collins Fount, 1977)
Lewis 1947	C. S. Lewis, *Miracles: A Preliminary Study* (1947) (London: Collins Fount, 1977)
Lewis 1952	C. S. Lewis, *Mere Christianity* (1952) (London: Collins Fount, 1977)
Lewis 1955	C. S. Lewis, *Surprised by Joy* (1955) (London: Collins Fount, 1977)
Lewis 1977	C. S. Lewis, *Fern-Seed and Elephants, and Other Essays on Christianity* (London: Collins Fount, 1977)
Lewontin 1985	R. C. Lewontin, in N. Keyfitz (ed.), *Population and Biology* (Liege: Ordina, 1985), ch. 1.
MacKay 1979a	D. M. MacKay, *Freedom of Action in a Mechanistic Universe* (Cambridge: Cambridge University Press, 1979)
MacKay 1979b	D. M. MacKay, *Human Science and Human Dignity* (London: Hodder & Stoughton, 1979)
Macmurray 1961	J. Macmurray, *Persons in Relation* (London: Faber & Faber, 1961)
McGrath 1984	A. E. McGrath, '*Homo assumptus*? A Study in the Christology of the *Via Moderna* with Particular Reference to William of Ockham', *Ephemerides Theologicae Lovanienses* 60 (1984), pp. 283–297
McGrath 1986	A. E. McGrath, *The Making of Modern German Christology* (Oxford: Basil Blackwell, 1986)
Medawar 1984	P. Medawar, *The Limits of Science* (New York: Harper & Row, 1984)

Midgley 1985   M. Midgley, *Evolution as a Religion*
                        (London: Methuen, 1985)

Miguez Bonino 1975   J. Miguez Bonino, *Doing Theology in
                        a Revolutionary Situation*
                        (Philadelphia: Fortress Press, 1975);
                        also published under the title
                        *Revolutionary Theology Comes of
                        Age* (London: SPCK, 1975)

Miranda 1977   J. P. Miranda, *Being and the Messiah:
                        The Message of St John* (Maryknoll,
                        NY: Orbis Books, 1977)

Moltmann 1974   J. Moltmann, *The Crucified God*
                        (London: SCM Press, 1974)

Moltmann 1976   J. Moltmann, '"On Latin American
                        Liberation Theology": an Open
                        Letter to José Miguez Bonino',
                        Christianity and Crisis 36, 29 March
                        1976

Monod 1971   J. Monod, *Chance and Necessity*
                        (London: Collins, 1971)

Nebelsick 1984   H. R. Nebelsick, 'Article Review: Iain
                        Paul, *Science, Theology and
                        Einstein'*, *Scottish Journal of
                        Theology* 37 (1984), pp. 237–242

Newbigin 1983   L. Newbigin, *The Other Side of 1984:
                        Questions to the churches* (Geneva:
                        World Council of Churches,
                        1983)

Newbigin 1986   L. Newbigin, *Foolishness to the
                        Greeks: The Gospel and Western
                        Culture* (London: SPCK, 1986)

Niebuhr 1929   H. R. Niebuhr, *The Social Sources of
                        Denominationalism* (1929)
                        (Cleveland, OH: Meridian, 1957)

Pannenberg 1968   W. Pannenberg, *Jesus: God and Man*
                        (London: SCM Press, 1968)

Polanyi 1969   M. Polanyi, *Knowing and Being*
                        (London: Routledge & Kegan Paul,
                        1969)

Polkinghorne 1983   J. Polkinghorne, *The Way the World Is*
                        (London: SPCK, 1983)

Rahner 1961–81   K. Rahner, *Theological Investigations*
                        (London: Darton, Longman &
                        Todd, 1961–1981), 20 vols

Ramm 1983   B. Ramm, *After Fundamentalism*
                        (San Francisco: Harper & Row,
                        1983)

Reardon 1980   B. Reardon, *Religious Thought in the
                        Victorian Age* (London: Longman,
                        1980)

Robinson 1963   J. A. T. Robinson, *Honest to God*
                        (London: SCM Press, 1963)

Rogerson 1985   J. W. Rogerson, 'Using the Bible in
                        the Debate about Abortion' in
                        J. H. Channer (ed.), *Abortion and
                        the Sanctity of Human Life*
                        (Exeter: Paternoster Press, 1985),
                        ch. 4

Schleiermacher 1821   F. D. Schleiermacher, *The Christian
                        Faith* (1821) (Edinburgh: T. & T.
                        Clark, 1928)

Snow 1975   C. P. Snow, *The Two Cultures*
                        (Cambridge: Cambridge University
                        Press, 1975)

Solzhenitsyn 1976   A. Solzhenitsyn (ed.), *Under the
                        Rubble* (London: Fontana Books,
                        1976)

Suenens 1982   L.-J. Suenens, *Renewal and the Powers
                        of Darkness* (London: Darton,
                        Longman & Todd, 1982)

Thorpe 1978   W. H. Thorpe, *Purpose in a World of
                        Chance* (Oxford: Oxford University
                        Press, 1978)

Toon 1986   P. Toon, *Longing for the Heavenly
                        Realm* (London: Hodder &
                        Stoughton, 1986)

Toon 1987   P. Toon, *From Mind to Heart* (Grand
                        Rapids, MI: Baker Book House,
                        1987)

Torrance 1969   T. F. Torrance, *Theological Science*
                        (Oxford: Oxford University Press,
                        1969)

Torrance 1986   T. F. Torrance, 'The Legacy of Karl
                                  Barth (1886–1986)', *Scottish Journal
                                  of Theology* 39 (1986), pp. 289–308

Troeltsch 1902   E. Troeltsch, *The Absoluteness of
                                  Christianity and the History of
                                  Religion* (1902) (London: SCM
                                  Press, 1972)

Walker 1987   A. Walker, *Enemy Territory: The
                                  Christian Struggle for the Modern
                                  World* (London: Hodder &
                                  Stoughton, 1987)

Ward 1986   K. Ward, *The Turn of the Tide:
                                  Christian Belief in Britain Today*
                                  (London: BBC Publications, 1986)

Whitehead 1929   A. N. Whitehead, *Process and Reality*
                                  (London: Macmillan, 1929)

Wilson 1984   I. Wilson, *Jesus: The Evidence*
                                  (London: Weidenfeld & Nicolson,
                                  1984)

Zizioulas 1985   J. Zizioulas, *Being as Communion*
                                  (London: Darton, Longman &
                                  Todd, 1985)

Notes on contributors

Metropolitan Anthony is the head of the Patriarchal Russian Orthodox Church in Great Britain and Ireland. Formerly the Exarch of the Russian Patriarchate in Europe, Metropolitan Anthony is widely known for his works on spirituality and prayer. He is the author of *School for Prayer* (London: Darton, Longman & Todd, 1970), *Living Prayer* (London: Darton, Longman & Todd, ²1980), *God and Man* (London: Darton, Longman & Todd, ²1983) and *The Essence of Prayer* (London: Darton, Longman & Todd, 1986), and numerous other works on the spiritual life.

Peter L. Berger is Director of the Institute for the Study of Economic Culture, Boston University, Massachusetts, and is the author of numerous works on the sociology of knowledge and the sociology of religion, including *Invitation to Sociology: A Humanistic Perspective* (Harmondsworth: Penguin Books, 1966), *A Rumour of Angels: M .ern Society and the Rediscovery of the Supernatural* (Harmondsworth: Penguin Books, 1971), *The Homeless Mind: Modernization and Consciousness*, with Brigitte Berger and Hansfried Kellner (Harmondsworth: Penguin Books, 1974), *Facing up to Modernity: Excursions in Society, Politics and Religion* (Harmondsworth: Penguin Books, 1979), *The Heretical Imperative: Contemporary Possibilities of Religious Affirmation* (London: Collins, 1980).

R. J. Berry is Professor of Genetics at University College, London. He is currently President of the British Ecological Society; from 1982–1985 he was President of the Linnaean Society, and from 1968–1988 Chairman of the Research Scientists' Christian Fellowship (now Christians in Science). He is the author of *Teach Yourself Genetics* (London: Hodder & Stoughton, 1965), *Inheritance and Natural History* (London: Collins, 1977), *Natural History of Orkney* (London: Collins, 1985), etc. His most recent book is *God and Evolution* (London: Hodder & Stoughton, 1988).

Gavin D'Costa is an Indian Roman Catholic theologian and lectures in Religious Studies at the West London Institute of Higher Education. He is Secretary to the British Council of Churches Committee for Relations with People of Other Faiths: Theological Issues Consultative Group, and a member of the Roman Catholic Committee for Other Faiths (England and Wales). He is the author of *Theology and Religious Pluralism* (Oxford: Basil Blackwell, 1986) and *John Hick's Theology of Religions* (New York/London: University Press of America, 1987). His most recent work is an edited collection of essays, *Faith meets Faith: A Volume of Interfaith Essays* (London: BFSS RE Centre, 1988).

James D. G. Dunn is Professor of Divinity at the University of Durham, he was formerly Reader in Theology at the University of Nottingham. He is the author of *Baptism in the Holy Spirit* (London: SCM Press, 1970), *Unity and Diversity in the New Testament* (London: SCM Press, 1977), *Jesus and the Spirit* (London: SCM Press, 1978), *Christology in the Making* (London: SCM Press, 1980), *Evidence for Jesus* (London: SCM Press, 1985), and *New Testament Theology in Dialogue*, with James P. Mackey (London: SPCK, 1987). His most recent book is *The Living Word* (London: SCM Press, 1987).

Billy Graham, an evangelist with a world-wide ministry, is the holder of several honorary degrees in literature and theology, the Templeton Foundation Prize for Religion (1982), and the President's Medal of Freedom Award (1983). His numerous books include *Angels: God's Secret Agents* (London: Hodder & Stoughton, 1976), *Till Armageddon: A Perspective on Suffering* (London: Hodder & Stoughton, 1983), *Approaching Hoofbeats: The Four Horsemen of the Apocalypse* (London: Hodder & Stoughton, 1983), *How to be Born Again* (London: Hodder & Stoughton, 1984).

Colin E. Gunton is Professor of Christian Doctrine at King's College, London, and is Associate Minister of Brentwood United Reformed Church. He is the author of *Becoming and Being: The Doctrine of God in Charles Hartshorne and Karl Barth* (Oxford: Oxford University Press, 1978), *Yesterday and Today: A Study of Continuities in Christology* (London: Darton, Longman and Todd, 1983) and *Enlightenment and Alienation: An Essay Towards a Trinitarian Theology* (Basingstoke: Marshall, Morgan & Scott, 1985). His most recent book is *The Actuality of Atonement* (Edinburgh: T. & T. Clark, 1989).

Alasdair I. C. Heron is Professor of Reformed Theology at the University of Erlangen, West Germany. He was formerly Lecturer in Christian Dogmatics at the University of Edinburgh. He is the author of *A Century of Protestant Theology* (Guildford: Lutterworth, 1980) and Editor of *The Scottish Journal of Theology*. His most recent book is *Table and Tradition: Towards an Ecumenical Understanding of the Eucharist* (Edinburgh: Handsel Press, 1983).

Graham Leonard, the Bishop of London since 1981, is the author of several books, including *God Alive: Priorities in Pastoral Theology* (London:

Darton, Longman & Todd, 1981), *Firmly I Believe and Truly* (Oxford: Mowbray, 1985) and *Life in Christ* (Oxford: Mowbray, 1986).

Alister E. McGrath is Lecturer in Historical and Systematic Theology at Wycliffe Hall, Oxford, a member of the Oxford University Faculty of Theology, and Bampton Lecturer at Oxford for 1990. He is the author of *The Making of Modern German Christology* (Oxford: Basil Blackwell, 1986) and *Iustitia Dei: A History of the Christian Doctrine of Justification*, 2 vols (Cambridge: Cambridge University Press, 1986), and his most recent popular book is *Explaining Your Faith* (Leicester: IVP, 1988).

Lesslie Newbigin is a minister in the United Reformed Church. He was formerly a bishop in the Church of South India. He is the author of *The Other Side of 1984: Questions for the Churches* (Geneva: WCC, 1983) and *Foolishness to the Greeks: The Gospel and Western Culture* (London: SPCK, 1986). His most recent book is *Mission in Christ's Way* (Geneva: WCC, 1987).

Thomas A. Smail is the Rector of Sanderstead, Surrey. He was formerly Vice-Principal of St John's College, Nottingham. He is the author of *The Forgotten Father* (London: Hodder & Stoughton, ²1987), and his most recent book is *The Giving Gift* (London: Hodder & Stoughton, 1988).

Leon-Joseph Suenens, a Cardinal since 1962, was formerly the Archbishop of Brussels-Malines. He was a Moderator of the Second Vatican Council and the winner of the 1976 Templeton Foundation Prize for Religion. He is the author of *A New Pentecost?* (London: Darton, Longman & Todd, 1975), *Renewal and the Powers of Darkness* (London: Darton, Longman & Todd, 1982) and *Nature and Grace: A Vital Unity* (London: Darton, Longman & Todd, 1986).

Peter Toon is Vicar of Staindrop, Durham, and a visiting lecturer at St John's College, Durham, and at several American seminaries. He was Tutor in Theology at Oak Hill Theological College, London, and is the author and editor of many theological books. His latest are *Meditating Upon God's Word* (London: Darton, Longman & Todd, 1988), and *What is Spirituality?* (London: Darton, Longman & Todd, 1989).

Alan J. Torrance is Professor of Systematic Theology, Theological Hall, Knox College, in the University of Otago. Prior to this he was Academic Assistant to the Chair of Reformed Theology at the University of Erlangen, West Germany. He is a regular contributor to learned theological journals, and his recent work includes the following: 'Forgiveness? The Essential Socio-political Structure of Personal Being', *Journal of Theology for Southern Africa* 56 (September 1986); 'The Self-Relation, Narcissism and the Gospel of Grace', *Scottish Journal of Theology* 40/4 (1987); and

'Christian Experience and Divine Revelation in the Theologies of Friedrich Schleiermacher and Karl Barth' in I. Howard Marshall (ed.), *Christian Experience in Theology and Life* (Edinburgh: Rutherford House, 1988).

Thomas F. Torrance is the Emeritus Professor of Christian Dogmatics in the University of Edinburgh, and was formerly Moderator of the General Assembly of the Church of Scotland for the year 1976–1977. He is the author of *Theological Science* (Oxford: Oxford University Press, 1969), *Space, Time and Incarnation* (Oxford: Oxford University Press, 1969), *Space, Time and Resurrection* (Edinburgh: Handsel Press, 1976), and his latest book is *The Trinitarian Faith* (Edinburgh: T. & T. Clark, 1988).

Andrew Walker, a lay theologian in the Orthodox tradition, is the founder and Director of the C. S. Lewis Centre and teaches theology and sociology at the West London Institute of Higher Education. He was a Fellow in the Department of Christian Doctrine at King's College, London, 1986–1987 and Visiting Professor at the Perkins School of Theology, Southern Methodist University, Dallas, in the summer of 1988. He is the author of *Restoring the Kingdom* (London: Hodder & Stoughton, [2]1988) and has contributed articles and essays to several academic journals and symposia. His most recent book is *Enemy Territory* (London: C. S. Lewis Centre/ Hodder & Stoughton, 1987).

Keith Ward is an ordained priest of the Church of England and is Professor of the History and the Philosophy of Religion at King's College, London. He was formerly F. D. Maurice Professor at King's College, London. He is the author of several books, including *Holding Fast to God: A reply to Don Cupitt* (London: SPCK, 1982), *The Battle for the Soul* (London: Hodder & Stoughton, 1985), *Rational Theology and the Creativity of God* (Oxford: Basil Blackwell, 1985), *The Turn of the Tide: Christian Belief in Britain Today* (London: BBC Publications, 1986) and *Images of Eternity* (London: Darton, Longman & Todd, 1987).

The C. S. Lewis Centre

The C. S. Lewis Centre for the Study of Religion and Modernity is a Christian research organisation working in partnership with Hodder and Stoughton to publish thought-provoking material concerning the relationship between the Christian faith and the modern world. Following C. S. Lewis' example, it is the Centre's policy to reach a broad market, speaking to 'everyman' in an intelligent and informed way, and responding to the challenge presented to orthodox belief by the secular culture of our contemporary society.